BENTWATERS & WOODBRIDGE

Please return/renew this item
by the last date shown.

Suffolk Libraries
01473 584563

www.suffolk.gov.uk/libraries/

First edition, published in 2007 by

WOODFIELD PUBLISHING
Bognor Regis, West Sussex PO21 5EL
United Kingdom
www.woodfieldpublishing.com

© Graham Haynes, 2007

All rights reserved.
No part of this publication may be reproduced
or transmitted in any form or by any means,
electronic or mechanical, nor may it be stored
in any information storage and retrieval system,
without prior permission from the publisher.

The right of Graham Haynes
to be identified as author of this work
has been asserted in accordance with
the Copyright, Designs and Patents Act 1988

ISBN 1-84683-032-X

Bentwaters & Woodbridge

An illustrated history of the USAF twin base complex in East Anglia

GRAHAM HAYNES

Woodfield

Suffolk County Council

Libraries & Heritage

	WOfP	07/08
942.646		

For Rebecca, Euan and Chloe

CONTENTS

Foreword iii

Acknowledgements iv

1. Bentwaters History 1
2. Chapter 2 – Woodbridge History 11
3. Unit Histories 18
   - 81st Tactical Fighter Wing 18
   - 78th Tactical Fighter Squadron 24
   - 91st Tactical Fighter Squadron 27
   - 92nd Tactical Fighter Squadron 29
   - 509th Tactical Fighter Squadron 33
   - 510th Tactical Fighter Squadron 35
   - 511th Tactical Fighter Squadron 37
   - 527th Aggressor Squadron 39
   - 87th Fighter-Interceptor Squadron 42
   - 512th Fighter-Interceptor Squadron 44
   - 79th Tactical Fighter Squadron 46
   - 67th Special Operations Squadron 49
   - 21st Special Operations Squadron 52
4. 'Twin-Bases' Aircraft 55
5. Thoughts about Wheelus 131
6. The Ultimate Dilemma: a reflection on Victor Alert at Bentwaters 137
7. A Pilot's Story: Flying the F-86A & F-84F from Bentwaters 142
8. Chapter 8 – Twin Bases Wall Art 149
9. Around the Twin-Bases 159
10. Preserving the Memory: Bentwaters 'Cold War' Museum 168

Foreword

At the conclusion of the Gulf War in 1991, I returned from Saudi Arabia to my usual duty at RAF Alconbury as the Vice Commander of the 10th Tactical Fighter Wing. I had been advised that I was to receive a new assignment but it was unclear what that was to be. This was my second posting in the United Kingdom. My wife, Suzanne and I brought our infant sons to Suffolk in 1977 where I flew F-111Fs at RAF Lakenheath. Now, I was flying the A-10 Thunderbolt II. We had truly enjoyed our time in England, and we hoped to stay a little longer.

Since the early 1950s thousands of U.S. Air Force airmen had been privileged to call RAF Bentwaters and RAF Woodbridge home. The countryside was beautiful and the citizens of Suffolk were magnificent hosts. Finally, the 81st Tactical Fighter Wing, the host United States unit at the "Twin Bases," had a storied heritage as a great organization. Assignments to the Bentwaters/Woodbridge complex were highly prized.

One morning in mid-June, my commander at Alconbury informed me that I was to take command of the 81st Wing in mid-July 1991. This was a fighter pilot's dream come true. I did not sleep well for days. Ahead of us was a great challenge. The face of the U.S. military presence in Europe was about to change rapidly. The "Cold War" was over. As I took command I knew that in two years, I would lower the United States flag and the USAF role in the Woodbridge area would come to an end.

The story of "Mission Completion" at the Twin Bases is a happy one – though tinged with sadness. The Americans did a noble job in taking apart a great military organization, and our British hosts could not have been more helpful. It was a team effort that went very smoothly.

Suzanne and I drove away from Bentwaters in August of 1993. My eyes grow a little misty as I think back on that day. My time in command of the 81st Wing marked the highlight of my career. I was to trade my colonel's eagles for the two stars of a major general before I left the Air Force. But, I would not trade my two years leading the Twin Bases for anything. I miss the 81st team and my British friends. To all who read these words, thank you for all you gave Suzanne and me. God Bless You.

Major General Roger R. Radcliff USAF (ret)
Last Commander of 81st Tactical Fighter Wing
RAF Bentwaters and RAF Woodbridge
August 2004

Major General Roger R. Radcliff.

Acknowledgements

I would like to thank Vernon Drane of Rendlesham Projects Ltd. for allowing me access to Bentwaters on numerous occasions during my initial research in 1999 and for providing me with information relating to the base infrastructure. My thanks also go to the current owners of Bentwaters - the Kemball family – in particular, Bill and Sarah, for their assistance. Other people that contributed to this book are SSgt George E. Cox Jr., historian for the 81st Training Wing at Keesler AFB, Mississippi; CMSgt Les Della Maestra (ret), former Senior Enlisted Advisor to the 81st TFW; the Air Force Historical Research Agency at Maxwell AFB, Alabama; Harry Eckes, former 81st Wing F-86A/F-84F pilot; George Berke, former 81st Wing F-84F/F-101 pilot and David Baker, Ashley Annis and Mick Sudds who allowed me access to their incredible photo collections. I am also indebted to Major General Roger R. Radcliff (ret), former Commander of the 81st TFW, for writing the Foreword; words cannot express my gratitude. There are also numerous other people who helped me along the way but, in particular, I must thank George Pennick for providing me with information and photographs that had proved difficult, if not impossible, to obtain from other sources. His excellent photographs have helped to redress the historical balance of this work and without his help this project would probably never have got off the ground.

Graham Haynes 2007

1. Bentwaters History

The RAF Bentwaters site was first discovered by the Air Ministry in August 1942 and was immediately identified as a suitable location for the development of an airfield. The area was ideal for wartime flying operations, being flat, remote, sparsely populated and only a few miles from the coast. At this time the search for suitable airfield locations was taking on a real sense of urgency due to the imminent build-up of the United States Army Air Force's Eighth Air Force in England.

The airfield was originally given the name 'Butley', after the village situated a mile or so to the southeast and allocated the USAAF identity 'Station 151.' Construction work began in late 1942 but by March the following year this had ceased with the workforce transferring to other airfields in East Anglia whose completion was considered a much higher priority. The workforce returned in late 1943 and the airfield was renamed 'Bentwaters.' The name was taken from two cottages ('Bentwaters Cottages') that had stood on the site of the main runway.

The construction work became less urgent in mid 1944 and the future use of Bentwaters as an airfield was placed in doubt. This doubt was heightened during May when the last USAAF Bomb Group arrived in England and took up residence at Debach, about seven miles to the west of Bentwaters. This brought to an end the planned build-up of the Eighth Air Force. As a consequence of this, Bentwaters was no longer required by the USAAF and, after construction was completed, the airfield was placed under 'Care and Maintenance' whilst its future was considered.

Bentwaters became a welcome sight for Allied aircrew returning from missions in battle-damaged aircraft. The deserted airfield provided them with the opportunity to make an emergency landing instead of attempting to make it back to their home bases. The first aircraft to use Bentwaters for this purpose was a Snetterton Heath-based Boeing B-17G Flying Fortress. The 96th Bomb Group aircraft made a successful emergency landing on 20th July 1944, somehow avoiding the obstructions that had been deliberately placed on the runway to prevent its unauthorised use. In October, a second B-17 attempted an emergency landing but this time was less fortunate. The aircraft hit some of the runway obstructions causing considerable and unnecessary damage to the airframe. After this incident the runway was cleared and Bentwaters was designated an official Emergency Landing Ground. On 24th October three USAAF North American P-51D Mustangs, belonging to the 359th Fighter Group at East Wretham, became the first aircraft to land at Bentwaters after removal of the obstructions when they were forced to divert after running low of fuel.

In the latter part of 1944 the Eighth Air Force handed over control of Bentwaters to the Air Ministry. After RAF Bomber Command declined its use the airfield was taken over, on 22nd November 1944, by No. 11 Group of RAF Fighter Command and became the last RAF airfield to be activated during the Second World War.

On 11th December 1944 the first aircraft to be based at Bentwaters arrived in the shape of the North American Mustang IIIs belonging to No. 129 Squadron. Four days later, on 15th December, two more squadrons, Nos. 118 and 165 arrived at the base. Both of these squadrons were equipped with the Supermarine Spitfire, albeit different versions. No. 118 Squadron flew the Mk. LFVb and the Mk. VII, whilst No. 165 Squadron flew the Mk. IX. The Spitfire's days at Bentwaters were short-lived because both squadrons converted to the Mustang III before the end of January 1945. A fourth Mustang III squadron, No. 234, followed on 17th December with the number rising to five on the 29th December when No. 64 Squadron relocated from Bradwell Bay, Essex. The sixth and final Mustang III squadron arrived the following day when No. 126 Squadron, also from Bradwell Bay, flew in to Bentwaters. The task of commanding the Bentwaters Mustang wing was given to Wing Commander H.A.C. Bird-Wilson.

The first wartime mission from Bentwaters took place on 23rd December 1944 when the Mustang IIIs escorted over 150 Avro Lancasters on a bombing raid to the railway yards at Trier, Germany, a few miles east of the border with Luxembourg. Numerous other escort missions were flown by the Mustang wing prior to the end of the war. Among the most notable of these was that of 21st March 1945 when Nos. 64 and 126 Squadrons were involved in Operation Carthage. This mission saw 28 Mustangs escort 18 Fersfield-based Mosquito FB.IVs on a daylight raid to the Gestapo headquarters located in the Shellhuss, Copenhagen. Although deemed a success, 4 Mosquitos and 1 Mustang failed to return to their respective home bases.

Also in March 1945, No. 234 Squadron converted to the Mustang IV and on 1st May the squadron relocated to Peterhead, Aberdeenshire, reducing the number of operational squadrons at Bentwaters to five.

On 4th May 1945, the Mustang wing was tasked with escorting Beaufighters on an anti-U-Boat raid in the Great Belt off Denmark. This was to be the RAF's last wartime mission from Bentwaters and by early September of that year all of the Mustang squadrons had been withdrawn. The first squadron to leave was No. 129 on 26th May, followed three days later by No. 165, which relocated to Dyce, Aberdeenshire. Nearly three months passed before the next squadrons prepared to depart. No. 118 Squadron left Bentwaters on 11th August 1945 followed four days later, on the 15th August, by No. 64 Squadron. The Mustang III era at Bentwaters was brought to a close on 5th September 1945 when the final squadron, No. 126, left the Suffolk base to take up residence at Hethel, Norfolk.

Prior to the departure of the Mustang squadrons, another two units had arrived at Bentwaters. No. 65 Squadron arrived on 15th May 1945 equipped with the Spitfire LF XVIe and they were followed two months later by No. 234 Squadron. The latter was a former resident at Bentwaters whilst equipped with the Mustang III but 234's second stint at the base saw it operate the Spitfire HF IX.

The RAF remained resident during the early post-war years, using the airfield for flying training with a number of aircraft types. On 6th October 1945, 16 Gloster Meteor IIIs arrived at the base, heralding Bentwaters' entrance into the jet-age. The Meteors were assigned to 1335 Conversion Unit (No. 124 (Shadow) Squadron) and had relocated from RAF Molesworth, Cambridgeshire. The Meteor III was not the only type operated by 1335 CU. The unit was split into four flights, the other three flights being equipped with the de Havilland Hornet F.1, Hawker Tempest II and the de Havilland Vampire FB.1. These were busy times for the Suffolk base!

The 12th February 1946 saw No. 234 Squadron depart Bentwaters and relocate to Molesworth for conversion to the Meteor III. A few weeks later, on 1st April 1946, the Meteor Flight of 1335 CU was re-numbered as No. 56 Squadron and ceased to be part of the conversion unit. Otherwise known as the 'Firebirds,' No. 56 Squadron had previously flown the Hawker Tempest V from Fassberg, Germany and in converting to its new mount, had become the first 'front-line' squadron in the RAF to receive the Mk. III version of the Meteor.

The remaining three flights of 1335 CU carried on with their training role at Bentwaters for a further four months until the unit was disbanded during August 1946. The personnel and aircraft of 1335 CU were used to form No. 226 Operational Conversion Unit (OCU) at Molesworth on the 15th of that month.

June 1946 saw No. 65 Squadron begin replacing it's Spitfire LF XVIe's with the de Havilland Hornet F.1 prior to a move to Linton-on-Ouse, Yorkshire a few months later.

De Havilland Vampire FB.1 VF/309 of 226 Operational Conversion Unit pictured at Bentwaters circa 1948.
(photo: via Bentwaters 'Cold War' Museum archives)

June 1946 also saw the Meteor IIIs of No. 245 Squadron take up residence at Bentwaters alongside those of No. 56 Squadron. 245's stay was to be very brief as they departed for Boxted during the middle of August 1946. The Meteors of No. 56 Squadron followed them four weeks later, on 16th September, when they too relocated to the Essex base.

The departure of No. 56 Squadron left Bentwaters with no resident units remaining. This was to be short-lived as 10th October 1946 saw No. 226 Operational Conversion Unit move in from Molesworth. No. 226 OCU were tasked with training pilots for the day-fighter and fighter-reconnaissance role and to this end were equipped with various aircraft types. Among the aircraft assigned were the Avro Anson I, North American Harvard I, de Havilland Vampire FB.1, de Havilland Mosquito T.III, Hawker Tempest II and the Gloster Meteor F.4.

No. 226 OCU remained at Bentwaters until 26th August 1949 when it began the process of relocating to RAF Driffield in Yorkshire. With the relocation of No. 226 OCU complete, Bentwaters was deactivated and placed under Care and Maintenance on 1st September 1949.

On 16th March 1951 control of Bentwaters was handed over to the United States Air Force. During May, a detachment of the Shepherds Grove-based 1980th Airways & Air Communication Service became established at the base to prepare the site for the arrival of the first aircraft.

The first aircraft arrived two months later, on 1st July 1951, when C-Flight of the 9th Air Rescue Squadron settled in at Bentwaters bringing with it the largest aircraft that would ever be stationed at the base - the Boeing SB-29. Nicknamed 'Super Dumbo,' the SB-29 was basically a B-29 Superfortress modified for the air rescue role by the addition of an air-droppable lifeboat. In addition to the SB-29, C-Flight also brought the Grumman SA-16A Albatross amphibian to Bentwaters. The unit's stay at the base was, however, relatively short as it departed for a more permanent location at Burtonwood, Cheshire on 14th November 1952.

On 5th September 1951, two months prior to the departure of C-Flight, the 81st Fighter-Interceptor Wing became the new host unit for the base. On 26th September, three weeks after taking control of the base, the wing's first aircraft arrived in the form of North American F-86A Sabres belonging to the 91st Fighter-Interceptor Squadron. The 91st FIS was assigned to the 81st Fighter-Interceptor Group, the primary operational component of the 81st FIW. The 81st's role was to assist No. 11 Group, RAF Fighter Command, with the air defence of the U.K.

On 22nd March 1952 another unit arrived to take up temporary residence at the base. This unit was the 7554th Target Tow Flight and, as the designation suggests, its role was to tow aerial targets used for gunnery practice by NATO fighter aircraft. The unit operated a number of Stinson L-5E Sentinels and Douglas TB-26C Invaders that were instantly recognisable by their high visibility 'candy-stripe' painted tail fins and horizontal stabilisers. The purpose of this colouring was to prevent attacking fighters from mistakenly shooting at the tow-aircraft instead of the target! The 7554th TTF remained at Bentwaters until 16th December 1952 when it relocated to RAF Sculthorpe. Although their stay at Bentwaters was short, the TB-26Cs and the L-5Es became a familiar sight in the skies around the base, flying several missions per day.

Hawker Tempest II MW765 and Gloster Meteor F.4 RA474 of 226 OCU seen outside Hangar 45 at Bentwaters during 1948. (photo: via Bentwaters 'Cold War' Museum archives)

In late 1952 Bentwaters became a temporary home for the Republic F-84G Thunderjets of the 79th Fighter-Bomber Squadron. The 79th's 25 F-84Gs had relocated from RAF Woodbridge whilst the construction of a weapon storage facility at that base was being carried out. The squadron moved back to Woodbridge on 1st October 1954.

After three years of Sabre operations the base was about to take on a very important change of role. This change began in October 1954 with the arrival of the first examples of the successor to the F-86As of the 91st FIS, namely the Republic F-84F Thunderstreak. The arrival of the new aircraft at Bentwaters brought about the end of the air defence duty that the F-86A had carried out since it arrived at Bentwaters, replacing it with the role of tactical nuclear strike. This change in role was formally completed in early 1955 when the 91st (redesignated a Fighter-Bomber Squadron) attained operational status with the Thunderstreak. The F-84F was a swept-wing derivative of the F-84G Thunderjet which, at the time, equipped the 79th FBS at Woodbridge. The F-84F could carry up to three times the amount of ordnance of the Thunderjet, at higher altitudes and greater speeds.

The 91st remained the only squadron at Bentwaters until 13th December 1954 when it was joined by the 87th FIS flying the all-weather interceptor version of the Sabre - the F-86D 'Sabre Dog.' The first examples of the F-86D arrived at the base eight days later, on 21st December. The 87th FIS was controlled directly from the Third Air Force headquarters for the duration of its stay at Bentwaters and not assigned to the 81st FIW.

The 87th FIS was deactivated on 8th September 1955 and its personnel and equipment were handed over to the 512th FIS. The 512th FIS, a component of the RAF Manston-based 406th Fighter-Interceptor Wing, continued flying the F-86D from Bentwaters until 24th March 1958 when it left to take up residence at Sembach AB, West Germany. Once again, the 91st FBS became the base's only resident squadron, although this time it was to be short-lived. On 30th April, the 91st was joined by the 92nd FBS, previously based at RAF Manston and also equipped with the F-84F. The arrival of this second squadron was in preparation for another change of aircraft type at the base - a type that would prove to be one of the most memorable for many people, both military and civilian alike.

Base personnel had their first experience of the new type on 7th July 1958 with the arrival of four McDonnell F-101C Voodoos from the 522nd TFS/27th TFW at Bergstrom AFB, Texas. These aircraft stopped off at Bentwaters on the return leg of a transatlantic proving flight to Bierset in Belgium. On the following day, in readiness for its conversion to the Voodoo, the 81st became a Tactical Fighter Wing and its component squadrons became Tactical Fighter Squadrons. An F-101 Mobile Training Detachment was set up in the area of the base occupied by the 92nd TFS. This training facility included an F-101 flight simulator that had been brought in from Bergstrom.

This photo was taken at Bentwaters on 8th July 1958, the day after the arrival of four visiting F-101C Voodoos from the 522nd TFS/27th TFW at Bergstrom AFB, Texas. This was the first visit of the F-101C to the U.K. The aircraft involved were 54-1491, 56-0026, 56-0027 and 56-0028. (photo: David Baker)

More changes came in July 1958. With East-West relations worsening as a result of the U.S. involvement in the Lebanon crisis, the 81st TFW became involved with Operation Blast Off. In a bid to reduce reaction times for strike aircraft getting airborne, Operation Blast Off introduced the concept of maintaining armed and fuelled aircraft, together with crews, round-the-clock, with the ability to be launched at a moments notice. By the end of 1958, Operation Blast Off was renamed to Victor Alert and by July 1959, eight purpose-built aircraft shelters had been built in a high-security area of the base in order to house the 'alert' aircraft. These shelters became known as Victor Alert 'barns.'

On Sunday 10th August 1958, a little over a month after the last visit, service personnel and civilian employees gathered at Bentwaters to witness the impressive arrival of seven 27th TFW F-101A/C Voodoos, breaking into the circuit following an upward bomb-burst. The aircraft were drawn from all four of the 27th's component squadrons - one from the 522nd TFS and two each from the 481st, 523rd and 524th TFSs. The pilots that carried out this record-breaking flight were Maj Walter Eichelberger, Maj Brian Lincoln, Maj Adrian Drew, Capt Charles Cleveland, Capt Carl Mackenzie, Capt Howard Maree and Capt Jim Ramsey. This was the culmination of an eleven-hour, 5199-mile, transatlantic flight during which they had refuelled twice from KC-135 tankers and established a distance record for formation flying. The purpose of this visit was to allow base personnel the opportunity to get acquainted with the aircraft that was soon to replace the 81st TFW's Thunderstreaks. The seven Voodoos returned to Bergstrom AFB on Friday 15th August 1958.

December 1958 saw both the 91st TFS and the 92nd TFS begin to receive deliveries of the Voodoo, with the first five examples (F-101As) arriving at the base on the 4th of that month. By the end of the year the 81st TFW had received a total of 48 Voodoos, a mixture of 'A' and 'C' variants. This number had risen to 75 by March 1959, with 25 of these being assigned to the 78th TFS at Woodbridge. During this conversion period, the majority of the surplus Thunderstreaks were transferred to the Luftwaffe. With conversion to the F-101 completed, the remaining F-84Fs were flown back to the U.S. where they were assigned to Air National Guard units. The Voodoo, or 'One-O-Wonder' as it became known, was to remain at Bentwaters for the next seven years.

The 13th June 1962 saw a brief visit of two aircraft that were to become a familiar sight at the base in future years. The visitors were a pair of U.S. Navy McDonnell Douglas F-4B Phantom IIs on loan to the USAF and given the designation F-110A. (This designation would be scrapped in favour of F-4 before the type entered USAF service). The F-110As had flown in from Ramstein AB, West Germany whilst on a European tour, the purpose of which was to allow USAFE personnel a chance see the new aircraft first-hand.

A view of the Bentwaters Contol Tower during the 1965 'Armed Forces Day.' Note the four 81st TFW Voodoos performing their display routine. (photo: via Mick Sudds)

On 4th October 1965 the first example of the McDonnell Douglas F-4C Phantom II (64-0828) for the 81st TFW touched down at Bentwaters having flown in from Shaw AFB, South Carolina via Moron AB in Spain. Further deliveries of the F-4C - the close air support and ground attack version of the Phantom - arrived in quick succession and the wing's full complement was reached by 26th April 1966. The 81st TFW's last five Voodoos left Woodbridge on 3rd January 1966, bound for the U.S. where they were to be given a new lease of life, along with most of the other ex-81st machines, as RF-101Gs and RF-101Hs operating in the photo reconnaissance role.

After eight years of flying the F-4C, August 1973 saw the type begin to get phased out in favour of the superior F-4D version of the Phantom. The 'D' was virtually identical in appearance to the earlier 'C,' with most of the modifications being confined to an updated avionics suite. The changeover was complete by October when both the 91st TFS and the 92nd TFS had re-equipped with the F-4D. The surplus F-4Cs were either reassigned to the 401st TFW at Torrejon AB, Spain or transferred to the Spanish Air Force. By January 1974 Bentwaters was home to around 50 F-4Ds.

On 18th February 1978 the now customary visit by a future Bentwaters aircraft type occurred when four Fairchild Republic A-10A Thunderbolt IIs from the 57th Tactical Training Wing at Nellis AFB, Nevada, arrived at the base. The A-10s (75-0258/WA, 75-0261/WA, 75-0262/WA & 75-0297/WA) were en route back to the U.S. having participated in 'Coronet Jay,' an exercise in West Germany to test the suitability of the Maverick missile for the anti-tank role. The visit enabled base personnel and the press to get a taste of what was to come in the near future. It also enabled local residents to witness how much quieter this aircraft was compared to its predecessors. The four A-10s departed for home on the 23rd February. This visit was not, however, the first time an A-10 had landed at Bentwaters. During the previous year (on 8th September 1977), two 355th TFW A-10s (75-0287/DM, 75-0290/DM) from Davis Monthan AFB, Arizona, stopped off briefly whilst returning to the U.S. from Sembach AB, Germany. The pair were amongst six of the type that had taken part in exercise 'Coronet Bantam.'

Another A-10 (75-0296/WA) visited Bentwaters on 19th June 1978 having flown direct from Loring AFB, Texas. The purpose of this visit was to test out systems at the base prior to the arrival of the first of the 81st TFW's own 'Warthogs.' The aircraft returned to the U.S. on 24th June.

Republic F-84Fs pictured at Bentwaters during the winter of 1954/1955, shortly after delivery to the 81st FBW. Some of the Thunderstreaks are carrying what are believed to be ferry numbers on the fin. The 81st's F-84Fs were delivered via two routes. Some of the aircraft were flown across the Atlantic by ferry crews to Lisbon, Portugal, a journey that required in-flight refuelling en route. From here the F-84Fs were handed over to 81st crews who then flew the final leg of the delivery flight to either Bentwaters or Shepherds Grove. The remaining aircraft were transported from the U.S. via ship to Sydenham, Northern Ireland. Once off-loaded, they were flown by 81st crews to their respective bases. (photo: George Pennick)

512th FIS F-86D-50-NA (52-10035) photographed at Bentwaters circa 1958.
(photo: late Peter Hutting (USAF retd) via George Pennick)

F-84F of the 91st FBS/81st TFW makes a spectacular 'Jet-Assisted Take-Off' (JATO) departure from Bentwaters, circa 1955. Of note in this photo is the rarely seen nuclear training 'shape' on the inboard port wing pylon.
(photo: Harry Eckes)

Pictured at Bentwaters in May 1965 are three T-33As of the 81st TFW. Nearest the camera is 57-0691 with 53-5819 behind and 53-5137 in the background. (photo: Mick Sudds)

In early 1978 major construction work began which would provide Hardened Aircraft Shelters and other facilities deemed necessary for the base's future role. The project was dogged by problems with British workers going on strike in July 1978 over a pay dispute and, as a consequence, a deep political argument was started between the Ministry of Defence and the Trade Unions. This dispute was not confined to Bentwaters; it also included the bases at Woodbridge, Lakenheath and Alconbury. The contract for erecting the steel reinforcing for the HASs had been awarded by NATO to an Italian firm, Costruzioni Cimolai Armando S.p.A., who in turn had sub-contracted the hiring of labour to Carter Horsley, a British company. The protest strike led to the sacking of 50 workers resulting in picket lines being set up at the entrances to the four bases. The situation worsened when Italian labour was drafted in to complete the work sparking off several confrontations between the pickets and the foreign workers. In early October a settlement was finally reached, the Italian workers left, the sacked British workers were reinstated and a new pay deal was struck. Construction work recommenced after a delay of 3 months.

On 24th August 1978 the first three 81st TFW A-10s (77-0192/WR, 77-0193/WR & 77-0194/WR) were delivered to Bentwaters to allow maintenance training to begin prior to the main batch of deliveries arriving. The next four aircraft (77-0227/WR, 77-0230/WR, 77-0232/WR & 77-0233/WR) arrived three months later, on 8th December.

At approximately 14:00 hours on 25th January 1979 the first main batch of fourteen A-10s arrived at a snow-covered Bentwaters after a five-and-a-half hour flight from the Azores. The lead aircraft was flown by the 81st TFW's commander, Col Rudolph F. Wacker, and after their arrival the aircraft were handed over to Commander Allied Forces in Central Europe, Col John Pauly. This event marked the activation of the 92nd TFS as the first operational A-10 squadron in Europe.

Following conversion to the A-10 the base gained three more squadrons, the 509th, 510th and 511th Tactical Fighter Squadrons but lost the 91st TFS when it moved to Woodbridge to operate the new type alongside the already-resident 78th TFS.

Bentwaters and the 81st TFW very nearly didn't receive the A-10. In late 1976 the 36th TFW at Bitburg AB, Germany, were busy preparing to replace its F-4E Phantoms with the McDonnell Douglas F-15A/B Eagle. In December of that year, personnel associated with the F-4E squadrons were told that they would be transferring to Bentwaters, commencing in January 1977. The 36th TFWs surplus F-4Es were destined to replace the 81st TFWs F-4Ds. Personnel and their families spent that Christmas in transient quarters with all their belongings packed and en route to Bentwaters. By January, as a concession resulting from arms reduction talks with the Soviet Union, the transfer was cancelled. Bitburg's F-4Es were to remain in Germany, being split between the 86th TFW at Ramstein AB and the 50th TFW at Hahn AB.

The 15th April 1988 saw the base lose one of its squadrons when the 509th TFS was transferred to the 10th TFW at RAF Alconbury. This was followed eleven weeks later, on 1st July 1988, by the loss of a second squadron when the 511th TFS was also transferred to the 10th TFW. This left Bentwaters with only two remaining A-10 squadrons, the 92nd TFS and the 510th TFS.

In between the departure of the 509th TFS and the 511th TFS, the base gained another squadron when the 527th Aggressor Squadron arrived after transferring from the 10th TFW. The first two of an intended complement of eighteen General Dynamics F-16C Fighting Falcons arrived at Bentwaters on 14th June 1988. The complement had reached twelve on the 16th January 1989 when one F-16C was delivered from Spangdahlem AB, Germany.

Unfortunately the sight of these F-16Cs at Bentwaters was short-lived and, in November 1989, the 527th AS began disposing of its aircraft in preparation for deactivation, having never reached its full complement. The first two F-16Cs to leave were flown to Spangdahlem AB on the 29th November 1989. The 527th AS had reassigned its entire fleet of 12 aircraft by early 1990 and deactivated later that year.

In July 1989 the U.S. Secretary of State for Defence, George Younger, gave official confirmation of a plan to base the General Dynamics F-111G in the U.K. and identified Bentwaters as a possible location. The F-111G was a modified FB-111A - the strategic bomber version of the F-111 - and the conversion program had only just commenced at the time. It was very soon apparent that certain elements of the USAF were not happy with the proposal although both the U.S. and U.K. governments were very keen for it to go ahead. The plan was destined never to take place as the F-111Gs remained stateside and were delivered to the 27th TFW at Cannon AFB, New Mexico.

Some twelve months later Bentwaters was short-listed as a possible base for the McDonnell Douglas F-15E Strike Eagle. Again Bentwaters lost out, possibly due to protests around the base by certain factions such as CND and some 'local' pressure groups. The F-15E ended up being based at RAF Lakenheath and this decision was almost certainly the final nail in Bentwaters' coffin. Had this decision turned out in favour of Bentwaters it would undoubtedly have secured the base's future, possibly at the expense of Lakenheath. It is ironic to note that, on 15th February 1992, the first F-15E to be delivered to Lakenheath from the U.S. actually landed at Bentwaters prior to making the short trip to its new home!

Flying operations from Bentwaters finally came to an end on 23rd March 1993 when the last two A-10s departed for their new home at Spangdahlem AB in Germany. The aircraft were flown by Col Roger R. Radcliff, the 81st TFW Commander and his Deputy Commander for Operations (DCO), Col Wally Berg. The base was opened to the public to enable local residents to witness this historical and emotional event.

Bentwaters was formally closed on 1st July 1993 after the deactivation of the 81st TFW. This ended the American presence at the base, which had lasted just over 42 years.

On the morning of Monday 19th September 1994 the sound of jet engines could once again be heard around Bentwaters as the first wave of Harrier GR.7s approached Runway 25 for the start of the two-week 'Hazel Flute' deployment.

Prior to the first aircraft arriving, Bentwaters was a hive of activity with the Royal Engineers and RAF personnel preparing the derelict base for flying operations. This involved bringing in supplies, such as fuel and water, by road and setting up mobile generators to supply electricity. Accommodation for the many service personnel was in the form of tents, some of which were actually set up outside the perimeter fence in woodland near Friday Street, south-west of the base. There were around 1000 personnel involved in Hazel Flute under the command of RAF Laarbruch's station commander, Group Captain Peter Harris. The majority of these personnel came from 3(F) and 4(F) Squadrons at RAF Laarbruch with the rest coming from 1(F) Squadron at RAF Wittering.

Harrier GR.7 (ZD470/01) of 1(F) Sqn, RAF Wittering, pictured at Bentwaters during Hazel Flute 94. (photo: Author)

A mobile air traffic control centre was set up on the grass near the centre of the main runway. In addition to VHF/UHF communications, the ATCC was equipped with a TACAN (TACtical Air Navigation) beacon and a Plessey Watchman mobile airfield surveillance radar. The radar had been flight-checked by a BAe Andover E3A from 115 Squadron at RAF Benson during the week leading up to the deployment. This was to ensure that the system had been set up correctly and provided the coverage required to conduct air operations safely. Although this air traffic control centre was used throughout the exercise, the immediate zone around Bentwaters remained under the control of Wattisham Airfield due to Army Air Corps helicopter operations at RAF Woodbridge.

About 22 Harrier GR.7s were involved in Hazel Flute with eight coming from 1(F) Squadron, six from 3(F) Squadron and another eight from 4(F) Squadron. At various times during the two-week deployment Harriers from 20(R) Squadron (the Harrier Operational Conversion Unit) at RAF Wittering made visits to the base.

Not only was this the first time all three front-line Harrier squadrons had trained together it was also the first time for four years that the UK had hosted a mobile deployment on such a large scale. The aim of Hazel Flute was to enable the Royal Air Force Harrier wing to prepare for their new role as part of NATO's Reaction Forces (Air) from 1995.

Bentwaters provided the Harrier wing with an ideal variety of dispersal options, with 1(F) and 3(F) Squadrons setting up individual rural hides within the trees to the south of the base and 4 (F) Squadron opting for an urban operation amongst the Hardened Aircraft Shelters to the east (Wantisden) side .The main logistics area, manned by RAF personnel and Royal Engineers, was located near the redundant weapons storage facility.

Takeoffs were restricted to the eastern half of the 3000 metre main runway in an attempt to reduce noise and fuel consumption. Two options for landing were available to the Harrier pilots on their return to Bentwaters after the day's sorties. Approaches could be made to the main runway or direct to the hides, each squadron site having its own landing pad in place for vertical recoveries. Hazel Flute was conducted in two parts, the first week saw normal Harrier sorties carried out and the second week saw a build up to a full-scale war scenario. During the two-week period the base was also subjected to mock airfield attacks by Sepecat Jaguars from RAF Coltishall.

Although the Harrier GR.7 is capable of night operations, these were not conducted during the exercise in an attempt to reduce the noise impact to local residents. All operations were conducted between 6 o'clock in the morning and 6 o'clock in the evening, with air-to-air sorties being flown on the morning of Saturday 24th September.

The theory that this deployment was to determine the suitability of Bentwaters for the location of the Harrier wing after withdrawal from Germany was unfounded. When RAF Laarbruch was eventually closed in 1999, 3(F) and 4(F) Squadrons were transferred to their new home at RAF Cottesmore along with 1(F) Squadron from RAF Wittering to form part of Joint Force Harrier - a combined Royal Air Force Harrier and Royal Navy Sea Harrier rapid reaction force.

Following several years that saw an uncertain future for the base, Bentwaters is now owned by the Kemball family who operate their Bentwaters Parks business from the site. The bsase will still hold an interest for aviation enthusiasts with the planned opening of the Bentwaters 'Cold War' Museum within the next few years. The bulk of the base infrastructure remains and the runway does see occasional use from light aircraft and warbirds. All in all the future of Bentwaters looks secure, with the base likely to become a future attraction for those with an interest in 'Cold War' history.

An early-morning photo showing two of the many rural hides that were set up in the dispersal areas to the south of the base. (photo: Author)

2. Chapter 2 – Woodbridge History

During 1941 the Air Ministry identified the requirement for a number of emergency runways on the east coast of England after RAF Wittering began to be used for this purpose. The 4500 yard grassed runway at the Cambridgeshire airfield soon became blocked by damaged aircraft that had made emergency landings. This severely hampered the station's normal flying operations and consequently its contribution to the war effort. On the 5th August 1942 a meeting at the Air Ministry in London decided that three emergency runways would be built at Woodbridge in Suffolk, Carnaby in Yorkshire and Manston in Kent.

The site chosen for RAF Woodbridge, or RAF Sutton Heath as it was originally named, was in the middle of Tangham and Rendlesham Forests. The locality was ideal for an airfield, being sparsely populated with a clear, unobstructed approach from both the east and the west and, more importantly, fog did not appear to be a big problem in the area. There was one major obstacle that did need to be overcome however, over one million trees needed to be felled and cleared away before construction could begin. This was met with protests by local residents who were unhappy with the prospect of such a large plantation being destroyed. Nevertheless the felling and clearing was carried out and construction of the massive 3000-yard long, 250-yard wide and 160-acre concrete runway began. In addition to the concrete runway, provision was made for two grassed areas at either end of the runway, each 500 yards long, to deal with the possibility of an aircraft under- or overshooting.

The main runway was to be split into three lanes for emergency landings. The north lane was to be illuminated by yellow lights and the centre lane by white lights. These two lanes could only be used by aircraft under the direction of Flying Control. The south lane, illuminated by green lights, was to be designated as the emergency lane. Aircraft could use this lane without having prior contact with Flying Control.

It was estimated that the construction work would be completed by October 1942 although this was soon considered far to ambitious and was revised to January 1943. The airfield was actually completed ten months later and officially opened in November 1943 although by this time several emergency landings had already been carried out, the first of these was on 18th July 1943.

Within two weeks of its 'official' opening a further 54 emergency landings had been made, around 20 of these were due to bad weather conditions over the home airfields. On the night of 16/17th December 1943 a tragic series of events unfolded which was to result in a dramatic change in the way that Woodbridge operated as an emergency airfield. The incident involved several Halifaxes of Tempsford-based Nos. 138 and 161 Squadrons which had been forced to abort a mission over France due to low cloud over their target areas. Apart from one Halifax which made it safely back to its home airfield, the remaining aircraft attempted to recover to Woodbridge, which was itself the victim of fog and low cloud. Only one of the bombers made a safe landing, the others were less fortunate. One struck a pylon after failing to find the runway killing three of the crew and injuring three others; another crashed into trees near the airfield, again after failing to locate the runway; another crashed into the river Deben with the loss of one of its crew and two ditched into the sea off Ipswich. The remaining Halifax crashed into the sea off the Lincolnshire coast. The net outcome of this night of tragedy was that the visibility of the runway needed to be improved in bad weather and this was achieved by the installation of 'Fog Investigation and Dispersal Operation' otherwise known as FIDO.

A typical FIDO installation comprised of pipelines running either side and each end of the runway into which petrol was injected under pressure. The petrol was ejected through small holes in the pipe and then ignited by burners fitted at certain intervals along its length. The resultant fire produced heat so intense that it literally burned the fog away from the vicinity of the runway. Woodbridge was one of fifteen airfields in England to be equipped with FIDO.

It may appear strange that a FIDO installation was needed at Woodbridge; after all the main reason for locating an emergency airfield there in the first place was because fog was not deemed to be a problem. Nevertheless the FIDO installation commenced in early January 1944 and was to take about five months to complete. This would turn out to be the biggest FIDO project ever carried out by the Air Ministry. Four 350,000-gallon fuel tanks were built on the northeast side of the runway to house the vast quantity of petrol that FIDO would consume. To avoid the problem of large convoys of fuel bowsers causing congestion on the narrow roads around the airfield, a 4-mile long underground pipeline was installed which ran initially to existing railway sidings at Dock Lane, Melton.

The existing sidings were used as a temporary measure until 6th May when construction of a purpose-built railway siding, also at Dock Lane, was completed. Storage tanks, far smaller than those at Woodbridge itself, were built at the new railway siding and the petrol would be pumped from here to the airfield tanks. Once the new siding was in use it was anticipated that one trainload of petrol would be delivered per day until 25th May, by which time all of the installation tanks would be at full capacity.

Initial testing of the fuel system and burner units began on 17th April, the day after the first trainload of petrol was pumped from the temporary sidings to the airfield tanks. Final testing of the entire installation was completed by 29th April, the same day that another 800 tons of petrol was brought into the sidings. After completion of the final tests the system could be made operational for a limited period of time if required, although it wasn't declared fully operational until the end of May.

FIDO was used operationally for the first time at Woodbridge on 23rd June 1944 when a Lancaster from No. 7 Squadron at Oakington was forced to land at the base having been badly damaged by Luftwaffe night-fighters. The bomber, piloted by Flt Lt Brian Frow, was returning from a raid on V1 installations near Pas de Calais, France.

In early July 1944 a unit of USAAF B-17 Flying Fortresses arrived from Knettishall, near Thetford, to take up temporary residence at Woodbridge. The aircraft belonged to 562 Squadron of the 388th Bombardment Group. These were by no means 'ordinary' B-17s; they were specially modified examples that were to be used for 'Operation Aphrodite' missions. This operation, personally authorised by General Doolittle, was an American attempt to eliminate the threat of Germany's V-1 'Doodle Bug' and V-2 rockets, which were being launched at targets in the United Kingdom. Operation Aphrodite involved the use of war-weary B-17s as 'robots', stripped of their defensive armament, packed with 10 tons of explosives and steered via radio control by another B-17 acting as a 'mother' ship. The robot was effectively a guided missile and was to be used against the V-1 and V-2 launch sites in Northern France. The robot would be flown by a crew of two for takeoff and the initial stages of the mission but, after setting a course for the target area and arming the explosives, they would bail out leaving the mother ship in control. On the 10th July, Mr Duncan Sandys, the Joint Parliamentary Secretary to the Ministry of Supply and Chairman of the Committee for Countermeasures Against Pilotless Aircraft, visited Woodbridge for a progress report on the squadron's preparations.

On the 12th July 1944 crews were briefed for the first Aphrodite mission but this was aborted at the last minute due to heavy rain and low cloud. No Aphrodite mission was ever to be flown from Woodbridge because, after this first aborted attempt, the unit moved up to Fersfield, near Diss in Norfolk. The first mission was launched from Fersfield on Friday 4th August 1944 and involved two robots and two mothers. One of the robots got in to difficulty as it passed overhead Woodbridge town and eventually crashed into Wattling Wood just outside the village of Sudbourne with an explosion that is claimed to be the largest ever known in England. The flight engineer TSgt Elmer Most bailed out and landed in the grounds of Chillesford church but the pilot, 1st Lt John W. Fisher Jnr., went down with the stricken aircraft and was never found. Some of the later Aphrodite missions met with a similar fate but, although some robots did make it across the North Sea, none ever hit their intended targets. The U.S. Navy also contributed a small number of aircraft and crews to a similar operation alongside the USAAF at Fersfield. Known as 'Project Anvil' by the Navy, the operation utilised Consolidated B-24 Liberators instead of B-17s. Perhaps the most famous failure of this type of mission occurred at 18:20 on Saturday 12th August 1944 when a Project Anvil B-24 exploded in mid-air south of Blythburgh, killing Lt Wilford Willy and Lt Joseph P. Kennedy Jr., the brother of the future president of the United States. Operation Aphrodite was eventually cancelled on 20th January 1945 after another failed mission.

On 13th July 1944 a Luftwaffe Junkers Ju 88G-1 night-fighter from Volkel in Holland was an unexpected but extremely welcome visitor to Woodbridge. The crew had become disorientated after failure of their navigational equipment and were convinced that they had landed at an airfield near the Danish and German border. This aircraft was of great interest to the RAF because, as well as being completely intact, it was fitted with the latest Lichtenstein SN-2 interceptor radar and Flensburg and Naxos radar detectors. Within a matter of days the Royal Aircraft Establishment had developed countermeasures for these pieces of equipment. This single mistake provided the RAF and its Allies with examples of some of Germany's most closely guarded secrets.

From 19th to 24th March 1945 the airfield took on a new role. Woodbridge was temporarily closed for emergency landings due to its involvement in the build-up for Operation Varsity - the airborne support for the U.S. Ninth and British Second Armies crossing of the Rhine. The enormous air armada consisted of more than 1,500 USAAF aircraft and gliders and 1,200 RAF aircraft and gliders. Fighter cover was provided by 880 aircraft from both the USAAF and RAF. The size of this operation can only be appreciated when you consider that there was a time-span of two-and-a-half hours covering the first and last aircraft. 60 Halifax tow aircraft from Nos. 298 and 644 Squadrons and 60 gliders (48 Hamilcars and 12 Horsas), containing troops, tanks and other armoured vehicles, departed from Woodbridge at 06:00 on 24th March, all were airborne within 40 minutes. Although Operation Varsity was deemed a success there were substantial Allied casualties.

The last three months of the war saw 230 aircraft use the airfield for emergency landings but, by the end of July 1945, the number of landings had dramatically reduced. By the end of the war a total of 4200 Allied aircraft had made emergency landings at Woodbridge with a far greater number of aircrews lives saved.

The RAF continued to use Woodbridge after the war, mainly for experimental work. One of the units resident at the base was the Blind Landing Experimental Unit. Equipped with Avro Lancasters, the BLEU carried out the groundwork for the development of what we know today as the Instrument Landing System (ILS). Another Lancaster-equipped unit was tasked with development work for the 'Grand Slam' bomb. During the course of this work several of the 26ft long, 22,000lb bombs were dropped on nearby Orford Ness. The RAF had ceased using Woodbridge by March 1948, at which time the base was considered surplus to requirements and placed under 'Care and Maintenance.'

On 1st June 1952 the airfield received a new lease of life as the USAF's 79th Fighter-Bomber Squadron moved in, although it wasn't until the 6th June that the first of its Republic F-84G Thunderjets arrived direct from Langley AFB, Virginia. The 79th FBS was assigned to the 20th Fighter-Bomber Group (FBG), the primary operational component of the 20th Fighter-Bomber Wing (FBW), headquartered at RAF Wethersfield in Essex. Initially the squadron received logistical support from the 81st FBW at RAF Bentwaters but, in September 1952, logistical support was handed back to the 20th FBW. Not long after arriving at Woodbridge, the 79th FBS temporarily relocated to Bentwaters whilst construction work on a suitable weapon storage facility was completed. The squadron moved back to Woodbridge on 1st October 1954.

On 8th February 1955, major restructuring saw the removal of operational groups within the USAF, after which the 79th FBS found itself reporting directly to the 20th FBW. During the autumn of 1955 the 79th converted to the swept-wing Republic F-84F Thunderstreak.

During June 1957, after nearly two years of operating the Thunderstreak, the 79th FBS began transitioning to the North American F-100D/F Super Sabre and, on 8th July 1958, the 79th FBS was renamed the 79th Tactical Fighter Squadron (TFS) when its parent wing, the 20th FBW, became the 20th Tactical Fighter Wing (TFW). On the same day, the 20th TFW handed over control of Woodbridge to the 81st TFW. Even though its parent unit no longer controlled Woodbridge, the 79th TFS were destined to remain at the base for another twelve years.

Although the 81st TFW took over operational control of Woodbridge on 8th July 1958, it wasn't until 22nd December 1958 that its first aircraft arrived. These were Republic F-84F Thunderstreaks belonging to the 78th TFS, which had relocated from RAF Shepherds Grove in preparation for the arrival of their new mount, the McDonnell F-101A/C Voodoo. By March 1959 the 78th TFS had received 25 Voodoos.

Republic F-84F-40-RE Thunderstreak (52-6539), of the 79th FBS/20th FBW. (photo: Ashley Annis)

Monday 29th December 1958 witnessed a tragic accident involving a 79th TFS F-100D. The F-100D involved (56-2985), was being flown by Lt Charles Prescott and was one of a pair undertaking a routine training sortie. The pilot of the other Super Sabre, and leader of the mission was Lt Guary Walker. The 09:53 takeoff from Runway 27 was uneventful but 2 minutes into the flight Lt Walker noticed that the rear of Lt Prescott's aircraft was engulfed in flames. After realising there was no chance of recovering to Woodbridge, Lt Prescott ejected from the stricken aircraft. The blazing aircraft went into a dive and struck the Falcon Caravans dealership in Kesgrave, on the outskirts of Ipswich, killing a female office worker. The resulting explosion levelled the garage destroying a dozen caravans in the process. An adjacent bungalow was also destroyed in the incident and several other properties were damaged. Lt Prescott witnessed the events unfolding below him as he descended by parachute, eventually landing two miles away in the village of Martlesham. He was found suffering from shock; his only injury was a cut on the face.

In July 1961 the 79th TFS hosted the first ever NATO 'Tiger Meet' at RAF Woodbridge. This event brought together NATO squadrons that had a Tiger depicted in their unit badge and was seen as a means of providing an opportunity to further relationships between the participating air forces. The other units involved in this first meeting were No.74 Squadron, RAF, who made the short trip from Coltishall and EC1/12 of France's Armee de l'Air. This first meeting was so successful that the 79th TFS decided to host it again, the following year. This time eight squadrons representing six NATO countries attended and from that day on the NATO Tiger Meet has become an annual event with each Tiger Squadron taking its turn to be the host unit. RAF Woodbridge saw its last Tiger Meet in 1969.

RAF Woodbridge witnessed the arrival of another aircraft type during the autumn of 1965. This was the Kaman HH-43B Huskie helicopter operated by a detachment (Det.12) of the 40th Aerospace Rescue and Recovery Wing (ARRW). The base received a pair of these small but noisy helicopters for short range fire fighting and rescue duties and they remained at Woodbridge until October 1972 when they were withdrawn from use. By the time of their withdrawal both Huskies had been converted to HH-43F standard but had still proved inadequate for their main role of air-sea rescue due to their size. Both of Woodbridge's examples were eventually sent to a scrap yard at Snailwell, north of Newmarket.

67th ARRS HC-130N Hercules (69-5825) and two HH-53C Super Jolly Green Giants demonstrate the technique of in-flight refuelling during an 'Armed Forces Day' at Bentwaters. (photo: Author)

The final months of 1965 saw the 78th TFS begin conversion to the McDonnell Douglas F-4C Phantom II. The first aircraft to arrive was flown direct from Tucson, Arizona by Lt Col Robert R. Fredette, squadron commander of the 78th. The last five Voodoos left Woodbridge on 3rd January 1966, bound for the U.S. where they were destined to be converted to photo-reconnaissance RF-101Gs and RF-101Hs along with the majority of the other ex-81st machines. The departure of these five Voodoos was significant as, not only were they the last of the 78th TFS's aircraft, they were also the very last of the 81st TFW's F-101s to leave the 'Twin Bases.'

On 23rd April 1969, after three years of operating the F-4C, the 78th TFS began exchanging the type for the more advanced F-4D version of the Phantom (the first of the 81st TFW's squadrons to do so). The F-4Ds had been acquired from the Hahn-based 50th TFW when that unit upgraded to the F-4E. The 78th's F-4Cs were transferred to the Ejercito del Aire (Spanish Air Force) where they were assigned to Ala 12 (12 Wing) at Torrejon AB.

In December 1969 Woodbridge gained another squadron when the 67th ARRS arrived, equipped with the Lockheed C-130 Hercules and the Sikorsky HH-3E Jolly Green Giant. The 67th ARRS flew three versions of the Hercules, namely the HC-130H, HC-130N and the HC-130P. As well as its general rescue role, the 67th ARRS also operated with the U.S. Special Forces on clandestine missions, and provided specialist rescue cover for NASA's space missions.

On 15th January 1970 the 79th TFS relocated to RAF Upper Heyford and converted to the General Dynamics F-111E, becoming the first squadron to be operational with the new aircraft in Europe.

On 6th November 1971 the 67th ARRS commenced replacement of its HH-3Es when the first two examples of the bigger, more powerful Sikorsky HH-53C Super Jolly Green Giant arrived at the base.

In 1978 the 78th TFS received its first Fairchild Republic A-10A Thunderbolt IIs to replace the venerable Phantom. At the same time the 91st TFS relocated to Woodbridge from Bentwaters after it had completed the transition from F-4 to A-10.

It is perhaps fairly sad that, despite all of the history associated with the base, RAF Woodbridge is probably best remembered for a series of events that started in the early hours of Friday 26th December 1980. It all began when a Security Police patrol at the East Gate spotted some strange lights in Rendlesham Forest. The sighting of these lights heralded the start of a series of incidents involving a UFO that occurred over two nights. This alleged 'close encounter' has evolved into one of the most documented and controversial UFO mysteries ever, only being surpassed by the famous 'Roswell incident.' I have no intention of writing in detail about this event as there are plenty of publications available that tell the story (albeit different versions!). As the 25th anniversary of this event approaches, it is still not known whether this UFO was of 'alien' or U.S. military origin but one thing is certain, something did happen in Rendlesham Forest during those two nights. There were many reliable civilian witnesses to the events, as well as military ones, and as such the UFO encounter must be mentioned in any work documenting the history of the base.

On 3rd June 1988, after a major restructuring of the USAF which saw the Aerospace Rescue and Recovery Service merge with the Special Operations Forces, the 67th ARRS was reassigned to become the 67th Special Operations Squadron (SOS). During this process the 67th lost its fleet of Super Jolly Green Giants and these were assigned to a new squadron which was activated on the same day at Woodbridge, this being the 21st SOS.

On 23rd October 1988, the 21st SOS received the first of six Sikorsky MH-53J Pave Low IIIEs to replace its HH-53s. This was airlifted into Woodbridge on board a Lockheed C-5A Galaxy. Further deliveries of the MH-53J were received on 3rd December.

1992 witnessed the beginning of the USAF withdrawal from Woodbridge. On 5th January, as part of the 'Mission Completion' programme, the first eight 78th TFS A-10s left the base bound for the U.S. On 15th May, with the 78th TFS withdrawal completed, the squadron was deactivated.

Special operations forces located in Europe were the subject of a major reorganisation during 1992 which was to have a significant effect on Woodbridge. On 15th January, the 67th and 21st SOS's parent unit, the 39th Special Operations Wing, moved its headquarters from Rhein-Main AB, Germany to RAF Alconbury. As a consequence of this move, both squadrons left Woodbridge on 20th May, to take up residence at Alconbury.

The one remaining squadron, the 91st TFS, had completed its withdrawal by August and was officially deactivated on the 14th of that month. This move was a significant and historic event by virtue of the fact that it ended the 40-year USAF presence at the base.

Unlike Bentwaters, Woodbridge remains in use today as a training base for 3 and 4 Regiment of the Army Air Corps, based at Wattisham Airfield. Although less glamorous but, it has to be said, no less important than the USAF aircraft that preceded them, the AAC helicopters are now a regular sight and sound over the base and surrounding villages, day and night. The AAC currently operate two types of helicopter from Wattisham, these being the Westland Lynx AH.7 and the Westland Gazelle AH.1. During 2000 the AAC received its first examples of an updated version of the Boeing AH-64 Apache, the Westland-built WAH-64D Apache Longbow. The type will be known in AAC service as the Apache AH.1. 3 Regiment are due to commence conversion to the Apache AH.1 in March 2005 with both 3 and 4 Regiments completing conversion in September 2007. The type should therefore become a common and fairly formidable sight around Woodbridge in future years.

In addition to helicopter training, Woodbridge is also due to become home to 23 Engineer Regiment (Air Assault), in 2007. The base is currently undergoing major construction work with many of the existing buildings being demolished to make way for new ones. By the time the construction work is finished, Woodbridge will be virtually unrecognisable to those people who once lived, worked or just visited the base during the USAF years. A sad fact but one that we will all have to get used to.

Aerial photo of RAF Woodbridge taken in 1975. Note the C-130s and F-4s parked at their dispersals and the C-141 on the taxiway. (U.S. Air Force photo)

Woodbridge-based Kaman HH-43B Huskie (62-4521) from Det. 12 of the 40th ARRW, pictured at RAF Thorney Island in June 1969. (photo: Mick Sudds)

Suitably dressed Lockheed CF-104 Starfighter (12883) of 439 Sqn, Canadian Armed Forces seen during the 1969 Tiger Meet at Woodbridge. (photo: George Pennick)

Busy scene at the Runway 27 'end of runway' (EOR) checkpoint with a locally based 91st TFS A-10 alongside three 4450th Tactical Group (TG) A-7D Corsairs. Based at Nellis AFB, Nevada, the 4450th TG deployed to Woodbridge on two occasions - 31st October to 14th November 1984 and 8th to 22nd May 1986. This photo was taken during the latter deployment. There has always been a veil of secrecy surrounding these deployments with many believing that they were linked to a 'black' project (or more precisely, avionics development trials for the Lockheed F-117A Stealth Fighter). (photo: Erroll Frost)

3. Unit Histories

81st Tactical Fighter Wing

Established in 1948, the 81st Tactical Fighter Wing's distinguished history dates back to World War II, when the 81st Pursuit Group (Interceptor) was activated in February 1942 at Morris Field, North Carolina. In May 1942, the unit was redesignated as the 81st Fighter Group and received the Bell P-39 Airacobra. Later that year, the group's ground echelon arrived in French Morocco with the force that invaded North Africa on 8th November 1942. Its air echelon, which had trained in England, arrived in North Africa in December 1942 and, under the Twelfth Air Force, supported Allied ground operations against the Axis forces in Tunisia. After this the 81st patrolled the coast of Africa and protected Allied shipping in the Mediterranean Sea. The group also provided cover for ship convoys that landed troops on the islands of Pantelleria and Sicily and at Anzio, Italy.

In February 1944, the 81st transferred to India and began conversion training with the Curtiss P-40 Warhawk and Republic P-47 Thunderbolt. The group moved to China in May and became part of the Fourteenth Air Force. The 81st continued training, but in January 1945, it returned to combat duty. The group's aircraft attacked enemy airfields and installations and aided Chinese ground forces by attacking Japanese troop concentrations, ammunition dumps, communication lines, and other strategic targets. The 81st FG was inactivated in China on 27th December 1945.

The 81st Fighter Group was reactivated on 15th October 1946 at Wheeler Field, Hawaii, and equipped with North American P-51 Mustangs. On 1st May 1948, the 81st Fighter Wing was also activated at Wheeler Field, and the 81st Fighter Group became its primary operational component. Although the wing's Mustang fighters were replaced with P-47N Thunderbolt aircraft, the 81st continued to defend Hawaiian airspace until mid 1949. In June of that year, the 81st moved to Kirtland AFB at Albuquerque, New Mexico, where it began flying the Lockheed F-80C Shooting Star jet fighter. On 20th January 1950, the wing was redesignated the 81st Fighter-Interceptor Wing and re-equipped with the North American F-86A Sabre. Having converted to the F-86A, the wing moved to Moses Lake (later Larson) AFB, Washington, a few months later. Upon arrival, the 81st was assigned to the Western Air Defense Force and given the new mission of air defence of the Pacific Northwest.

On 5th September 1951 the 81st FIW, together with its component groups and fifty F-86As, arrived in the U.K. For the men and women of the 81st (except the pilots ferrying the aircraft), this was the end of an eight-day voyage across the Atlantic on board the USS General Maurice Rose – a voyage that began from Staten Island, New York on 29th August. On arrival in the U.K., the wing was split between two bases, RAF Bentwaters, which was selected as the wing's headquarters, and RAF Shepherds Grove, both in Suffolk. The 81st's primary operational component at this time was the 81st Fighter-Interceptor Group. As part of the Third Air Force under the command of United States Air Forces in Europe, the 81st became the first F-86 Sabre unit in Europe. Its role was to assist No.11 Group, RAF Fighter Command, with the air defence of the U.K. and to support offensive air operations against Warsaw Pact forces. The squadrons assigned to the wing were the 91st FIS (Bentwaters), 92nd FIS and 116th FIS (Shepherds Grove).

The 116th FIS arrived in the U.K. ahead of the rest of the wing, having left Moses Lake AFB on 15th August

1951. The unit's twenty-five F-86's routed via Goose Bay, Bluie West One in Greenland, Iceland and Stornoway, eventually settling in at Shepherds Grove on 27th August. Their arrival at Shepherds Grove was later than had been anticipated due to bad weather en route. The 92nd FIS arrived at Shepherds Grove on 5th September and the 91st FIS arrived at Bentwaters via Shepherds Grove on 26th September. The 116th FIS was a U.S. Air National Guard unit that had been recalled to active service, but its assignment to the 81st FIG was to be fairly short-lived. The unit was deactivated 15 months later, on 1st November 1952, coinciding with the activation of the 78th FIS, which acquired personnel and equipment from the 116th.

The 18th March 1953 saw the 92nd FIS embark on a three-week deployment to Fürstenfeldbruck in Germany. This deployment of twelve F-86As came in the aftermath of the shooting down of a USAF F-84 by Czech Air Force fighters. The 92nd FIS were tasked with policing the border between East and West Germany, intercepting any hostile aircraft that ventured too close. The remaining 81st FIG squadrons also deployed to Fürstenfeldbruck in rotation. The 92nd FIS were replaced by the 91st, who in turn were replaced by the 78th. At the end of this deployment, no hostile aircraft had been encountered by any of the wing's Sabres.

The next reassignment occurred on 1st April 1954 when the 81st FIW became the 81st Fighter-Bomber Wing to reflect its future nuclear strike capability and 'Cold War' mission. The wing's primary operational group followed suit by becoming the 81st Fighter-Bomber Group and the component squadrons became Fighter-Bomber Squadrons. This reassignment was in preparation for the imminent arrival of a new aircraft type. During October 1954 the first examples of the Republic F-84F Thunderstreak were delivered to the wing but the 81st continued to use the F-86A Sabre until 1955 when it was completely phased out in favour of the F-84F. The last F-84F was delivered to the 81st FBW in May 1955.

On 8th February 1955 a major reorganisation of the USAF, which saw the demise of the 'group' structure, resulted in the 81st FBG becoming absorbed by the 81st FBW. The 78th FBS departed Shepherds Grove on 31st May 1956 for a relatively brief stay at RAF Sculthorpe, Norfolk, before returning back to Shepherds Grove on 3rd May 1957. The 92nd FBS left Shepherds Grove on 28th March 1955 to take up residence at RAF Manston, Kent and on 30th April 1958 moved again, this time to Bentwaters.

On 8th July 1958 the 81st FBW became the 81st Tactical Fighter Wing in readiness for re-equipping with its next aircraft type. The squadrons assigned to the 81st TFW at this time were the 78th TFS at Shepherds Grove and the 91st TFS and 92nd TFS at Bentwaters.

The wing first used RAF Woodbridge on 22nd December 1958 when the 78th TFS transferred from RAF Shepherds Grove, in preparation for delivery of the first examples of the McDonnell F-101A/C Voodoo. At around the same time both the 91st TFS and 92nd TFS began converting to the F-101. These 'new' aircraft were actually unwanted second-hand examples that had equipped Tactical Air Command's 27th TFW at Bergstrom AFB, Texas. The 81st TFW were not at all happy about flying the Voodoo as they had been expecting to receive the same aircraft that equipped five other fighter units within USAFE, namely the North American F-100D Super Sabre. Indeed, the 81st TFW had even published an F-100 Conversion Plan.

North American F-86A Sabres of the 91st FIS/81st FIG arrive at RAF Shepherds Grove after completing the final leg of their transatlantic flight on 5th September 1951. The 91st FIS moved to Bentwaters on 26th September. An aircraft of the 116th FIS, a unit that arrived in the U.K. two weeks before the 91st, can be seen (in the background) second from left. (photo: George Pennick)

The USAFE Commander at the time, General Frank F. Everest let his feelings be known to the Air Force executives at the Pentagon. He was not happy at the prospect of having a unique wing of aircraft putting further pressure on his already stretched supply chain. It soon became apparent that the decision had already been taken and no amount of protest could reverse it. By the end of 1958 the 81st TFW had received a total of 48 Voodoos, a mixture of 'A' and 'C' variants, but during the conversion period for the new aircraft the wing remained combat ready with the Thunderstreak.

Once fully operational with the Voodoo the 81st's primary role was the same as it was when it flew Thunderstreaks. This was the tactical nuclear strike mission and was to involve each aircraft carrying a single atomic weapon to a specific target, release it and then return home. The 'return home' part of the mission was unlikely ever to have been completed and, in fact the 81st TFW Voodoo pilots considered their mission to be a one way trip. As all of the 81st's allocated targets were in close proximity to each other it was likely that some of its Voodoos would be taken out before reaching their targets due to the fact that they would be flying into the atomic bursts created by the aircraft ahead of them. Thankfully this was never to be proven. The Voodoo was to remain a familiar sight in the skies around the 'Twin Bases' for the next six years.

The 81st TFW became part of the USAF's Seventeenth Air Force in 1961, but in September 1963, the wing found itself back under the control of the Third Air Force.

The 81st's next change of aircraft type commenced during 1965 when the first deliveries of the McDonnell Douglas F-4 Phantom heralded the beginning of the end for the Voodoo. The wing's tactical nuclear strike mission continued with the new type although the F-4 added an additional close air support and ground attack capability. The Phantom was destined to be an even more familiar sight than the F-101 in the skies over Suffolk for the next thirteen years. The initial version of the Phantom flown by the 81st TFW was the F-4C but, by 1975 (beginning in April 1969 with the 78th TFS), this was superseded by the upgraded F-4D. The 91st TFS and 92nd TFS received their first F-4Ds in September 1973. Following transition to the F-4D, the majority of the 81st TFW's F-4Cs were exported to Spain under the 'Peace Alfa' programme where they were assigned to Ala 12 (12 Wing) of the Ejercito del Aire (Spanish Air Force) at Torrejon AB.

The impressive Phantom began to be phased out in favour of the quieter, slower but more agile Fairchild A-10A Thunderbolt II in November 1978 when the wing began to receive its first deliveries of the new type. The arrival of the A-10 saw the 91st TFS move from Bentwaters to Woodbridge to take up residence alongside the 78th TFS. The new aircraft type brought with it a new role for the 81st TFW. The wing was now tasked to provide close air support and battlefield interdiction in support of NATO ground forces. Three new squadrons were added to the wing with the arrival of the A-10, these were the 509th TFS, 510th TFS and the 511th TFS. It was at this point, with six squadrons and 120 aircraft on strength, that the 81st TFW became the largest wing within the entire USAF.

F-101C-50-MC Voodoo (56-0020) of the 81ˢᵗ TFW, pictured at the 1963 Bentwaters 'Armed Forces Day.'
(photo: via Mick Sudds)

From early 1978, the principle objective of all USAF A-10 activity was to get the 81st operational as soon as possible. The 355th Tactical Fighter Training Wing at Davis Monthan AFB, Arizona took a leading role in the 'Operation Ready Thunder' (later known as 'Operation Ready Bentwaters') programme. Using experience gained in European tests and Joint Attack Weapons System (JAWS) trials, the 355th TFTW was tasked with processing pilots and new aircraft. The 81st was to receive only factory-fresh A-10s to the latest build standard. Pilots for the 81st TFW were drawn from four groups, in roughly equal numbers. These consisted of new graduates from T-38 training; T-38 instructor pilots, ready for their first operational wing; the 81st's own F-4D pilots, with European experience; and pilots returning to flight status from other assignments. The F-4 pilots and the latter group brought with them a lot of combat support and Forward Air Control experience gained in Vietnam, but this did not prevent younger, less experienced pilots from being denied the chance of leadership within the unit. The first squadron to complete training was the 92nd TFS and, due to the specialised training by the 355th TFTW, with the help of senior 81st TFW personnel, the 92nd was considered fully operational as soon as it arrived at Bentwaters.

The 81st TFW continued to be the priority A-10 unit. As its aircraft became due for major servicing, the wing's pilots would ferry them back to the Air Logistics Center at McClellan AFB, Sacramento, the centre of all A-10 overhaul and modification, and then travel to Fairchild Republic's facility at Hagerstown to collect a factory-fresh replacement. In this way the 81st became the first unit to have all of its A-10s fitted with an Inertial Navigation System (INS) and other important features.

Maintaining six squadrons of A-10s at the twin-bases necessitated regular ferry flights to and from the U.S. but in later years a large percentage of major servicing was also carried out in the U.K. by USAF personnel at RAF Kemble in Gloucestershire.

Although there were 120 A-10s based at Bentwaters and Woodbridge, at least one third of them were always deployed to one of four Forward Operating Locations (FOLs) in West Germany. Each FOL detachment consisted of eight aircraft and about a hundred personnel. The FOL for Det 1 was Sembach AB, operated by USAFE. The other three FOLs were at bases operated by the Luftwaffe. Det 2 was at Leipheim, Det 3 at Ahlhorn and Det 4 was at Norvenich. The squadrons were usually assigned to the same FOLs on each detachment, the 78th TFS to Det 4, 91st TFS to Det 3, 92nd TFS to Det 2 and the 510th TFS to Det 1. The 511th TFS was usually assigned to either Det 1 or Det 2 and the 509th TFS to Det 3 or Det 4. Two additional FOLs were planned at Jever and Wiesbaden but these were never used.

Due to its large size, the 81st TFW logged thousands of flying hours and sorties. This was emphasised during 1982 when the wing completed a total of 53,391 flying hours to set a peacetime tactical air forces record for hours flown by a wing.

The 509th TFS was transferred to the 10th TFW at RAF Alconbury on the 15th April 1988 and was followed eleven weeks later, on 1st July, by the 511th TFS when it too was transferred to the 10th TFW. This left the 81st TFW with only four A-10 squadrons, the 78th TFS and 91st TFS at Woodbridge and the 92nd TFS and 510th TFS at Bentwaters.

81st TFW A-10A Forward Operating Locations

The wing gained another squadron during 1988 when the 527th Aggressor Squadron arrived at Bentwaters after transferring from the 10th TFW at RAF Alconbury. The squadron's first General Dynamics F-16C Fighting Falcons landed at the base on 14th June. The squadron's assignment to the 81st TFW was not to last, however. In November 1989, the 527th AS began relinquishing its aircraft in preparation for deactivation, having never reached its full complement. The 527th AS had reassigned its entire fleet of 12 aircraft by early 1990 and deactivated later that year.

The final operational mission flown by the 81st TFW was carried out on 19th February 1993 when four A-10s performed farewell flypasts over several East Anglian air bases. Flight operations by the 81st finally came to an end on 23rd March 1993 when the last two A-10s departed for their new home at Spangdahlem AB in Germany. The aircraft were flown by the 81st TFW

Commander, Col Roger R. Radcliff and his Deputy Commander for Operations (DCO), Col Wally Berg.

The 81st TFW's formal inactivation ceremony was held at Bentwaters on 21st May 1993 with actual deactivation occurring on 1st July 1993. This day finally brought to an end the wing's forty-two year presence in the U.K.

The 81st was reactivated as the 81st Training Wing at Keesler AFB, Mississippi, on the 1st July 1993; the same day it was deactivated at Bentwaters. The wing, now no longer part of USAFE, was assigned to Air Education & Training Command. The 81st's new role was the training of USAF personnel in over 650 resident and non-resident courses including electronics, computers, information management, personnel support, aerospace command and control, and various advanced pilot training courses. For the latter courses the 81st TW was assigned the 45th Airlift Squadron. The 45th AS were equipped with two aircraft types, namely the Beech C-12C/F Super King Air and the Gates C-21A Learjet.

At the time of writing (2004) the 81st TW and the 45th AS remain at Keesler AFB. The 45th AS trains approximately 275 student pilots annually, both in classrooms and cockpits of the C-12C/F and C-21A. The students who filter into the 45th AS are either one of two types, undergraduate pilots or qualified combat aircraft pilots. Pilots graduate through either the initial qualification, instructor upgrade, or differences training course. The initial qualification course runs approximately three weeks with both the instructor upgrade and the differences training course running for two weeks. The 45th AS performs its role with 22 instructor pilots training in 3 C-12C/F aircraft and 5 C-21A aircraft.

The 'WR' tailcode that, since the late 1960s, has always been associated with the 81st TFW at Bentwaters and Woodbridge is still in use today. Rightly or wrongly (depending on your views), 'WR' is now associated with 93rd Air Control Wing at Robins AFB (formally Warner-Robins AFB), in Georgia. The code is applied to the unit's E-8C J-STARS (Joint Surveillance Target Attack Radar System) aircraft.

81st Wing Commanders (1948 - 2002)

(Note: Bold text indicates commanders for the period when the wing was resident at Bentwaters)

Col Thomas W. Blackburn	1st May 1948
Lt Col Francis R. Royal	21st May 1949
Col Thomas W. Blackburn	28th June 1949
Col Gladwyn E. Pinkstone	28th April 1950
Col Robert F. Harris	22nd August 1951
Col Gladwyn E. Pinkstone	**27th September 1951**
Col Robert F. Harris	3rd January 1953
Col Gladwyn E. Pinkstone	20th February 1953
Col Robert J. Garrigan	20th June 1953
Col Gladwyn E. Pinkstone	20th August 1953
Col Harold N. Holt	2nd June 1954
Col Ivan W. McElroy	10th June 1955
Col Lester L. Krause Jr.	18th June 1957
Col Henry L. Crouch Jr.	8th July 1957
Col James R. DuBose Jr.	6th May 1960
Col Eugene L. Strickland	9th July 1960
Col William C. Clark	9th July 1962
Col Robin Olds	9th August 1963
Brig Gen DeWitt R. Searles	26th July 1965
Col Ramon R. Melton	28th July 1967
Col George S. Dormon	5th July 1968
Col Devol Brett	25th September 1968
Col David J. Schmerbeck	29th August 1969
Col John C. Bartholf	6th March 1970
Col James W. Enos	4th September 1970
Col Dwain L. Weatherwax	22nd June 1971
Brig Gen Charles E. Word	16th August 1972
Col John R. Paulk	19th April 1974
Brig Gen Clyde H. Garner	14th March 1975
Col Gerald D. Larson	11th February 1976
Brig Gen Rudolph F. Wacker	6th May 1977
Col Gordon E. Williams	7th August 1979
Brig Gen Richard M. Pascoe	24th April 1981
Maj Gen Dale C. Tabor	2nd August 1982
Col Lester P. Brown Jr.	20th March 1984
Col William A. Studer	26th March 1986
Col Harold H. Rhoden	30th July 1987
Col Tad J. Oelstrom	5th August 1988
Col Roger E. Carleton	13th July 1990
Col Roger R. Radcliff	**12th July 1991**
Brig Gen Karen S. Rankin	1st July 1993
Brig Gen Andrew J. Pelak Jr.	7th November 1995
Brig Gen John M. Speigel	4th August 1997
Brig Gen Elizabeth A. Harrell	14th July 1999
Brig Gen Roosevelt Mercer Jr.	September 2000
Brig Gen Michael W. Peterson	2nd May 2002

Emblem

Description: Or a dragon salient wings displayed and addorsed Azure, armed and langued Gules, incensed proper, holding in its dexter claw a stylised boll weevil Sable.

Significance: The Wing's mission is symbolised by the fabled fiery dragon, a creature adopted in medieval times with the thought of intimidating enemies. The dragon's breath of fire renders all opposition useless, while the stylised boll weevil clutched in the dragon's claw is suggestive of the enemy. Approved for the 81st Group on 2nd March 1943 and the 81st Wing on 14th May 1956.

Motto: *Le Nom-Les Armes-La Loyaute* (The Name, The Arms, The Loyalty).

78th Tactical Fighter Squadron

The 'Bushmasters' were formed on 28th February 1918 as the 78th Aero Squadron at Waco Field, Texas, but moved to Taliaferro Field, Texas, that same day. The role of the 78th Aero Squadron was the training of personnel for flying squadrons. The unit was redesignated Squadron A on 23rd July 1918, and was deactivated on 13th November 1918.

On 18th October 1927, a second 78th Squadron (the 78th Observation Squadron) was formed. The 78th Observation Squadron was redesignated as the 78th Pursuit Squadron on 8th May 1927.

On 1st April 1931, the 78th Pursuit Squadron was assigned to the 20th Pursuit Group and attached to the 6th Composite Group. It was then activated at France Field in the Panama Canal Zone without any aircraft. The 78th moved within the Canal Zone to Albrook Field on 15th October 1932, and began operating P-12 aircraft. The squadron was then assigned to the 3rd Attack Wing, but remained attached to the 6th Composite Group. However, the 78th was reassigned to the 16th Pursuit Group that December and remained in the Canal Zone. The U.S. War Department, realising the existence of another 78th squadron, reconstituted and consolidated both squadrons on 25th April 1933. The squadron, unequipped with aircraft for nearly a year, was deactivated again on 1st September 1937.

The squadron was redesignated the 78th Pursuit Squadron (Interceptor) and reactivated on 1st February 1940, at Wheeler Field, Hawaii. The 78th, now assigned to the 18th Pursuit Group, began flying operations with P-26 and P-36 aircraft. The 78th temporarily moved to Bellows Field for gunnery training in October 1941, returning to Wheeler Field a month prior to the Japanese attack on Pearl Harbor.

The 78th's newly acquired P-40s were destroyed or damaged on the ground in the surprise attack on 7th December 1941 but by the next morning the squadron's groundcrew had made four P-40's available for patrol duties. The squadron moved to Kaneohe Naval Air Station two days later as part of the defence-dispersal and to provide a smoother landing field while preparing for the arrival of 12 new P-39s.

After the declaration of war, the squadron's principal mission was to train pilots for other combat units in the Pacific Theatre. A ground echelon sailed from Honolulu on 12th January 1943, to prepare for the arrival of the aircraft and pilots on Midway Island. The 78th's pilots then flew non-stop 1,100 nautical miles from Barking Sands, Kauai, to Midway, replacing the 73rd Squadron that was on patrol duty. The squadron continued to provide aerial defence for Midway until April 1943, when it returned to Hawaii and was reassigned to the 15th Fighter Group.

Over the next 18 months the 78th moved to five bases throughout Hawaii, finally arriving at Bellows Field on 8th June 1944. During that time the squadron converted to the Republic P-47 Thunderbolt and began training for extreme long-range escort missions. That program continued through 1944 and was marked by the 78th's conversion to the North American P-51 Mustang at the end of the year.

During 1944, members of the 78th awaited transfer to a combat theatre. A move in September 1944, was cancelled, however, new orders sent the squadron into combat with the 15th Fighter Group in January 1945. The first section of the squadron's ground echelon arrived at Iwo Jima on 19th February, during the invasion landings on the island.

After the island was secured on 2nd March, the first echelon disembarked and set up camp. The second ground echelon arrived three days later and were followed by the aircraft on 8th March. The remaining squadron members arrived five days later. Almost immediately the squadron began flying combat patrol missions in support of the Marines on Iwo Jima. By the end of the month the squadron had begun flying missions against enemy airfields and other installations on islands in the Bonin Group.

On 7th April 1945, the 78th, along with other components of the 15th Fighter Group, flew their first escort missions to Japan, earning a Distinguished Unit Citation for escorting the Boeing B-29 Superfortresses that bombed the Masashino Plant aircraft factory at Nakajima near Tokyo. During the remaining months of the war the squadron flew fighter sweeps against Japanese airfields and escorted B-29s on long-range strikes.

The squadron remained on Iwo Jima until 25th November 1945, at which time it returned, without personnel or equipment, to Bellows Field. The squadron absorbed the personnel and equipment of the 468th Fighter Squadron. The 78th moved to Wheeler Field on 6th February 1946, and deactivated again nine months later on 15th October 1946.

The 'Bushmasters' were reactivated as the 78th Fighter-Interceptor Squadron (FIS) at RAF Shepherds Grove, England on 1st November 1952 taking over personnel and equipment from the 116th FIS and flying the North American F-86A Sabre. On the 1st and 10th December 1953, the 78th FIS received nine F-86F versions of the Sabre to replace some of its ageing F-86As. The 78th FIS seemed almost certain to replace it's entire fleet of -As with the superior -F model, but this was not to be the case. The squadron transferred to RAF Sculthorpe on 31st May 1956 before arriving back at Shepherds Grove a year later. The 'Bushmasters' became the 78th Fighter-Bomber Squadron (FBS) on the 1st April 1954 and began to receive the Republic F-84F Thunderstreak in October of that year. Whilst converting to the Thunderstreak, the 78th were still receiving deliveries of the F-86F Sabre. This continued until October 1954.

In July 1958 the squadron was redesignated as the 78th Tactical Fighter Squadron (TFS). On 22nd December of that year the 78th relocated to RAF Woodbridge to prepare for the imminent replacement of its F-84F Thunderstreaks with the McDonnell F-101A/C Voodoo.

The Voodoo was replaced by the McDonnell Douglas F-4C Phantom II in 1965 and these were superseded by the F-4D version of the Phantom from 23rd April 1969. The next major change occurred on 1st January 1979 when the first deliveries of the Fairchild Republic A-10A Thunderbolt II arrived to replace the Phantom. The 78th TFS eventually received a full complement of 18 A-10s.

'Bushmasters' F-4D-29-MC (66-0272/WR) seen at its dispersal at Woodbridge on 21st April 1971. (photo: Don Gilham)

As well as operating from Woodbridge, the A-10s regularly deployed to a Forward Operating Location (FOL) at Norvenich in West Germany. The 'Bushmasters' also deployed to Incirlik Air Base, Turkey in 1991 in support of Operation Provide Comfort, flying relief missions for Kurdish refugees in Iraq.

The 78th TFS was unique out of all of the mainstay squadrons assigned to the 81st TFW as it was the only one never to have been based at Bentwaters. The squadron was deactivated on 15th May 1992 at RAF Woodbridge and reactivated as the 78th Fighter Squadron on 3rd January 1994 as part of the 20th Fighter Wing at Shaw AFB, South Carolina, flying the Lockheed F-16C/D Fighting Falcon. After flying the F-16 for nine years, the squadron was deactivated at Shaw on 23rd May 2003. The unit was reactivated as the 78th Reconnaissance Squadron on 30th June 2006, at Nellis AFB, Nevada. Now a Reserve unit, the 78th RS is assigned to the U.S. Air Force Warfare Centre.

Stations

Waco Field, Texas	28th February 1918
Taliaferro Field, Texas	28th Feb – 15th Nov 1918
France Field, CZ	1st April 1931
Albrook Field, CZ	15th Oct 1932 – 1st Sept 1937
Wheeler Field, TH	1st February 1940
Kaneohe, TH	c. 9th December 1941

Midway	23rd January 1943
Barking Sands, TH	23rd April 1943
Haleiwa Field, TH	31st July 1943
Stanley Field, TH	6th January 1944
Mokuleia Field, TH	c. 1st April 1944
Bellows Field, TH	8 June 1944 – 24 Jan 1945
South Field, Iwo Jima	2nd March 1945
Bellows Field, TH	25th November 1945
Wheeler Field, TH	9th Feb – 15th Oct 1946
RAF Shepherds Grove, UK	1st November 1952
RAF Sculthorpe, UK	31st May 1956
RAF Shepherds Grove, UK	3rd May 1957
RAF Woodbridge, UK	**22 Dec 1958 – 15 May 1992**
Shaw AFB, South Carolina	3 Jan 1994 – 23 May 2003
Nellis AFB, Nevada	30th June 2006 –

Decorations

Distinguished Unit Citation: Japan, 7th April 1945.
Air Force Outstanding Unit Award: 1st July 1961 – 30th June 1963.

Emblem

Description: On a Blue disc with a wide Yellow border a Bushmaster's head proper. Approved on 14th September 1933.

F-84F-35-RE Thunderstreak (52-6499) of the 78th FBS/81st FBW. (photo: J Williams via D Menard and George Pennick)

78th TFS commander's A-10A (81-0978/WR) pictured at Woodbridge in 1990. (photo: Kenny Read)

91st Tactical Fighter Squadron

The 'Blue Streaks' were formed on 13th January 1942 as the 91st Pursuit Squadron (Interceptor), just over two months after the Japanese attack on Pearl Harbor. The 91st was activated at Morris Field, North Carolina, on 9th February 1942, and equipped with the Bell P-39 Airacobra. The 91st were given assignments all around the world, being based in places such as French Morocco, Tunisia, Algeria, Sicily, India and China. Whilst in Tunisia, the 91st were heavily involved in the famous battle for Kasserine Pass and the subsequent action.

The squadron was redesignated as the 91st Fighter Squadron on 15th May 1942 and continued to operate the P-39. The 91st was later equipped with the Lockheed P-38 Lightning, the Curtiss P-40 Warhawk and the Republic P-47 Thunderbolt before deactivating on 27th December 1945.

The 91st was reactivated on 15th October 1946, again flying the P-47. In early 1949 the squadron moved into the jet age when it received deliveries of the Lockheed F-80 Shooting Star. Having spent less than six months flying the F-80, the 91st converted to the North American F-86A Sabre in July 1949 at Kirtland AFB, New Mexico. The squadron was redesignated 91st Fighter-Interceptor Squadron on 20th January 1950, and moved to Moses Lake AFB, Washington on 1st May 1950.

The 91st FIS transferred across the Atlantic to take up temporary residence at RAF Shepherds Grove, England on 5th September 1951. Less than two weeks later, on 26th September, the 'Blue Streaks' relocated to its permanent home at RAF Bentwaters. The squadron was assigned to the 81st Fighter Interceptor Group (FIG) upon its arrival in the U.K. The F-86A continued in service until 1955, being progressively replaced by the Republic F-84F Thunderstreak from October 1954.

The 91st FIS became the 91st Fighter-Bomber Squadron on 1st April 1954 and was later redesignated as the 91st Tactical Fighter Squadron on 8th July 1958. The squadron continued to operate the F-84F until 1959 when it was retired in favour of the McDonnell F-101A/C Voodoo, deliveries of which had begun the previous year. The F-101 continued in service until 1965, when it was replaced by the McDonnell Douglas F-4C Phantom II, examples of which were received from 1965 onwards. After only a few months of flying the F-4C, the 91st TFS, along with the other 81st TFW squadrons, deployed more than half of its pilots to South East Asia during 1966 1967 due to pilot shortages in that theatre.

The F-4C was later replaced by the F-4D and this version of the Phantom continued to serve with the 91st TFS until 1978 when the first examples of the Fairchild Republic A-10A Thunderbolt II were received. The 'Blue Streaks' transferred to RAF Woodbridge to operate the A-10 and remained there for the next 15 years. The 91st regularly deployed its A-10s to a Forward Operating Location (FOL) at Ahlhorn in West Germany.

The squadron was deactivated as part of the 81st TFW's 'Mission Completion' programme on 14th August 1992.

Stations

Morris Field, North Carolina	9th February 1942
Dale Mabry Field, Florida	1st May 1942
Muroc, California	27th June - 4th October 1942
Port Lyautey, French Morocco	10th November 1942
Fedala, French Morocco	16th December 1942
Mediouna, French Morocco	c. 3rd January 1943
Thelepte, Tunisia	23rd January 1943
Le Kouif Airfield, Algeria	17th February 1943
Youks-les-Bains, Algeria	22nd February 1943

Le Kouif Airfield, Algeria	24th February 1943
Thelepte, Tunisia	5th March 1943
Bone, Algeria	5th April 1943
Sfax, Tunisia	23rd May 1943
Sidi Ahmed, Tunisia	5th August 1943
Castelvetrano, Sicily	12th October 1943
Montecorvino Airfield, Italy	6th December 1943 - 15th February 1944 (operated from Capodichino, Italy, 13th Dec. 1943 - 1st Feb. 1944)
Karachi, India	25th February 1944
Fungwanshan, China	c. 1st June 1944 (operated from Hsian, China, 9th April - 15th August 1945)
Huhsien, China	c. 17th August - 27th December 1945
Wheeler Field, TH	15th October 1946 - 21st May 1949
Kirtland AFB, New Mexico	17th June 1949
Moses Lake AFB, Washington	c. 1st May 1950 - 21st August 1951
RAF Shepherds Grove, England	5th September 1951
RAF Bentwaters/ Woodbridge, England	**26th September 1951 - 14th August 1992**

Decorations

Air Force Outstanding Unit Award: 1st July 1961 - 30th June 1963.

Emblem

Description: On a disc of thirteen alternating vertical stripes, White and Red, a horizontal upper division Blue. The disc piped Yellow, thereon, a wing and a cloud, White, pierced with a lightning flash Yellow. Approved 14th June 1951.

91st FBS Republic F-84F Thunderstreak touches down on Runway 07 at Bentwaters, circa 1955. (photo: Harry Eckes)

Fairchild A-10A Thunderbolt II of the 91st TFS 'Blue Streaks.' (photo: Kenny Read)

92nd Tactical Fighter Squadron

The 'Skulls' were constituted on 13th January 1942 as the 92nd Pursuit Squadron (Interceptor) and activated at Morris Field, North Carolina, on 9th February 1942, equipped with the Bell P-39 Airacobra.

The squadron was redesignated as the 92nd Fighter Squadron on 15th May 1942 and continued to operate the P-39. The 92nd FS was later equipped with the Lockheed P-38 Lightning, the Curtiss P-40 Warhawk and the Republic P-47 Thunderbolt before deactivating on 27th December 1945.

The squadron was reactivated on 15th October 1946, again flying the P-47 Thunderbolt. In early 1949 the 92nd received its first jet aircraft in the form of the Lockheed F-80 Shooting Star. Operations with the F-80 were to be short-lived. Having spent less than six months flying the F-80, the squadron converted to the North American F-86A Sabre during July 1949 at Kirtland AFB, New Mexico. The 92nd was redesignated as a Fighter-Interceptor Squadron on 20th January 1950, and moved to Moses Lake AFB, Washington on 30th April 1950.

The 92nd FIS transferred across the Atlantic to RAF Shepherds Grove, England on 5th September 1951. The 92nd FIS were assigned to the 81st Fighter-Interceptor Group (FIG) upon its arrival in the U.K. Redesignated as the 92nd Fighter-Bomber Squadron (FBS) on 1st April 1954, the squadron continued to use the Sabre until the first deliveries of the Republic F-84F Thunderstreak arrived during October 1954. The squadron relocated to RAF Manston on 28th March 1955.

After nearly four years of operating the F-84F, the 92nd FBS relocated from Manston to RAF Bentwaters on 30th April 1958. This move was in preparation for the delivery of the first examples of the squadron's next aircraft type, the McDonnell F-101 Voodoo, later that year.

On 8th July 1958, the 92nd FBS was redesignated as a Tactical Fighter Squadron (TFS), in readiness for the delivery of the McDonnell Douglas F-101A/C Voodoo. The 92nd TFS received its first Voodoos in December 1958 and continued to fly the type in the tactical nuclear strike role for another eight years. 1965 saw the beginning of the end of the Voodoo era with the arrival of the first McDonnell Douglas F-4C Phantom IIs for the 92nd TFS. The Voodoo was retired in favour of the new type the following year.

Having operated the F-4C for eight years, the type was superseded by the more advanced F-4D version of the Phantom in September 1973. The 92nd TFS flew the Phantom for another five years before first deliveries of the Fairchild Republic A-10A Thunderbolt II were received in November 1978. Once the conversion process from the F-4 to the A-10 was completed, the 92nd TFS became the first operational A-10 squadron in USAFE (United States Air Forces in Europe). The squadron operated the 'Warthog' for some fifteen years from Bentwaters and regularly deployed to a Forward Operating Location (FOL) at Leipheim in West Germany.

The squadron was deactivated as part of the 81st TFW's 'Mission Completion' programme on 12th March 1993 and had the honour of being the last squadron to leave Bentwaters. From its conception in 1942 to its deactivation in 1993, the 92nd had been part of the 81st Tactical Fighter Wing (in its various forms).

The squadron was reactivated at Lackland AFB, Texas on 1st November 2000 as the 92nd Information Warfare Aggressor Squadron with the official activation ceremony taking place at Kelly AFB, Texas on 6th November 2000. At the time of writing (2002), the 92nd IWAS still resides at Lackland AFB.

Line up of F-86A Sabres from the 92nd FIS/81st FIG pictured during a stopover at Keflavik, Iceland whilst en route to RAF Shepherds Grove, U.K. in September 1951. (photo: Col S. H. Pile via George Pennick)

Fairchild A-10A Thunderbolt II of the 92nd TFS pictured at Bentwaters in July 1990. (photo: Trevor Rose)

The 92nd IWAS is assigned to the 318th Information Operations Group, a subordinate unit of the Air Force Information Warfare Centre and is primarily tasked with employing information warfare adversary tactics. The squadron's secondary role is to provide information warfare vulnerability assessments, manage the Air Force operations security training and Air Force tactical deception training programmes and is the AFIWC focal point for counter-deception operations, psychological operations and command and control attack analysis. In order to carry out these tasks, the 92nd IWAS is split up into four flights. These are the Network Operations Flight, the Systems Vulnerability Flight, the Aggressor Operations Flight and the Counter-Information Programs Flight.

It is perhaps a sign of the times that a number of similar information warfare units now exist in today's USAF. To quote Lt Col Jerry Cummin, Operations Officer of the 92nd IWAS on the first anniversary of the squadron's reactivation: "The fact that the 92nd has shifted from a fighter squadron to an information warfare squadron is an indication of where wars are headed."

Stations

Morris Field, North Carolina	9th February 1942
Dale Mabry Field, Florida	1st May 1942
Muroc, California	27th June – 4th Oct 1942
Port Lyautey, French Morocco	11th November 1942
Louis Gentile Field, French Morocco	16th December 1942
Mediouna, French Morocco	c. 5th January 1943
Thelepte, Tunisia	12th January 1943
Le Kouif Airfield, Algeria	17th February 1943
Youks-les-Bains, Algeria	22nd February 1943
Le Kouif Airfield, Algeria	24th February 1943
Thelepte, Tunisia	6th March 1943
Youks-les-Bains, Algeria	29th March 1943
Maison Blanche, Algeria	6th April 1943
Warner, Algeria	12th May 1943
Sidi Ahmed, Tunisia	15th August 1943
Castelvetrano, Sicily	13th October 1943
Capodichino, Italy	17th Jan – 14th Feb 1944
Karachi, India	22nd March 1944
Kwanghan, China	15th May 1944
Fungwanshan, China	12th February 1945
Huhsien, China	20th August 1945
Hsian, China	c. Oct – 27 Dec 1945
Wheeler Field, TH	15 Oct 1946 – 21 May 1949
Kirtland AFB, New Mexico	17th June 1949
Moses Lake AFB, Washington	30 Apr 1950 – 21 Aug 1951
RAF Shepherds Grove, UK	5th September 1951
RAF Manston, UK	28th March 1955
RAF Bentwaters, UK	**30 Apr 1958 – 12 Mar 1993**
Lackland AFB, Texas	1st November 2000 -

Decorations

Air Force Outstanding Unit Award: 1st July 1961 - 30th June 1963.

Emblem

Description: An irregular shaped figure, divided palewise by cloud-like formation, Yellow and Ultramarine Blue, charged in sinister segment with a White skull facing toward dexter, and having an Orange lightning flash issuing from the mouth and a like flash from the eye, all within a border divided palewise, Ultramarine Blue and Light Green. Approved 30th June 1945.

F-101C-45-MC Voodoo (56-0006) of the 92nd TFS/81st TFW, pictured at RAF Lakenheath during 1961. (photo: Mick Sudds)

A-10A 81-0992/WR of the 92nd TFS/81st TFW taxies back to its Hardened Aircraft Shelter (HAS) at Bentwaters in June 1990. Note the two travel pods carried on this aircraft. This was usually indicative of a return from a Forward Operating Location (FOL) in Germany. (photo: Ashley Annis)

509th Tactical Fighter Squadron

The 509th TFS ('Pirates') was constituted as the 624th Bombardment Squadron (Dive) on 4th February 1943 and was activated on 1st March 1943 at Drew Field, Florida. The squadron was a component of the 405th Bombardment Group and flew three aircraft types in its first year of operations, namely the Douglas A-24 Dauntless dive-bomber, Bell P-39 Airacobra and the Republic P-47 Thunderbolt. On 10th August 1943 the squadron was redesignated as the 509th Fighter-Bomber Squadron.

The 509th transferred to Europe on 7th March 1944, its first base being Christchurch in the U.K. The squadron was again redesignated as the 509th Fighter Squadron on 30th May 1944. The squadron moved to Picauville, France on 29th June and then to St. Dizier, also in France, on 13th September. The next move came on 9th February 1945 when the 509th relocated to Ophoven, Belgium. At the end of the Second World War and following two moves to Kitzingen and Straubing in Germany, the unit returned to Camp Shanks, New York, on 14th October 1945 where it deactivated the following day.

On 15th October 1952 the squadron was reactivated as the 509th Fighter-Bomber Squadron at Godman AFB, Kentucky, flying the Republic F-84F Thunderstreak. The 509th FBS moved to Langley AFB, Virginia, on 17th April 1953 where it re-equipped with the North American F-100 Super Sabre. The squadron operated the F-100 for some five years before it was deactivated on 1st July 1958.

The squadron was reactivated as the 509th Fighter-Interceptor Squadron on 11th March 1959 at Clark AB, Luzon and equipped with the North American F-86D Sabre Dog. Having operated the F-86D for only one year, the type was superseded by the Convair F-102A Delta Dagger. The 509th FIS continued operating the F-102 until it deactivated on 15th November 1969.

The squadron was reactivated at RAF Bentwaters as the 509th Tactical Fighter Squadron on 1st October 1979 and was equipped with the Fairchild Republic A-10A Thunderbolt II. The 509th TFS became the sixth and final A-10 squadron assigned to the 81st TFW. The 'Pirates' remained at Bentwaters until 15th April 1988 when the squadron commenced a transfer to the 10th TFW at RAF Alconbury - its first two aircraft arriving that same day. The move to Alconbury was completed two months later. The 509th TFS was tasked with providing close air support for NATO's Northern Air Group and regularly deployed to the Forward Operating Locations at Ahlhorn and Norvenich in West Germany for this purpose.

The squadron remained at Alconbury until October 1991 when it began returning to the U.S. for deactivation. The withdrawal was completed in early 1992. This action was significant as it was the first of many subsequent withdrawals from the U.K. as a direct result of the end of the 'Cold War.' Upon their return to the U.S., the majority of the squadron's A-10s were flown to the Aerospace Maintenance and Regeneration Center (AMARC), otherwise known as the 'Desert Boneyard,' at Davis Monthan AFB, Arizona where they were placed in long-term storage.

Stations

Drew Field, Florida	1st March 1943
Walterboro AAFld, South Carolina	14th September 1943 - 14th February 1944
Christchurch, England	7th March - 22nd June 1944
Picauville, France	29th June 1944
St Dizier, France	c. 13th September 1944
Ophoven, Belgium	9th February 1945

Kitzingen, Germany	23rd April 1945
Straubing, Germany	8th May - 2nd July 1945
Camp Shanks, New York	14th - 15th October 1945
Godman AFB, Kentucky	1st December 1952
Langley AFB, Virginia	17th April 1953 - 1st July 1958
Clark AB, Luzon	9th April 1959 - 15th November 1969
RAF Bentwaters, England	**1st October 1979**
RAF Alconbury, England	15th June 1988 - c. February 1992

Decorations

- Distinguished Unit Citation: France, 24th September 1944.
- Cited in the Order of the Day, Belgian Army: 6th June - 30th September 1944.
- Air Force Outstanding Unit Award: 1st November 1960 - 30th June 1961.

Emblem

Description: On a Light Silver Grey disc bordered Black, in base a mound of earth, Dark Grey; imbedded in the earth and lying on its side a White skull, gaping eye sockets, nose and mouth Black; springing up through the upper eye socket and extending over the border in bend, a Red rose, stem and leaves Green; all outlines and details Black throughout. Approved 30th January 1957.

Fairchild A-10A Thunderbolt II of the 509th TFS 'Pirates.' (photo: Ian Powell)

510th Tactical Fighter Squadron

The 510th TFS ('Buzzards') was constituted as the 625th Bombardment Squadron (Dive) on 4th February 1943 and was activated on 1st March 1943 at Drew Field, Florida. The squadron was a component of the 405th Bombardment Group and flew three aircraft types in its first year of operations. It was initially equipped with the Douglas A-24 Dauntless dive-bomber. The A-24 gave way to the Bell P-39 Airacobra, which in turn was superseded by the Republic P-47 Thunderbolt. On 10th August 1943 the squadron was redesignated the 510th Fighter-Bomber Squadron. Ten days later the unit was redesignated to 510th Fighter-Bomber Squadron, Single Engine.

The 510th transferred to Europe on 6th March 1944, its first base being Christchurch in the U.K. The squadron was again redesignated on 30th May 1944, this time it became the 510th Fighter Squadron, Single Engine. The 510th moved to Picauville, France on 30th June and then to St. Dizier, also in France, on 11th September. The next move came on 6th February 1945 when the 510th relocated to Ophoven, Belgium. At the end of the Second World War and following two moves to Kitzingen and Straubing in Germany, the unit returned to Camp Kilmer, New Jersey, on 25th October 1945. Deactivation came two days later, on 27th October 1945.

On 15th October 1952 the squadron was reactivated as the 510th Fighter-Bomber Squadron at Godman AFB, Kentucky, flying the Republic F-84F Thunderstreak. The 510th FBS moved to Langley AFB, Virginia, on 17th April 1953 where it re-equipped with the North American F-100 Super Sabre. The squadron deactivated on 1st July 1958.

The squadron was reactivated as the 510th Tactical Fighter Squadron on 9th April 1959 at Clark AB, Luzon, again equipped with the F-100. On 16th March 1964 the squadron moved to England AFB, Louisiana. The 510th TFS deployed to Bien Hoa AB, South Vietnam, between 10th November 1965 and 15th November 1969. During this period the 510th flew more than 27,200 combat missions in Southeast Asia in support of United States and Allied operations. The squadron was deactivated on 15th November 1969.

On 1st October 1978 the 510th TFS was reactivated to operate the Fairchild Republic A-10A Thunderbolt II from RAF Bentwaters as part of the 81st TFW, and was then one of six squadrons operational within the wing. It continued to operate the type for fourteen years from RAF Bentwaters although the squadron regularly deployed to a Forward Operating Location at Sembach AB, Germany.

The 'Buzzards,' along with the 78th, 91st and 92nd TFSs, were involved in Operation Provide Comfort, providing air cover for Allied aircraft over Northern Iraq and helping escort aircraft drop supplies to the Kurdish refugees stranded in the Iraqi mountains.

The 510th TFS left Bentwaters during the latter half of 1992 and took up residence at Spangdahlem AB, Germany, as part of the 52nd Fighter Wing. This move was completed by 13th November of that year. The 510th TFS was deactivated at Spangdahlem on 1st February 1994 and its A-10s were handed over to the 81st FS (not to be confused with the 81st TFW). The squadron was reactivated as the 510th Fighter Squadron on 1st July 1994 as part of the 31st FW at Aviano AB, Italy, flying the Lockheed F-16C/D Fighting Falcon.

Stations

Drew Field, Florida	1st March 1943
Walterboro AAFld, S. Carolina	13 Sept 1943 – 14 Feb 1944
Christchurch, England	6 March – 22 June 1944
Picauville, France	30th June 1944
St Dizier, France	11th September 1944
Ophoven, Belgium	6th February 1945
Kitzingen, Germany	23rd April 1945

Straubing, Germany	14 May – 2nd July 1945
Camp Kilmer, New Jersey	25–27 October 1945
Godman AFB, Kentucky	1st December 1952
Langley AFB, Virginia	17 Apr 1953 - 1 Jul 1958
Clark AB, Luzon	9 Apr 1959 – 15 Nov 1969
RAF Bentwaters, England	**1st October 1978**
Spangdahlem AB, Germany	13 Nov 1992 – 1 Feb 1994
Aviano AB, Italy	1st July 1994 –

Decorations

- Distinguished Unit Citation: France, 24th September 1944.
- Cited in the Order of the Day, Belgian Army: 6th June - 30th September 1944.
- Air Force Outstanding Unit Award: 1st November 1960 - 30th June 1961.

Emblem

Description: On a disc per bend Royal Purple and Black; between a bendlet White, a falcon's head, erased fesswise, of the last, shaded Light Blue, eye and pupil indicated in Black; his beak open; and issuing from base a demi-sphere Light Blue, outline and grid lines White; centered on the bendlet an atomic symbol of three entwined White elliptical rings around a Red atom; the perimeter of the rings marked with six smaller atoms; three lightning bolts radiating downward from the symbol over the sphere all White; a diminutive border around the shield of the second. Approved on 14th February 1957; replaced emblems approved on 8th September 1953 and 7th July 1944.

Fairchild A-10A Thunderbolt II of the 510th TFS 'Buzzards.' (photo: Ashley Annis)

A-10A 80-0195/WR of the 510th TFS photographed during 1986. Note the gun gas deflector that was evaluated in this year. The deflector was intended to divert the gun gas away from the engines during a firing pass in an attempt to prevent a compressor stall. The trials did not prove successful and the deflector was subsequently not adopted.
(photo: Ashley Annis)

511th Tactical Fighter Squadron

The 511th TFS ('Vultures') was constituted as the 626th Bombardment Squadron (Dive) on 4th February 1943 and was activated on 1st March 1943 at Drew Field, Florida. The squadron was a component of the 405th Bombardment Group and flew three aircraft types in its first year of operations, these being the Douglas A-24 Dauntless dive-bomber, Bell P-39 Airacobra and the Republic P-47 Thunderbolt. On 10th August 1943 the squadron was redesignated as the 511th Fighter-Bomber Squadron.

The 511th, along with the 510th FBS, transferred to Europe on 6th March 1944, its first base being Christchurch in the U.K. The squadron was again redesignated as the 511th Fighter Squadron on 30th May 1944. The squadron moved to Picauville, France on 29th June and then to St. Dizier, also in France, on 14th September. The next move came on 9th February 1945 when the 511th relocated to Ophoven, Belgium. At the end of the Second World War and following two moves to Kitzingen and Straubing in Germany, the unit returned to Camp Patrick Henry, Virginia, on 19th October 1945 where it was deactivated.

On 15th October 1952 the squadron was reactivated as the 511th Fighter-Bomber Squadron at Godman AFB, Kentucky, flying the Republic F-84F Thunderstreak. The 511th FBS moved to Langley AFB, Virginia, on 17th April 1953 where it re-equipped with the North American F-100 Super Sabre. The squadron operated the F-100 for some five years before it was deactivated on 1st July 1958.

The squadron was reactivated as the 511th Tactical Fighter Squadron at RAF Bentwaters on 1st January 1980 as part of the 81st TFW when the latter increased its squadron complement from three to six. The squadron remained at Bentwaters for a little over eight years but was transferred to the 10th TFW at RAF Alconbury on 15th September 1988, where it joined the already resident 509th TFS. The 511th performed close air support tasks for the Northern Air Group of NATO and detached aircraft and personnel to the Forward Operating Locations at Sembach and Leipheim in West Germany to carry out this task.

On 27th December 1990 the 'Vultures' were deployed to the Persian Gulf to carry out offensive air operations in support of 'Desert Storm.' The squadron operated from King Fahad International Airport, Saudi Arabia, for the duration of the conflict returning to Alconbury in June 1991. During this deployment, Capt. Todd 'Shanghai' Sheehy made history by scoring an air-to-air kill whilst flying A-10A 81-0964/AR. On 15th February 1991, Capt. Sheehy downed an Iraqi Mil Mi-8 'Hip' helicopter with his Warthog's GAU-8/A cannon and in doing so became one of only two pilots to have scored an air-to-air kill with an A-10.

During early 1992 the 511th began withdrawing from Alconbury and returning to the U.S. On 30th March 1992 the withdrawal was completed when the last 7 A-10s departed. Upon their return to the U.S. the 511th TFS was deactivated and the majority of the squadron's A-10s were flown to the Aerospace Maintenance and Regeneration Center (AMARC), at Davis Monthan AFB, Arizona where they were placed in long term storage.

Stations

Drew Field, Florida	1st March 1943
Walterboro AAFld, South Carolina	14th Sept 1943 – 14th Feb 1944
Christchurch, England	6th March - 22nd June 1944
Picauville, France	29th June 1944
St Dizier, France	14th September 1944
Ophoven, Belgium	9th February 1945
Kitzingen, Germany	23rd April 1945
Straubing, Germany	c. 13th May - 2nd July 1945

Camp Patrick Henry, Virginia	19th October 1945
Godman AFB, Kentucky	1st December 1952
Langley AFB, Virginia	17 April 1953 – 1 July 1958
RAF Bentwaters, UK	**1st January 1980**
RAF Alconbury, UK	15 Sept 1988 – 30 Mar 1992

Decorations

- Distinguished Unit Citation: France, 24th September 1944.
- Cited in the Order of the Day, Belgian Army: 6th June - 30th September 1944.

Emblem

Description: On a disc grayed Light Blue Violet, thin border White, edged Black, a caricatured, Black vulture with Red beak, feet, and rough neck feathers, diving toward dexter base, having four machine guns in leading edge of each wing, and dropping two, large, Red aerial bombs in direction of flight, while losing feathers from the tail as result of near hits by two 'ack-ack' bursts in chief, proper. Approved 12th February 1945.

Fairchild A-10A Thunderbolt II of the 511th TFS 'Vultures.' (photo: Ashley Annis)

A-10A 80-0157/WR of the 511th TFS photographed at Bentwaters in May 1988, shortly before transferring to the 10th TFW at RAF Alconbury. (photo: Ashley Annis)

527th Aggressor Squadron

The 527th Aggressor Squadron was constituted as the 312th Bombardment Squadron (Light) on 13th January 1943 and activated on 10th February 1943 at Will Rogers Field, Oklahoma, equipped with the Douglas A-20 Havoc. The unit flew a total of three aircraft types in its first year of service. In addition to the A-20, the 312th operated the Douglas A-24 Dauntless, the Vultee A-31 Vengeance and the North American A-36 Apache. The unit was redesignated as the 312th Bombardment Squadron (Dive) on 3rd September 1942. Two more redesignations followed, the first occurring on 23rd August 1943 when the 312th became the 527th Fighter-Bomber Squadron. The second redesignation came on the 30th May 1944, this time the unit became the 527th Fighter Squadron and re-equipped with the Republic P-47 Thunderbolt. The 527th FS continued to operate the P-47 until it deactivated at Bolling Field, DC, on 31st March 1946.

The 527th FS was reactivated five months later, on 20th August 1946, at Nordholz, Germany, again flying the P-47. On 20th January 1950, the unit was redesignated as the 527th Fighter-Bomber Squadron and moved into the jet era when it re-equipped with the Republic F-84E Thunderjet. The 527th FBS operated the F-84E for three years from Neubiberg AB and Landstuhl AB in Germany until it re-equipped at the latter base with the North American F-86F Sabre. The unit was redesignated as the 527th Fighter-Day Squadron on 8th October 1954 and deactivated sixteen months later, on 8th February 1956, with personnel and equipment transferring to the 461st FDS.

After a break of some twenty years, the unit was reactivated as the 527th Tactical Fighter Training Aggressor Squadron (TFTAS) on 1st April 1976 at RAF Alconbury. The squadron was part of the 10th Tactical Reconnaissance Wing (later to become the 10th Tactical Fighter Wing), operating the Northrop F-5E Tiger II in the Dissimilar Air Combat Tactics (DACT) training role.

The first batch of eight aircraft were air-freighted into Alconbury on the 21st May 1976 on board a Lockheed C-5A Galaxy direct from the production facility at Palmdale. Eight more Tigers arrived on the 14th June with the final batch of four following 10 days later, on the 24th June. These aircraft were also air-freighted on board a C-5A. The 527th was fully operational a few months later with the first DACT course commencing in October 1976.

The siting of an ACMI (Air Combat Manoeuvring Instrumentation) range at Decimomannu in Sardinia resulted in the 527th maintaining a semi-permanent presence at this NATO base. This facility also enabled air forces other than the USAF to take advantage of the training provided by the 527th TFTAS. The Royal Air Force, France's Armee de l'Air, the Italian Air Force and the Luftwaffe were amongst those that benefited.

The squadron, which was redesignated as the 527th Aggressor Squadron (AS) on 14 April 1983, remained at Alconbury until 1988, flying its last mission with the F-5E on 22nd June of that year. The control of the 527th AS was transferred to the 81st TFW at RAF Bentwaters and the F-5Es were replaced with the larger General Dynamics F-16C Fighting Falcon during 1988.

The first two of an intended complement of eighteen F-16Cs arrived at Bentwaters on 14th June 1988. These were single examples taken from the 52nd TFW at Spangdahlem AB and the 86th TFW at Ramstein AB. The squadron was officially activated on the 1st July 1988, with the first four months dedicated to pilot conversion for the new aircraft. The 527th AS resumed their aggressor role in November 1988 when six McDonnell Douglas F-15C Eagles from the 36th TFW at Bitburg AB, Germany arrived at Bentwaters for the start of a three week DACT course. The 527th's complement of aircraft had reached twelve on the 16th

January 1989 when one more F-16C was delivered from Spangdahlem AB.

The F-16Cs made their first deployment to Decimomannu on the 30th March 1989 when six aircraft deployed to the ACMI range for two weeks.

The 527th AS was to become a victim of cuts in U.S. defence spending and a rethink regarding the role of Aggressor Squadrons within the USAF. In November 1989, having never achieved its original planned complement of 18 aircraft, the 527th AS began disposing of its F-16Cs in preparation for deactivation the following year. The first two aircraft to leave were flown to Spangdahlem AB, West Germany on the 29th November 1989. The 527th AS had reassigned its entire fleet of 12 aircraft by mid 1990 and was officially deactivated on 30th September of that year.

The squadron was reactivated as the 527th Space Aggressor Squadron during a ceremony at Peterson AFB, Colorado, on 23rd October 2000 and became the USAF's first ever 'space aggressor' squadron. The 527th SAS is located at Schriever AFB, also in Colorado, and is assigned to the Space Warfare Center. The unit provides realistic training to other Space Command units and operates similar to an air aggressor squadron, but without the aircraft. The 527th's mission is to make USAF war planners aware of how much they rely on space assets and how they could counteract an enemy's attempt to deprive them of the use of those assets.

The squadron is divided into four sections: the Imagery Exploitation Flight, the Electronic Warfare Flight, the Red Attack Flight and the Space Control Flight. The Imagery Exploitation Flight explores the Internet for the commercial satellite imagery available to anyone with a computer and a credit card. From these freely available images an untrained analyst could locate U.S. aircraft, equipment, barracks and perimeter fences and gain important information relating to the movement of U.S. forces. It is now possible for anyone (including foreign governments) with access to the internet to purchase satellite imagery of U.S. military installations so long as they have a credit card.

The Electronic Warfare Flight uses known adversary technology to jam U.S. systems using the Global Positioning System and satellite communications during exercises. Once more, it only uses the equipment and doctrine known to be in potential adversaries' hands. The Red Attack Flight utilises these disruptive abilities and instigates plans to direct them against the regular Air Force's command and control capabilities during an exercise. The Space Control Flight uses information gained from these exercises to develop the countermeasures, new tactics and procedures to protect from a space-based offensive operation. The 527th SAS will play an important role in the defence of the U.S. and the rest of the free world for many years to come.

Northrop F-5E Tiger II of the 527th AS pictured during a deployment to Bentwaters in 1985. (photo: Kenny Read)

A pair of 527th AS F-16Cs line-up for takeoff at Bentwaters in 1989. (photo: Kenny Read)

Stations

Will Rogers Field, Oklahoma	10th February 1942
Hunter Field, Georgia	15th June 1942
Key Field, Mississippi	c. 7th August 1942 - 19th March 1943
La Senia, Algeria	11th May 1943
Mediouna, French Morocco	15th May 1943
Tafaraoui, Algeria	11th June 1943
Korba, Tunisia	1st July 1943
Gela, Sicily	20th July 1943
Barcelona, Sicily	27th August 1943
Sele Airfield, Italy	c. 16th September 1943
Serretella, Italy	c. 11th October 1943
Pomigliano, Italy	c. 20th October 1943
Marcianise, Italy	30th April 1944
Ciampino, Italy	12th June 1944
Orbetello, Italy	c. 19th June 1944
Poretta, Corsica	c. 12th July 1944
Grosseto, Italy	c. 17th September 1944
Pisa, Italy	c. 26th October 1944
Tantonville, France	c. 23rd February 1945
Braunschardt, Germany	17th April 1945
Schweinfurt, Germany	20th September 1945 - 15th February 1946
Bolling Field, District of Columbia	15th February - 31st March 1946
Nordholz, Germany	20th August 1946
Lechfeld, Germany	c. 1st December 1946
Bad Kissingen, Germany	5th March - 25th June 1947
Langley Field, Virginia	25th June - 30th December 1947
Neubiberg AB, Germany	30th December 1947
Landstuhl, Germany	1st August 1952 - 8th February 1956
RAF Alconbury, England	1st April 1976
RAF Bentwaters, England	**1st July 1988 - 30th September 1990**
Schriever AFB, Colorado	23rd October 2000 -

Decorations

- Distinguished Unit Citation: Italy, 25th May 1944.
- Distinguished Unit Citation: Germany, 20th April 1945.
- Air Force Outstanding Unit Award: 31st October 1955 - 8th February 195

87th Fighter-Interceptor Squadron

The 87th was activated as the 87th Aero Squadron on 18th August 1917. The unit was redesignated Squadron B on 25th July 1918 whilst operating from Park Field, Tennessee. The unit was reconstituted and consolidated with a second 87th squadron - the 87th Pursuit Squadron - on 1st December 1936. This second squadron was constituted on 19th February 1935, organised on 1st March and then deactivated on 1st September 1936. The combined unit was deactivated on 1st January 1938.

The 87th was reactivated as the 87th Pursuit Squadron (Interceptor) on 9th February 1942 at Dale Mabry Field, Florida. Three months after activation, on 15th May 1942, the unit was redesignated the 87th Fighter Squadron. By this time the unit had relocated to Morris Field, North Carolina and was flying the Curtiss P-40 Warhawk.

In 1944 the 87th converted to the Republic P-47 Thunderbolt and pressed the Axis forces up the Italian peninsula following their dynamic support at the invasions of Sicily and Anzio. The end of World War II found the 87th moving from Southern France, Italy and Austria before returning to the U.S. where it was deactivated at Langley Field on 15th July 1947.

On 1st November 1952, the 87th was reactivated as the 87th Fighter-Interceptor Squadron at Sioux City, Iowa, flying the North American P-51 Mustang. The following year saw the unit move in to the jet age when the P-51 made way for the North American F-86D Sabre Dog. On December 1954, the 87th FIS relocated across the Atlantic to RAF Bentwaters, England. The unit remained here for nine months before deactivating on 8th September 1955 and transferring personnel and equipment to the 512th FIS.

On 8th April 1956, the 87th was reactivated as a part of the Aerospace Defence Command at Lockborne AFB, Ohio, still flying the F-86D. In 1958, while still at Lockborne AFB, the 87th FIS re-equipped with the Convair F-102 Delta Dagger and this was followed two years later by the McDonnell F-101B Voodoo. The unit continued operating the F-101 until deactivation in June 1968.

This deactivation was short-lived as the 11th FIS at Duluth IAP, Minnesota, was redesignated as the 87th FIS in October 1968, flying the Convair F-106 Delta Dart. In May 1971 the 87th moved to K. I. Sawyer AFB, Michigan, where it continued to operate the F-106 for some fourteen years. The unit was deactivated on 1st October 1985.

The squadron was reactivated on 2nd April 1990 as the 87th Flying Training Squadron at Laughlin AFB, Texas, as a component of the 47th Flying Training Wing. The squadron was equipped with the Northrop T-38A Talon advanced supersonic trainer. The 87th FTS's new mission was to train USAF and Allied officers to fly fast jet aircraft and this remains its role today.

Decorations

- Distinguished Unit Citation: North Africa and Sicily, March - 17th August 1943.
- Distinguished Unit Citation: Italy, 16th - 20th April 1945.
- Air Force Outstanding Unit Award: 1st July 1976 - 30th June 1978.
- Air Force Outstanding Unit Award: 4th May 1981 - 3rd May 1983.
- Air Force Outstanding Unit Award: 16th March 1989 - 15th March 1991.

Stations

Kelly Field, Texas	18th August 1917
Selfridge Field, Michigan	c. September 1917
Park Field, Tennessee	c. December 1917 - 1st December 1918
Maxwell Field, Alabama	1st March 1935 - 1st September 1936
Dale Mabry Field, Florida	9th February 1942
Morris Field, North Carolina	1st May 1942
Rentschler Field, Connecticut	25th June - 28th September 1942
Egypt	12th November 1942
Libya	24th January 1943
Tunisia	13th March 1943
Malta	4th July 1943
Sicily	17th July 1943
Southern Italy	15th September 1943
Salsola, Italy	4th October 1943

Madna Airfield, Italy	17th November 1943
Capodichino, Italy	17th January 1944
Pomigliano, Italy	1st May 1944
Corsica	11th June 1944
Southern France	22nd August 1944
Iesi, Italy	4th October 1944
Fano, Italy	6th December 1944
Cesenatico, Italy	21st March 1945
Horsching, Austria	27th July 1945 - 25th June 1947
Langley Field, Virginia	25th June - 15th July 1947
Sioux City Municipal Airport, Iowa	1st November 1952
RAF Bentwaters, England	**13th December 1954 - 8th September 1955**
Lockbourne AFB, Ohio	8th April 1956
Duluth International Airport, Minnesota	30th September 1968
K.I. Sawyer AFB, Michigan	1st May 1971 - 1st October 1985
Laughlin AFB, Texas	2nd April 1990 -

Emblem

On an Air Force disc Azure and Argent, a bull's head Gules edged Sable, depicted frontal view with head lowered and curved horns Or with highlights of the second and edged Black; emanating from base near his nostrils a streak of Yellow lightning on either side, also edged Black. Above his head on a field of the first three stylised White aeroplanes with vapour trails of the last. Approved on 12th February 1969; replaced emblems approved on 16th July 1956 and 1st August 1945. *Motto:* VIGILANTIA EST PAX (Vigilance is Peace). Approved on 16th July 1956.

Previous Emblem

On a disc, tri-parted, from dexter Dark Grey, Light Grey, and Air Force Yellow, over centre of the disc, two White lightning bolts in saltire, between three silhouetted Black aircraft radiating to centre, outlined White; on the Dark Grey segment, three White stars; on the Light Grey segment a White storm cloud with Black precipitation lines; on the Air Force Yellow segment, a silhouetted city sky line White, with Black outlines and detail, and Green base area. *Motto:* Below the disc on an Air Force Yellow scroll inscribed in Black: VIGILANTIA EST PAX (Vigilance is Peace). Approved on 16th July 1956.

512th Fighter-Interceptor Squadron

The 512th Fighter-Interceptor Squadron was constituted as the 628th Bombardment Squadron (Dive) on 4th February 1943. The unit was activated on 1st March 1943 at Key Field, Mississippi, equipped with the Douglas A-20 Havoc light bomber. The 628th's first year of service saw it operate no less than ten different aircraft types. In addition to the A-20, the unit flew the Douglas A-24 Dauntless, Curtiss A-25 Helldiver, Douglas A-26 Invader, Vultee A-35 Vengeance, North American A-36 Apache, Cessna UC-78 Bobcat, North American BC-1, Bell P-39 Airacobra and the Curtiss P-40 Warhawk.

The unit was redesignated as the 512th Fighter-Bomber Squadron on 10th August 1943 and relocated to Congaree AAFld the following month where it re-equipped with the Republic P-47 Thunderbolt. The 512th FBS moved to Europe in 1944 where it operated from bases in the U.K., France, Belgium and Germany. The unit was redesignated as the 512th Fighter Squadron on 30th May 1944 and deactivated on 20th August 1946 following the end of the Second World War.

On 10th July 1952 the 512th was reactivated as a Fighter-Bomber Squadron under the control of the 406th Fighter-Bomber Group at RAF Manston, England, and was equipped with its first jet aircraft - the Republic F-84G Thunderjet. The unit's F-84 era lasted less than a year before it re-equipped again, this time with the North American F-86D Sabre Dog. The 512th FBS was redesignated as the 512th Fighter-Interceptor Squadron on 1st April 1954 and, four months later on 8th August, was redesignated again as the 512th Fighter-Day Squadron.

The unit's next move came on 1st November 1954 when it transferred to Soesterberg in the Netherlands. Less than a year later the 512th FDS found itself on the move again when, on 8th September, it moved back to England and settled into the Suffolk countryside at RAF Bentwaters. On arrival at Bentwaters the unit was redesignated as the 512th Fighter-Interceptor Squadron and absorbed the personnel and equipment of the 87th FIS. The unit remained at Bentwaters until it transferred to the 86th Fighter-Interceptor Wing at Sembach AB, Germany, on 24th March 1958. The 512th FIS was deactivated sixteen months later, on 1st July 1959.

The 512th was reactivated as a Tactical Fighter Squadron on 15th November 1976 to operate the McDonnell Douglas F-4E Phantom II from Ramstein AB, Germany. Assigned to the 86th Tactical Fighter Wing, the unit flew the F-4 for some ten years until it was progressively phased out in favour of the General Dynamics F-16C/D Fighting Falcon. Conversion to the F-16 was completed on 26th March 1987 with the delivery of the final three aircraft. The 512th TFS was redesignated as the 512th Fighter Squadron on 1st October 1991 and continued to operate the F-16C/D from Ramstein AB for another three years. On 1st July 1994 the squadron relocated to Aviano AB, Italy. On its arrival at Aviano the unit was deactivated 'on paper' but in reality it was redesignated as the 510th FS.

Decorations

- Distinguished Unit Citation: France, 7th September 1944.
- Distinguished Unit Citation: Belgium, 23rd - 27th December 1944.
- Air Force Outstanding Unit Award: 31st October 1955 - 31st October 1958.
- Air Force Outstanding Unit Award: July 1956 - February 1958.

Stations

Key Field, Mississippi	1st March 1943
Congaree AAFld, South Carolina	18 Sept 1943 - 13 March 1944
Ashford, England	6th April 1944
Tour-en-Bassin, France	c. 27th July 1944
Cretteville, France	17th August 1944
St Leonard, France	c. 4th September 1944
Mourmelon-le-Grand, France	c. 20th September 1944
Metz, France	31st January 1945
Asch, Belgium	8th February 1945
Handorf, Germany	15th April 1945
Nordholz, Germany	c. 5 June 1945 - 20 Aug 1946
RAF Manston, England	10th July 1952
Soesterberg, Netherlands	1st November 1954

RAF Bentwaters, England	8th September 1955
Sembach, Germany	24 March 1958 - 1st July 1959
Ramstein, Germany	15th Nov 1976 - 1st July 1994
Aviano, Italy	1st July 1994 - 1st July 1994

Emblem

A disc divided equally by a vertical arched line Air Force Yellow and Black, from a cloud formation proper, over the upper section of the disc, a Green dragon, his head and neck moving over the arched division, with his head toward the base, breathing Red flames of fire, his eyeballs White, his eyes Black with Red pupils, all between two Black silhouetted jet aircraft flying across the Yellow area; and a White lightning bolt charging the Black area. *Motto:* VIGILARE PRO PACE (On Guard for Peace). Approved 9th September 1955.

North American F-86D-50-NA Sabre (52-10045) of the Bentwaters-based 512th FIS preparing for a training mission from Wheelus AB, Tripoli, in 1956. (photo: late Peter Hutting (USAF retd) via George Pennick)

512th FIS F-86D-50-NA (52-4203) being re-armed with Mighty Mouse rockets prior to a training mission from Wheelus AB in 1956. (photo: late Peter Hutting (USAF retd) via George Pennick)

79th Tactical Fighter Squadron

The 79th was formed on 22nd February 1918, as the 79th Aero Service Squadron at Waco Field, Texas, with a primary task of aerial gunnery. The squadron was redesignated as Squadron B at Taliaferro Field, Texas, on 23rd July 1918 and deactivated four months later, on 15th November. A second 79th squadron was formed on 18th October 1927, this was the 79th Observation Squadron. The 79th OS was redesignated as the 79th Pursuit Squadron on 8th May 1929 and moved to Barksdale Field, Louisiana, where it flew the Boeing P-12 biplane. Both 79th squadrons were reconstituted and consolidated on 25th May 1933 and activated on 1st April 1933.

In 1938 the squadron eventually moved to Hamilton Field, California, after several stops in North Carolina, Florida and Washington. During the interwar years, the squadron transitioned from Boeing P-26 Peashooter to Curtiss P-39 Mohawk and then to Curtiss P-40 Warhawk aircraft. After the attack on Pearl Harbor, the 79th began patrolling the San Francisco Bay area for detection of hostile aircraft or ships. The squadron was later assigned duties patrolling near Washington, D.C. In January 1943 the squadron moved to March Field, California, and completed intensive training in the P-39 aircraft.

In August 1943 the squadron moved to Kings Cliffe, England, for the duration of World War II. As part of Eighth Air Force, the 79th, and its newly acquired Lockheed P-38 Lightnings, escorted medium and heavy bombers on strikes over Europe. In March 1944, as part of a new Allied tactic, 79th pilots strafed target areas after the bombers had departed. The squadron then earned its nickname, 'Loco Squadron,' after a series of very successful raids against transportation targets set an Army Air Forces record of 193 trains destroyed.

On D-Day the 79th mass-launched 180 sorties for five consecutive days, protecting Allied ships involved with the invasion at Normandy, France. In July 1944 the squadron re-equipped with the much faster North American P-51 Mustang and carried out air support for the 3rd Army in the Battle of the Bulge and other strategic areas. The squadron was deactivated at Camp Kilmer, New Jersey, in October 1945.

The 79th was reactivated in July 1946 at Biggs Field in El Paso, Texas. Between 1946 and 1952 the squadron's history is filled with several moves and aircraft changes before the 79th moved to Shaw Field, South Carolina. The squadron then moved to Langley AFB, Virginia, transitioning to the jet age with the Republic F-84G Thunderjet.

The 79th moved back to England on 1st June 1952 and took up residence at RAF Woodbridge. Upon their arrival, the 79th joined the United States Air Forces in Europe, becoming an integral part of NATO's air arm. Not long after arriving at Woodbridge, the 79th FBS temporarily relocated to nearby RAF Bentwaters whilst construction work on a suitable weapon storage facility was completed. The squadron moved back to Woodbridge on 1st October 1954.

The 79th's Thunderjets were superseded by the Republic F-84F Thunderstreak during 1955. The Thunderstreak remained with the squadron for just over two years when, in 1957, the 79th began converting to the North American F-100 Super Sabre. One year later, on 8th July 1958, the squadron was redesignated a Tactical Fighter Squadron.

In July 1961 the 79th TFS hosted the first ever NATO 'Tiger Meet' at RAF Woodbridge. This meeting drew together NATO squadrons sharing a common theme of a Tiger in their unit badge. This first meeting was so successful that the 79th TFS decided to host another one the following year and from that day on the NATO

'Tiger Meet' has become an annual event with each Tiger Squadron taking its turn to be the host unit.

In 1970 the 79th TFS left RAF Woodbridge and moved to RAF Upper Heyford where it converted to the swing-wing fighter-bomber version of the General Dynamics F-111, the F-111E. The 79th became the first squadron to be operational with the new aircraft in Europe and the first in the world in the 'E' model.

In January 1991, as part of Joint Task Force Proven Force at Incirlik Air Base, Turkey, the 79th became the first squadron to employ the F-111E in combat while supporting Operation Desert Storm. The Loco Squadron flew 293 combat sorties without sustaining a loss.

The squadron was redesignated the 79th Fighter Squadron (FS) on 1st October 1991, as part of the USAF's restructuring. The 79th FS was deactivated at Upper Heyford on 30th June 1993, and reactivated at its present home, Shaw AFB, South Carolina, on 1st January 1994, flying the Lockheed F-16C/D Fighting Falcon.

Decorations

- Distinguished Unit Citation: Central Germany, 8th April 1944.
- Air Force Outstanding Unit Award: 1st July 1956 - 30th September 1957.
- Air Force Outstanding Unit Award: 1st May 1963 - 31st December 1964.
- Air Force Outstanding Unit Award: 1st January 1965 - 31st March 1966.
- Air Force Outstanding Unit Award: 1st July 1968 - 31st March 1970.
- Air Force Outstanding Unit Award: 1st September 1970 - 30th June 1972.
- Air Force Outstanding Unit Award: 31st March 1973 - 30th June 1974.
- Air Force Outstanding Unit Award: 1st July 1977 - 30th June 1979.
- Air Force Outstanding Unit Award: 1st July 1981 - 30th June 1983.
- Air Force Outstanding Unit Award: 1st July 1987 - 30th June 1989.
- Air Force Outstanding Unit Award: 1st July 1990 - 30th June 1992.

Stations

Waco Field, Texas	22nd February 1918
Taliaferro Field, Texas	28th February - 15th November 1918
Barksdale Field, Louisiana	1st April 1933
Moffett Field, California	19th November 1939
Hamilton Field, California	9th September 1940 (operated from Oakland, California, 8th December 1941 - 8th February 1942)
Wilmington, North Carolina	c. 21st February 1942
Morris Field, North Carolina	23rd April 1942
Paine Field, Washington	30th September 1942
March Field, California	c. 1st January - 11th August 1943
Kings Cliffe, England	c. 27th August 1943 - 11th October 1945
Camp Kilmer, New Jersey	16th - 18th October 1945
Biggs Field, Texas	29th July 1946
Shaw Field, South Carolina	c. 25th October 1946
Langley AFB, Virginia	19th November 1951 - 22nd May 1952
RAF Woodbridge, England	**1st June 1952 (initially operated from RAF Bentwaters on a temporary basis until 1st October 1954)**
RAF Upper Heyford, England	c. 15th January 1970 - 30th June 1993 (deployed to Incirlik AB, Turkey, 23rd October 1990 - 28th February 1991)
Shaw AFB, South Carolina	1st January 1994 -

Emblem

On a Light Blue disc, bordered Yellow, a tiger's face affronte proper, resting his jaw on his paw in base, all proper, the paw grasping a lightning bolt Red and Black, emitting six flashes Red, all highlighted Yellow. Approved on 31st January 1955; replaced emblem approved on 5th February 1943.

This 79th TFS F-100F-10-NA (56-3893) shares the Wheelus AB flightline with F-100Ds from the same squadron. The unit had deployed to Wheelus from Woodbridge for an Armament Practice Camp during June 1958. (U.S. Air Force photo)

67th Special Operations Squadron

The 67th Special Operations Squadron ('Night Owls') was constituted as the 67th Air Rescue Squadron on 17th October 1952 and activated on 14th November 1952 at RAF Sculthorpe as part of the 9th Air Rescue Group. The squadron was equipped with the Boeing SB-29 and the Fairchild C-82 Packet. On 7th November 1953, the 67th ARS relocated to Prestwick in Scotland where it received the Douglas SC-47 Skytrain. 1955 was a busy year for the unit with the arrival of first examples of the Douglas SC-54 Rescuemaster as a replacement for the SC-47. It was also in this year that the 67th ARS began operating its first rotary-wing type, the Sikorsky SH-19. The arrival of the SH-19 resulted in the withdrawal of the SB-29 from the unit's inventory in early 1956. The following year saw the first examples of the Grumman SA-16 Albatross amphibian arrive at Prestwick as a replacement for the SC-54. The 67th ARS was deactivated three years later, on 18th March 1960.

The 67th ARS was reactivated at Prestwick on 18th June 1961 as part of the Military Air Transport Service and equipped with the HC-54, SA-16 and the SH-19. The unit was redesignated 67th Air Recovery Squadron on 1st August 1965 and, five months later on 8th January 1966, its designation was changed again to 67th Aerospace Rescue and Recovery Squadron. The 67th's next move was to Moron AB, Spain, on 1st July 1966, having received its first examples of the Lockheed C-130 Hercules the previous year.

The 67th ARRS relocated to RAF Woodbridge on 15th January 1970. At the time of its arrival at Woodbridge the 67th ARRS was equipped with three versions of the Lockheed C-130 Hercules (HC-130H, HC-130N and HC-130P), and the Sikorsky HH-3E Jolly Green Giant. During this period of operations, the 67th ARRS was assigned to the 39th Aerospace Rescue and Recovery Wing (ARRW), based at Eglin AFB, Florida. The 39th ARRW was controlled by Military Airlift Command's Aerospace Rescue and Recovery Service whose headquarters was at Scott AFB, Illinois.

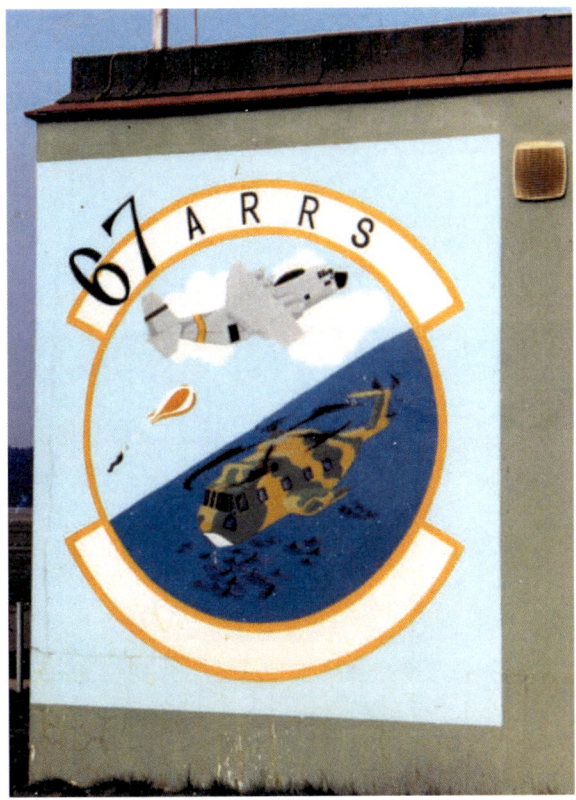

Artwork adorning the 67th ARRS operations building at Woodbridge in April 1979. (photo: George Pennick)

The 67th ARRS specialised in rescue and clandestine operations, including the delivery and retrieval of Special Forces personnel in foreign territory, and was one of the few units to be equipped with the spacecraft-recovery version of the Hercules, the HC-130P.

In early 1971 the 67th ARRS replaced its HH-3Es with the bigger, more powerful Sikorsky HH-53C Super Jolly Green Giant.

The Aerospace Rescue and Recovery Service merged with Special Operations Forces in 1988 and, on the 3rd

June in that year, the 67th ARRS was split up to form the 67th and the 21st Special Operations Squadrons (SOS). The 67th SOS was now assigned to Military Airlift Command's 39th Special Operations Wing (SOW) whose headquarters was located at Hulburt Field, Florida. After this restructuring the 67th SOS operated seven HC-130/N/P Hercules' having lost their HH-53Cs to the 21st SOS.

The first rescue mission for the 67th SOS came on 14th January 1989. Two of the squadron's HC-130Ns were tasked with providing refuelling support for two 21st SOS MH-53Js on a mission to rescue the crew of the 42,000 ton Cypriot registered bulk carrier 'Yarrawonga.' The ship had been damaged in heavy seas and a Force 8 gale and was drifting 400 miles off the west coast of Ireland. All 32 of the ship's crew were rescued successfully.

Special operations forces located in Europe were the subject of a major reorganisation during 1992, which saw the 39th SOW's headquarters move to RAF Alconbury on 15th January. As a consequence of this move, the 67th SOS departed RAF Woodbridge, along with the 21st SOS, to take up residence at RAF Alconbury on 1st April. On 1st December 1992, the 67th's parent unit, the 39th SOW, was deactivated and then reactivated as the 352nd Special Operations Group (SOG).

On 17th February 1995, the 67th SOS departed RAF Alconbury and relocated to the 352nd SOG's new headquarters at RAF Mildenhall. This is where the Night Owls reside today.

Lockheed HC-130N Hercules 69-5823 of the 67th ARRS pictured at Woodbridge in April 1979.
(photo: David Baker)

Decorations

- Air Force Outstanding Unit Award with Combat 'V' Device: 14th January - 23rd March 1991.
- Air Force Outstanding Unit Award: 1st July 1965 - 30th June 1967.
- Air Force Outstanding Unit Award: 8th February 1969 - 30th April 1970.
- Air Force Outstanding Unit Award: 1st May 1971 - 30th April 1972.
- Air Force Outstanding Unit Award: 1st July 1972 - 30th June 1974.
- Air Force Outstanding Unit Award: 1st July 1976 - 30th June 1978.
- Air Force Outstanding Unit Award: 1st July 1978 - 30th June 1980.
- Air Force Outstanding Unit Award: 1st June 1985 - 31st May 1987.
- Air Force Outstanding Unit Award: 24th March 1991 - 31st July 1992.
- Air Force Outstanding Unit Award: 1st August 1992 - 31st July 1993.
- Navy Meritorious Unit Commendation: 1st July 1967 - 26th July 1969.

Stations

RAF Sculthorpe, England	14th November 1952
Prestwick, Scotland	7th November 1953 - 18th March 1960
Prestwick, Scotland	18th June 1961
Moron AB, Spain	1st July 1966
RAF Woodbridge, England	**15th January 1970 (deployed to RAF Akrotiri, Cyprus, 13th - 27th June 1976; Incirlik AB, Turkey, 13th January - 18th March 1991 and 6th April - 10th June 1991)**
RAF Alconbury, England	1st April 1992 (deployed to Brindisi AB, Italy and Incirlik AB, Turkey, 2nd March - 12th July 1993)
RAF Mildenhall, England	17th February 1995 -

Emblem

Azure, two mullets of four points in chief bendwise, the sinister diminished by half between in dexter a decrescent Or and surmounted in base by a demi-owl issuant from base Gold Brown garnished Gold, all within a diminished bordure of the second. Approved on 16th June 1994; replaced emblem approved on 15th August 1985.

Mascot for the 67th SOS at Woodbridge was this Barn Owl seen posing for the camera in front of one of the squadron's HC-130Ns. (U.S. Air Force photo via Scott Jones)

21st Special Operations Squadron

The 21st Special Operations Squadron ('Dust Devils') was constituted as the 21st Pursuit Squadron (Interceptor) on 22nd December 1939 and activated on 1st February 1940 at Moffett Field, California. As a component of the 35th Pursuit Group, the 21st was equipped with the Curtiss P-40 Warhawk. The unit was deactivated on 2nd April 1946.

On 19th September 1955 the unit was consolidated with the 21st Helicopter Squadron, which was constituted on 24th February 1956. The 21st HS was activated at Donaldson AFB, South Carolina on 9th July 1956 equipped with the Piasecki H-21 Workhorse. This period of operation was to be short-lived as the unit was deactivated fifteen months later, on 15th October 1957.

After a ten year period of inactivity the unit was reactivated on 30th June 1967 at Shaw AFB, South Carolina, flying the Sikorsky CH-3. A redesignation occurred on 1st August 1968 when the unit became known as the 21st Special Operations Squadron. The 21st saw combat in Southeast Asia between November 1967 and August 1975, operating its CH-3s and later (from 1970) CH-53s from Nakhon Phanom RTAB, Thailand. The 21st SOS was deactivated on 22nd September 1975.

The 21st SOS was reactivated on the 3rd June 1988 at RAF Woodbridge using personnel and Sikorsky HH-53C Super Jolly Green Giant helicopters from the 67th ARRS and the 601st Tactical Air Support Squadron at Sembach AB, Germany. The 21st SOS was assigned to Military Airlift Command's 39th Special Operations Wing (SOW) whose headquarters was located at Hulburt Field, Florida. The squadron was tasked with combat search and rescue operations, deploying and retrieving special operations forces in clandestine operations as well as providing standby recovery support for NASA's space missions.

On 23rd October 1988 the 21st SOS received the first of six MH-53J Pave Low IIIEs to replace its HH-53s. This was airlifted in to RAF Woodbridge on board a Lockheed C-5A Galaxy. Further deliveries of the MH-53J were received on 3rd December. Some of the 21st's surplus HH-53s were airlifted back to Pensacola, Florida, to be converted to MH-53J standard.

The Dust Devils first rescue mission from Woodbridge came on 14th January 1989 when two of the squadron's MH-53Js rescued all 32 crew on board the 42,000 ton Cypriot registered bulk carrier 'Yarrawonga.' The ship was drifting in heavy seas and a Force 8 gale some 400 miles off the west coast of Ireland having been holed below the waterline. Both helicopters were refuelled several times by two HC-130Ns from the 67th SOS during the lengthy mission.

Special operations forces located in Europe were the subject of a major reorganisation during 1992 which saw the 39th SOW's headquarters move to RAF Alconbury on 15th January. As a consequence of this move, the 21st SOS departed RAF Woodbridge to take up residence at RAF Alconbury on 1st April. After arriving at Alconbury the 21st's parent unit, the 39th SOW, was deactivated and then reactivated as the 352nd Special Operations Group (SOG).

On 17th February 1995 the 21st SOS departed RAF Alconbury and relocated (along with the 67th SOS), to the 352nd SOG's new headquarters at RAF Mildenhall.

During 1999 the 21st SOS replaced its MH-53Js with the upgraded MH-53M Pave Low IV. This latest version of the MH-53 is externally identical to its predecessor but internally the cockpit has undergone a major upgrade. The MH-53M has been equipped with a 3D-colour moving map display, which can be relayed from the cockpit to other crewmembers located in the rear of the helicopter. This has the distinct advantage of allowing each crewmember to see their exact position whilst on a mission thus improving situational awareness. The MH-53M has also benefited from a new Lockheed Martin AP-102A weapons systems computer, updated avionics and new Multi-Functional Displays.

The 21st SOS put the MH-53M to good use in March 2000 when the squadron deployed to flood hit Central Mozambique to assist in the relief operation.

Decorations

- Distinguished Unit Citation (Philippine Islands): 7th December 1941 - 10th May 1942.
- Distinguished Unit Citation (Philippine Islands): 8th - 22nd December 1942.
- Distinguished Unit Citation (Philippine Islands): 6th January - 8th March 1943.
- Presidential Unit Citation (Southeast Asia): 1st November 1968 - 1st May 1969.
- Presidential Unit Citation (Southeast Asia): 1st October 1969 - 30th April 1970.
- Presidential Unit Citation (Southeast Asia): 1st April 1972 - 22nd February 1973.
- Air Force Outstanding Unit Award with Combat 'V' Device: 1st September 1970 - 30th April 1971.
- Air Force Outstanding Unit Award with Combat 'V' Device: 1st December 1971 - 29th February 1972.
- Air Force Outstanding Unit Award with Combat 'V' Device: 23rd February 1973 - 28th February 1974.
- Air Force Outstanding Unit Award with Combat 'V' Device: 24th January - 2nd May 1975.
- Air Force Outstanding Unit Award with Combat 'V' Device: 14th January - 23rd March 1991.
- Air Force Outstanding Unit Award: 24th March 1991 - 31st July 1992.
- Air Force Outstanding Unit Award: 1st August 1992 - 31st July 1993.
- Philippine Presidential Unit Citation (WWII).
- Republic of Vietnam Gallantry Cross with Palm: [27] November 1967 - 28th January 1973.

Sikorsky MH-53J Pave Low IIIE of the 21st SOS on a low level training mission over woodland.
(U.S. Air Force photo)

Stations

Moffett Field, California	1st February 1940
Hamilton Field, California	10th September - October 1941
Nichols Field, Luzon	c. 20th November 1941 (air echelon operated from Clark Field, c. 9th - c. 15th December 1941)
Lubao, Luzon	c. 25th December 1941
Bataan, Luzon	c. 4th January - April 1942 (a section of the air echelon operated from Mindanao, c. 9th April - c. 1st May 1942)
Donaldson AFB, South Carolina	9th July 1956 - 15th October 1957
Shaw AFB, South Carolina	15th July - 27th November 1967
Nakhon Phanom RTAFB, Thailand	27th November 1967 - 22nd September 1975 (air echelon operated from Ubon RTAFB, Thailand, 11th - 13th April 1975; the USS *Midway*, 20th April - 22nd September 1975; and U-Tapao RTNAF, Thailand, 2nd - 5th May and 14th - 16th May 1975)
RAF Woodbridge, England	**3rd June 1988 (deployed to Batman AB, Turkey, 13th January - 18th March 1991; Diyarbkir AB, Turkey, 6th April - 10th June 1991)**
RAF Alconbury, England	1st April 1992 (deployed to Brindisi AB, Italy and Incirlik AB, Turkey, 2nd March - 12th July 1993)
RAF Mildenhall, England	17th February 1995

Emblem

Gules, a funnel cloud bendwise Or shaded Sable detailed Brown supporting a devil's face Buff shaded Brown, highlighted White, detailed Sable; all within a diminished bordure Azure. Approved on 18th October 1967 and reinstated in 1996; replaced emblems approved on 5th June 1995 and 20th December 1941.

4. 'Twin-Bases' Aircraft

BOEING SB-29 'SUPER DUMBO'

*In-flight study of a Boeing SB-29 (44-69971) belonging to Military Airlift Command's Air Rescue Service.
(photo: D Menard via George Pennick)*

Fifteen B-29s and one B-29A were adapted for air rescue duty after the Second World War. Nicknamed 'Super Dumbo' and designated SB-29, these aircraft were modified to carry an air-droppable A-3 Edo lifeboat and remained in service throughout the Korean Conflict and into the mid 1950s.

It is not a widely acknowledged fact that this aircraft, along with the Grumman SA-16A Albatross, was the first USAF aircraft type to be based at Bentwaters, arriving on 1st July 1951. Although it was only to be a temporary stay at the Suffolk base, the Super Dumbos of C-Flight, 9th Air Rescue Squadron, preceded the arrival of the F-86A Sabres of the 91st Fighter-Interceptor Squadron by nearly three months.

The primary mission of the SB-29 was rescue support for units flying long distances over water. In the event of an aircraft ditching in the sea the SB-29 would be sent to the area to commence a search for survivors. After locating the aircrew to be rescued, the SB-29 released the lifeboat, which automatically deployed a parachute to slow its rate of descent. The boat, a self-righting type, was carried with the stern facing forward and, as well as the parachute, it featured two fins on the bow that would help glide to the sea. The 30ft long A-3 featured an inboard engine, could carry up to 14 people and had sufficient fuel for a 500-mile range in addition to a supply of food and water. The survivors would board the lifeboat and either await rescue from a ship or head toward land making use of the A-3s inboard engine.

The Super Dumbo was equipped with the same defensive armament as that of the production B-29 except for the forward lower gun turret. This was deleted in order to accommodate the radome for the AN/APQ-13 radar which was located aft of the nose landing gear.

The SB-29s operated by the 9th ARS were derivatives of the major production version of the Superfortress, the B-29, of which 2,513 were built. The first production B-29 rolled off the production line at Boeing's Wichita plant in September of 1943 with production finishing during October 1945.

Following the end of the Korean War, the B-29 was rapidly withdrawn from service. The last of the USAF's B-29 bombers had been replaced by the Boeing B-47 Stratojet by 1954. The KB-29M and KB-29P tankers were all replaced by the Boeing KC-97 by 1957. Other B-29s were modified for weather reconnaissance under the designation WB-29. A few were converted to TB-29 target towing and radar evaluation aircraft, and some became QB-29 target drones. The last B-29 (a TB-29) was retired from the USAF inventory on 21st June 1960.

Specification of the Boeing B-29 Superfortress

- Manufacturer: Boeing Aircraft Corp.
- Power Plant: Four Wright R-3350-23 Duplex Cyclone eighteen-cylinder air-cooled radial engines each with two General Electric superchargers, delivering 2,200hp for takeoff and having a war emergency rating of 2,300hp at 25,000 feet.
- Performance: Maximum Speed - 357mph at 30,000 feet and 306mph at sea level, Maximum Continuous Cruising Speed - 342mph at 30,000 feet, Economical Cruising Speed - 220mph at 25,000 feet, Initial Climb Rate - 900 feet per minute at combat weight. An altitude of 20,000 feet could be attained in 38 minutes.
- Service Ceiling: 33,600 feet.
- Range: Maximum - 3250 miles at 25,000 feet with 5,000lb bomb load, Practical Operational Radius - 1,600 to 1,800 miles, Maximum Ferry - up to 6,000 miles.
- Weights: Empty - 74,500lbs, Normal Loaded - 120,000lbs, Maximum Overload - 135,000lbs.
- Dimensions: Wingspan - 141 feet 3 inches, Length - 99 feet, Height - 27 feet 9 inches, Wing Area - 1,736 square feet.
- Armament: Twelve 0.50-inch machine guns in four remotely controlled turrets (two above and two below the fuselage) and in the tail, each with 1,000 rounds of ammunition. In addition, early production blocks had a single rearward-firing 20-mm M2 Type B cannon with 100 rounds in the tail position. Later, two more guns were provided for the forward top turret. Maximum internal short-range, low-altitude bomb load was 20,000 pounds. A load of 5,000lbs of bombs could be carried over a 1,600-mile radius at high altitude. A load of 12,000lbs of bombs could be carried over a 1,600-mile radius at medium altitude.

GRUMMAN SA-16A ALBATROSS

Grumman SA-16A Albatross (51-5305) of the 67th Air Rescue Squadron, photographed at Prestwick, Scotland in 1963. The SA-16A equipped C-Flight, 9th Air Rescue Squadron at Bentwaters from 1st July 1951 until 14th November 1952. (photo: Mick Sudds)

The Albatross was designed to meet a U.S. Navy requirement for a utility aircraft that could operate from land or water and, with skis, from snow and ice. Impressed by the performance of the Grumman Goose during the Second World War, the U.S. Navy asked Grumman to come up with a design for a larger amphibian that had a greater range.

In 1944, Grumman submitted and gained approval for Design No. G-64. Later renamed 'Albatross,' the G-64 design was for an aircraft operated by a crew of four and with a cabin capacity of 10 passengers, stretchers, or 5,000lbs of cargo, depending on the mission. The aircraft was of conventional all-metal construction consisting of a deep 'V' two-step hull and a shoulder mounted wing. In addition, there were pylons under the wing and outboard of the engines, which made it possible to carry drop tanks for increased range. In addition, fuel could be carried in the fixed underwing floats. To help reduce the Albatross's takeoff run, an important consideration when carrying heavy loads or when operating in open seas, snow or ice, provision was made for the fitting of Jet Assisted Takeoff (JATO) bottles either side of the rear fuselage.

Ordered by the Navy as a utility aircraft, the prototype, designated XJR2F-1, made its maiden flight on 24th October 1947. After satisfactory flight-testing the aircraft went into production with the designation UF-1. It wasn't long before the USAF realised the potential of the type and placed an order for 297. These aircraft were destined to be used in the air-sea rescue role with the designation of SA-16A. The majority of the SA-16As were assigned to Military Air Transport Service's (MATS) Air Rescue Service (ARS). Other USAF commands operating the type in the air-sea rescue role were Strategic Air Command (SAC), Tactical Air Command (TAC), Pacific Air Forces (PACAF), Air Force Reserve (AFRes) and the Air National Guard (ANG).

Experience with the UF-1 led to a number of modifications, such as more effective de-icing boots for the leading edges of airfoils, a 16.5-foot increase in wingspan with a leading edge camber replacing the slots of the earlier model. To compensate for the larger wing, additional aileron, fin and stabiliser area was provided. The revised model, introduced in 1955, was named UF-2.

In 1957 an improved USAF version equivalent to the Navy's UF-2 went into service as the SA-16B. 241 of the USAF's SA-16As were eventually converted to the 'B' configuration joining the 21 new-build B-models already in service.

In 1962 the U.S. Armed Services introduced a unified designation system for aircraft types. This resulted in the USAF's SA-16A and SA-16B being redesignated as the HU-16A and HU-16B respectively and the USN's UF-1 and UF-2 becoming the HU-16C and HU-16D. Navy aircraft specially winterised for Antarctic service (UF-1Ls) became LU-16Cs, and five dual control trainers initially designated UF-1T became TU-16C. Albatrosses assigned to the U.S. Coast Guard originally designated UF-1G were reclassified as HU-16E.

An anti-submarine warfare version (HU-16B MAD) was introduced in May 1961. This version was equipped with a nose radome housing an AN/APS 88 search radar, a retractable Magnetic Anomaly Detection (MAD) boom in the tail, electronic countermeasures (ECM) equipment and a 70 million candlepower searchlight. Fuselage stores included sonobuoys, marine markers and underwater sound signal charges, all with their own launching equipment. Underwing stores pylons were fitted to facilitate the carriage of torpedoes, rockets, depth charges and other ordnance. Although not purchased by the U.S. forces, it was used abroad, most notably by Norway which operated 18 of the type.

Grumman modified most USAF HU-16B airframes at their mid-life to a 'triphibian configuration.' This required the fitting of a keel skid to enable the aircraft to operate from sand or snow in addition to land and water.

Too late for service in World War II, the Albatross was used extensively in the Korean and Vietnam wars. During the Korean conflict Albatrosses rescued almost 1,000 United Nations personnel from coastal waters and rivers, often behind enemy lines. They also made numerous dramatic and hazardous rescues in South East Asia, often taxiing many miles over rough, open water when the prevailing conditions prevented the aircraft taking off.

A total of 464 Albatrosses were produced between 1950 and 1964. The type was retired by the USAF in 1974 but remained in service with the USN for another two years. The USCG retired its last Albatross in 1983.

The Albatross was exported to Canada, Mexico, Argentina, Germany, Brazil, Chile, Venezuela, Peru, Indonesia, Philippines, Thailand, Taiwan, Japan, Malaysia, Italy and Greece. The majority of these countries used the Albatross for search and rescue operations.

SA-16B Albatross Specifications

- Manufacturer: Grumman Aviation Corp.
- Primary Mission: Air-Sea Rescue.
- Crew: Four.
- Power plant: Two Wright R-1820-76A Cyclone each rated at 1,425hp (1,062kW).
- Performance: Maximum Level Speed 'Clean' at Sea Level - 205kts (236mph; 380km/h), Cruising Speed at Optimum Altitude - 149kts (172mph; 277km/h), Maximum Rate of Climb at Sea Level - 1,170ft (357m) per minute.
- Dimensions: Wingspan - 96 feet 8 inches (29.46m), Wing Area - 1,035.00 square feet (96.15m^2), Length - 62 feet 10 inches (19.15m), Height - 25 feet 10 inches (7.87m), Tailplane Span - 31 feet (9.45m).
- Ceiling: 23,500 feet (7,165m).
- Weights: Empty - 22,883lbs (10,380kg), Normal Takeoff - 30,353lbs (13,768kg), Maximum Takeoff - 34,000lbs (15,422kg) on water and 37,500lbs (17010kg) on land.
- Fuel Capacity: Internal - 1,088 U.S. gallons (4,119 litres), External - Up to two 295 U.S. gallon (1,117-litre) drop tanks.
- Range: Ferry - 3,010 nm (3,466 miles; 5,578 km), Normal - 1,490 nm (1,716 miles; 2,761 km).
- Armament: None.

NORTH AMERICAN F-86A SABRE

Fine air-to-air study of a 91st FIS/81st FIG F-86A Sabre, circa 1953. (photo: Harry Eckes)

The 26th September 1951 saw the arrival of the North American F-86A Sabres of the 91st FIS/81st FIG at Bentwaters, having relocated from RAF Shepherds Grove. The 81st FIG became the first foreign unit to assist in the air defence of the U.K. since the ending of the Second World War and the Group's F-86As were the first examples of the type in Europe.

The Sabre entered USAAF service in 1949 and earned the accolade of 'one of the greatest fighters of all time,' largely due to its outstanding performance during the Korean War. Following the end of that conflict the type went on to become front-line equipment with numerous Allied air forces.

The F-86 started off as North American Aviation's company project (named NA-134), designed to satisfy a U.S. Navy requirement for a carrier-based jet fighter. The project was authorised in 1943 by NAA president J. H. 'Dutch' Kindelberger and undertaken by a design team led by J. Lee Atwood and Ray Rice. The team came up with an aircraft having a short, rotund fuselage featuring a nose-mounted air intake for the jet engine and a straight, low-mounted wing.

The U.S. Navy, satisfied with the resultant design, ordered three prototypes of the NA-134 under the designation XFJ-1 on 1st January 1945. This was followed four months later, on 28th May, by a contract for 100 production FJ-1s (NA-141).

At around the same time that J. Lee Atwood, Ray Rice and their team began work on the XFJ-1, the USAAF issued a requirement for a medium-range day fighter capable of at least 600mph and also able to carry out escort and dive-bombing missions.

On 22nd November 1944, North American submitted a proposal to the USAAF that was based on the XFJ-1 and given the company designation of NA-140. The USAAF liked what they saw and issued a Letter Contract on 18th May 1945 that covered the production of three NA-140 aircraft under the designation XP-86.

Both the XFJ-1 and the XP-86 were designed around a General Electric J-36 axial flow turbojet fed by a nose intake and with a tailpipe exhaust exiting at the rear of the aircraft. A mock-up of the XP-86 was completed and approved on 20th June 20 1945 but early wind tunnel tests concluded that the airframe would not be able to attain the required speed of 600 mph. This would have been the end of the project under normal circumstances but developments arising from the end of the Second World War handed the XP-86 a lifeline.

Following the surrender of Germany in May 1945, the Allied forces were eager to get hold of any information relating to the latest German jet fighters as well as uncovering secret research on jet engines.

American teams were selected from industry and research institutions and sent into occupied Germany to investigate captured weapons research data, microfilm it, and ship it back to the U.S.A. Amongst the vast amount of captured data was a series of reports relating to the wind tunnel testing of numerous aerodynamic shapes. One report in particular, dated 1940, concluded that there were significant advantages offered by swept wings at speeds of around Mach 0.9. The report also stated that a straight-winged aircraft was severely affected by the compression effects of shock waves as supersonic speed was reached. The swept wing delayed this effect allowing better control at higher speeds. There was, however, one drawback with the use of a swept wing; it was highly unstable at low speeds.

F-86A-5-NA Sabre (49-1249) of the 92nd FIS/81st FIG pictured at RAF Shepherds Grove, circa 1953. (photo: via Mick Sudds)

The North American design team were keen to incorporate these findings into the XP-86 project. Whilst the swept wing did offer the possibility of attaining the 600mph mark, the company did not want to produce an aircraft that would be dangerous at low speeds. The cure for the problem would be the fitting of automatic wing leading edge slats which, when operated at low speeds, would increase lift and would thus lower the stalling speed.

In August 1945, project aerodynamicist L. P. Greene proposed to Raymond Rice that the P-86 should be changed to a swept-wing configuration. A series of wind tunnel tests in September 1945 confirmed the reduction in drag at high subsonic speeds in addition to the beneficial effect of the slats on low speed stability. As a result of incorporating the swept wing, the limiting Mach number was increased to 0.875. Drawing on the results from these tests, a revised proposal was submitted to the USAAF in the autumn of 1945. The revised XP-86 design gained approval on 1st November of that year.

The XFJ-1 made its maiden flight on 27th November 1946 but, due to design changes to its swept wing, the XP-86 still had some twelve months to go before it reached this milestone.

On 20th December 1946 the USAAF approved a Letter Contract for 33 production P-86As. The first of three prototypes, 45-59507, was completed on 8th August 1947 and was fitted with a Chevrolet-built J35-C-3 turbojet rated at 4,000lbs static thrust. The aircraft made its maiden flight on 1st October with company test pilot George Welch at the controls. This first flight was problem free up until the point that the undercarriage was lowered for the landing. The nose gear jammed in the retracted position and, after forty minutes of manoeuvring in an attempt to free it, George Welch decided to recover the XP-86 on just its main gear, keeping the aircraft's nose high for as long as possible once on the runway. Luck was to play its part eventually when the sudden impact of the XP-86's touchdown on the runway released the jammed nose gear resulting in a normal landing on all three wheels. The USAF granted final approval for the 33 P-86As, as well as an additional 190 P-86Bs, on 16th October 1947.

George Welch took the XP-86 through the sound barrier for the first time on 26th April 1948 after entering a shallow dive. This was the second time a U.S. aircraft had broken the sound barrier - the Bell X-1 flown by Capt. Chuck Yeager being the first to do so on 14th October 1947. Although the XP-86 was capable of attaining supersonic speed in a dive, production Sabre's would be limited to Mach 0.95 below 25,000 feet because of the aircraft's tendency to roll at such a speed.

On 30th November 1948 the first XP-86 (45-59597) was officially handed over to the USAF, although by this time it had been redesignated as XF-86. This aircraft was eventually written off in a crash during September 1952 after logging a total of 241 flying hours. The second and third prototypes (45-59598 and 45-59599) remained in the test programme until they were withdrawn from use in April 1953.

The first production version of the Sabre was the P-86A; the only difference between this and the XP-86 was the introduction of the 5,200lbs static thrust General Electric J47 in place of the J35. The order for the first 33 P-86A-1-NAs was placed on 16th October 1947 and these were allocated the NAA designation of NA-151.

F-86A-5-NA Sabre (49-1228) of the 78th FIS/81st FIG at RAF Shepherds Grove, circa 1953. (photo: via Mick Sudds)

The first P-86A-1-NA (47-0605) made its maiden flight on 20th May 1948, powered by a General Electric J47-GE-1 turbojet. Eight days later, the first and second production aircraft were officially accepted by the USAF although both remained at Inglewood to allow NAA to continue its development work. In June 1948 the USAF designation for the type changed from P-86 to F-86.

The F-86A-1-NAs could be distinguished by their curved windshields and the flush fitting, electrically operated doors that covered the muzzles of the six 0.5mm guns (three on either side of the nose). The muzzle doors opened automatically when the guns were fired, and closed automatically after each burst.

Although the F-86A-1-NA was 347lbs heavier than the XP-86, the increased power of the J47 produced a top speed of around 673mph at sea level (some 75mph faster), in addition to a climb rate figure more than double that of the prototype. The impressive performance of the F-86A-1-NA prompted the USAF to attempt to break the world air speed record at the National Air Races in Cleveland, Ohio, on 5th September 1948. At the time the record was held by a U.S. Navy Douglas D-558-1 Skystreak, which achieved a speed of 650.796mph on 25th August 1947. Unlike the F-86A, however, this aircraft was an experimental design and not a standard production aircraft.

In front of a crowd of around 80,000 spectators, Major Robert L. Johnson performed six low-level passes in the fourth production aircraft (47-0608) achieving an average speed of 669.480mph. Due to problems associated with the timing equipment the new record could not be officially endorsed by the Fédération Aéronautique Internationale. Success came ten days later, on 15th September, when Major Johnson set a new record of 670.981mph in F-86A-1-NA 47-0611 at Muroc Dry Lake.

The last of 33 F-86A-1-NAs (47-0637) was delivered in March 1949; all of these aircraft were used for test and evaluation purposes. F-86As from the second block (designated F-86A-5-NA) were the first to enter operational service with the USAF. The first of 188 of these J47-GE-7-powered aircraft was delivered in March 1949 with the final example handed over to the USAF six months later. The F-86A-5-NA differed from the A-1 in a number of areas. Amongst these was the fitting of a V-shaped armoured windscreen in place of the earlier curved example and the deletion of the electrically operated gun muzzle doors. The A-5 also introduced a jettisonable cockpit canopy, underwing pylons capable of carrying 500lb or 1,000lb bombs or 206 U.S. gallon fuel tanks, an improved canopy de-icing system, an anti-erosion coating on the nose intake duct and, from the 116th aircraft, a fully automatic wing slat mechanism.

On 29th May 1948 the USAF issued a letter contract for 333 additional F-86As, with final approval being reached on 23rd February 1949. Deliveries of these aircraft, powered by an improved General Electric J47-GE-13 engine rated at 5,200lbs static thrust, began in October 1949 and ended in December of the following year. The first 530 F-86As were fitted with a Mark 18 optical lead computing gunsight but this was later replaced by the more advanced A-1CM radar ranging sight that was coupled to an AN/APG-30 radar scanner installed in the upper lip of the nose intake. The last 24 A-5s to roll off the production line were fitted with the A-1CM radar ranging sight whilst earlier aircraft were retrofitted with the system in the field. These aircraft were redesignated F-86A-7-NA.

During February 1949 the first F-86A-5-NAs entered operational service. The first unit to receive the A-5 was the 1st Fighter Group based at March AFB in California, with the 94th Fighter-Interceptor Squadron being the first of the Group's three squadrons to take delivery of the new type. The 1st FG's remaining squadrons - the 27th FIS and the 71st FIS - had converted from the F-80 Shooting Star to the F-86A by the end of May 1949. The next two units to receive the type were the 4th Fighter Group at Langley AFB and the 81st Fighter Group, based at Kirtland AFB. The latter unit was tasked with the defence of the nuclear bomb facilities at Alamogordo, New Mexico.

On 4th March 1949 the F-86 was officially named 'Sabre;' the result of a contest held by the 1st Fighter Group to find a name for its new fighter.

The first Reserve unit to receive the Sabre was the 116th Fighter-Interceptor Squadron of the Washington Air National Guard, which received its first F-86As on 22nd December 1950.

December 1950 saw the 4th FG's F-86As enter the Korean War. During the first month of the conflict, the 4th FG flew 234 missions, engaged the enemy MiG-15s 76 times and scored eight victories with the loss of one aircraft. By May 1951 the unit had flown 3,550 sorties and scored 22 victories. During the following month another eight MiGs were shot down for the loss of three Sabres. July of 1951 saw the 4th FG begin to replace its F-86As with the improved F-86E; the final F-86A left the Korean theatre in June 1952.

The F-86A was replaced in active USAF service by the F-86E beginning in the autumn of 1951. The surplus F-86As were transferred to Air National Guard units beginning with the 198th FIS in Puerto Rico. The next units to receive the type were the 115th and 195th FISs at Van Nuys, California, the 196th FIS at Ontario, and the 197th FIS at Phoenix, Arizona.

F-86A-5-NA Specifications

- Manufacturer: North American Aviation Corp.
- Primary Mission: Single-seat day-fighter.
- Crew: One.
- Power Plant: One General Electric J47-GE-13 rated at 5,200lbs static thrust at sea level.
- Performance: Maximum Speed - 679mph at sea level and 601mph at 35,000 feet, Initial Climb Rate - 7,470 feet per minute at sea level (An altitude of 40,000 feet could be reached in 10.4 minutes).
- Dimensions: Wingspan - 37.12 feet, Wing Area - 287.9 square feet, Length - 37.54 feet, Height - 14.74 feet.
- Weights: Empty - 10,093lbs, Maximum Takeoff - 14,108lbs, Combat - 13,791lbs.
- Service Ceiling - 48,000 feet.
- Range: 1,270 miles (with drop tanks).
- Armament: Six 0.5-in (12.7-mm) fixed forward-firing machine guns, plus provision for two 1,000-lb (454-kg) bombs or various other bombs, rockets or other ordnance with or without two 200 U.S. gallon drop tanks.

F-86A Sabre of the 91st FIS/81st FIG, circa 1953. (photo: Harry Eckes)

1/Lt Harry Eckes at the controls of F-84F-45-RE 52-6783 of the 91st FBS/81st FBW. (photo: Harry Eckes)

STINSON L-5E SENTINEL

Stinson L-5E Sentinel of the 7554th Target Tow Flight photographed over the Norfolk/Suffolk coast whilst the unit was operating from RAF Sculthorpe. (photo: late Peter Hutting (USAF retd) via George Pennick)

Developed from the commercial three-seat Stinson Model 105 Voyager, the L-5 Sentinel was fitted with a more powerful Lycoming O-435 flat six-cylinder, air-cooled engine, rated at 190 hp. The fuselage was constructed of a tubular steel frame, covered by fabric, whilst the wing was of wood construction and also fabric covered.

The USAAF's need for a liaison aircraft led to a 1941 order of six commercial Stinson Voyagers for evaluation as YO-54s. The Army Air Force was so impressed with its performance that an order was immediately placed for 275 units. The aircraft was redesignated as O-62 in an initial Observation classification before the designation was changed again in April 1942 to L-5 (L for Liaison class).

The L-5's first flight was on 28th June 1941 and, by the end of final production in 1945, 3,608 had been built . This figure made the type second only to the Piper L-4 in terms of production figures for U.S. observation aircraft built during the Second World War. An additional 900 more were on order but these were eventually cancelled due to the ending of the war. 40 L-5As and 60 L-5Bs were delivered to the RAF to serve in Burma and India and 306 L-5Bs and L-5Es went to the US Navy, Coast Guard, and Marine Corps as OY-1s.

Of the 3,608 L-5s that were built, most were the L-5 or L-5A observer model whilst 679 of the L-5B ambulance model were produced. The L-5C had provision for a K-20 reconnaissance camera, and the L-5E added drooping ailerons, which operated in conjunction with the flaps to increase lift for even shorter landings and takeoffs. The final production version of the Sentinel was the L-5G.

The short field takeoff and landing capability of the L-5 made it suitable for a variety of roles. Among these were reconnaissance, removing litter patients from front line areas, delivering supplies to isolated units, laying communications wire, spotting enemy targets for attack aircraft, transporting and rescuing Allied personnel to and from remote areas not accessible by normal aircraft types. The L-5 could operate from dirt tracks, unprepared fields or anywhere that had about 300ft of relatively clear and flat surface to serve as a runway. The takeoff distance could be reduced to as little as 50ft with full flaps and this unique ability gave rise to its nickname of 'Flying Jeep.' Military service continued into the Korean War, where the U.S. Marines armed it with bazooka rocket launchers on the wing struts, before it was officially retired.

The aircraft remained in service with USAF units until 1953, and with the U.S. Army as late as 1962 when they were redesignated U-19 to conform to the new joint service identification system.

The L-5E version of the Sentinel was based at Bentwaters from 22nd March 1952 until the 16th December 1952 and was assigned to the 7554th Target Tow Flight.

L-5E Specifications

- Manufacturer: Stinson-Vultee Aircraft Corp.
- Power Plant: Lycoming 0-435-1 producing 190 horsepower.
- Performance: Maximum Speed - 130mph, Cruising Speed - 90mph.
- Dimensions: Wingspan - 34 feet, Wing Area - 155.00 square feet, Length - 24 feet 1 inch, Height: 8 feet 11 inches.
- Weight: Empty - 1,550lbs, Gross - 2,020lbs, Maximum - 2,050lbs.
- Range: 360 miles
- Service Ceiling: 15,600 feet.
- Armament: None

F-101A-35-MC Voodoo (54-1468) of the 92nd TFS, seen at Bentwaters 'Armed Forces Day' on 16th May 1959. (photo: Mick Sudds)

F-4C-24-MC Phantom of the 91st TFS/81st TFW taxies out for takeoff at Bentwaters during August 1970. (photo: Alan Haynes)

A pair of 510th TFS 'Buzzard' A-10s line up for takeoff at Bentwaters in 1989. (photo: Author)

Those were the days! A busy scene at the Runway 25 'End-Of-Runway' (EOR) checkpoint with a mixture of 510th TFS A-10s and 527th AS F-16s preparing for their next missions in March 1989. (photo: Author)

HC-130H Hercules (65-0962) of the 67th ARRS photographed at Woodbridge in April 1979. (photo: George Pennick)

HH-53C Super Jolly Green Giants of the 67th ARRS await their next mission at Woodbridge during 1985. (photo: Author)

DOUGLAS TB-26C INVADER

Douglas TB-26C-45-DT Invader (44-35667), 7554th Target Tow Flight, seen on temporary duty (TDY) at a base in Germany. (photo: H O Pritchard via D Menard and George Pennick)

Derived from the highly successful Douglas A-26C Invader light bomber of the Second World War, the primary mission of the TB-26C was that of towing aerial targets. TB-26Cs of the 7554th Target Tow Flight were based at Bentwaters for nine months between 22nd March and 16th December 1952 before relocating to RAF Sculthorpe.

The A-26 was originally conceived as a private venture by the Douglas Aircraft Corporation, with design work commencing in late 1940. The design team, headed by Edward Heinemann and Robert Donovan, carried out a preliminary study aimed at developing a light bomber/attack aircraft that would be seen as a common successor to the Douglas A-20 Havoc, Martin B-26 Marauder and the North American B-25 Mitchell.

The team had devised a proposal for the new aircraft, loosely based on the A-20 Havoc, by the end of January 1941. The proposal covered two different versions, a three-seat light bomber with a transparent nose for a navigator/bombardier (A-26C) and a two-seat radar-equipped, night-fighter with a solid nose fitted with forward-firing machine guns (A-26B). Apart from the different nose configurations, the two versions were to be identical.

The A-26 project suffered delays from the onset due largely to the USAAF being unsure as to what quantities of each version they required and what armament was to be fitted to the A-26B. While the AAF was pondering over the armament fitment to the 'B', Douglas continued with the development of the 'C.' It was this latter version that would eventually give rise to the TB-26C.

As mentioned previously, the A-26C was virtually identical in all respects to the A-26B except for the transparent nose and two forward-firing 0.50-inch machine guns on the starboard side. The positioning of a bombardier in the transparent nose enabled the A-26C to carry out accurate bombing from medium altitudes. The role of the bombardier was carried out by the second pilot who was able to move from the cockpit and take up his position in the nose during flight.

Production of the A-26C was initially carried out at both the Long Beach and Tulsa plants but, in late 1944, production of the C-model was switched solely to Tulsa with the B-model being built at Long Beach. A total of 1091 A-26Cs were eventually built, 1086 of them were built at Tulsa (A-26C-16-DT to A-26C-55-DT) and the remaining 5 at Long Beach (A-26C-1-DL and A-26C-2-DL). Invader production ended at Tulsa in August of 1945, when the end of the Second World War brought the cancellation of all further A-26C contracts.

The A-26 entered the European theatre with the Ninth Air Force in June 1944 with the first combat mission being carried out some three months later, on 17th September. This first mission, a low-altitude bombing strike involving a mixture of A-26Bs and A-20K Havocs, was carried out by the 553rd Bombardment Squadron of the 386th Bombardment Group, based at Great Dunmow in Essex, England.

The first operational unit in Europe to be fully equipped with A-26Bs was the 416th Bombardment Group who converted from Havocs to Invaders in November 1944. The last combat mission of the war in Europe involved some 124 A-26s on 3rd May 1945. By the end of the war in Europe, A-26s had flown a total of 11,567 missions.

In the Italian theatre, the 47th Bomb Group of the Twelfth Air Force flew A-26s alongside its A-20s during the last four months of the war. The 47th BG also received some A-26s in early 1945, but returned to the U.S. in July for training in the night attack role. The unit's overall black painted A-26Cs were equipped with radar and served for three years until being replaced by B-45 Tornados in 1948.

Regarded as the best twin-engined bomber in its inventory, the A-26 became the standard light bomber and night reconnaissance aircraft of the post-war USAAF, having replaced the B-25, B-26 and the A-20. The A-26 was the mainstay of the newly formed Tactical Air Command, established in 1946 by amalgamating the wartime 9th and 12th Air Forces. A-26s were also assigned to the Air National Guard and the Air Force Reserve with numerous other A-26s being sold as surplus, scrapped or stored for later use. A small number were transferred to the U.S. Navy for use as utility and target tow aircraft under the designation JD-1.

In June 1948, after deciding that it no longer had a requirement for light attack aircraft, the USAF withdrew the Attack designation category resulting in the two Invader variants becoming known as the B-26B and B-26C. This new designation did not clash with the Martin B-26 Marauder, as this aircraft was no longer in service.

The beginning of the war in Korea on 25th June 1950 saw the USAF critically short of light bombers. Of those 1,054 B-26s that were still officially in the USAF inventory, most were either in storage or operating in reserve units. The only B-26 unit that could be called upon for duty in Korea was the 3rd BG based at Johnson AB in Japan. The 3rd BG was equipped with both versions of the Invader, although it did have considerably more 'B's than 'C's on strength. The unit entered the action almost immediately, operating initially in the reconnaissance role. The 3rd BG's first offensive operation came on 28th June 1950 with an attack on a railway line supplying the North Korean forces. A second B-26 unit entered the Korean theatre in late 1950 when the 452nd BG (Light) of the Air Force Reserve arrived at Pusan in South Korea.

The 452nd BG flew its first combat mission on 27th October 1950 when it attacked supply dumps and troop concentrations near the city of Chong-Ju. The 3rd and 452nd BGs (later redesignated 3rd and 17th Bombardment Wing respectively) had carried out a total of 55,000 interdiction missions by the end of the war, the majority of these taking place at night.

The last combat mission of the Korean War was flown by a B-26 on 27th July 1953, 24 minutes before the cease-fire came into effect. Following the end of the Korean War, the B-26s began to be withdrawn from active service with TAC and were replaced by aircraft such as the Martin B-57 and the Douglas B-66. Following retirement from TAC the B-26 remained in service with the Air Force Reserve and the Air National Guard.

When American involvement in Vietnam was stepped up, B-26Bs and B-26Cs went into action in the counter-insurgency role with the Farm Gate detachment. With the Invader approaching the end of its operational life, airframe fatigue became a major concern. A number of catastrophic wing failures saw the majority of B-26s withdrawn from service. Those that remained in use underwent modifications to the wing spars in an attempt to extend their operational life. The USAF was so impressed with the success of the modifications that it placed orders for a reworked version of the B-26 that was to be tailored specifically for the counter-insurgency role. This aircraft was produced by the On Mark Engineering Company, California and was designated as the B-26K Counter Invader.

The last Invader to serve with the U.S. military was a VB-26B (44-34160) operated by the Air National Guard and was retired in 1972.

Douglas A-26C-30-DT Invader Specifications:

- Manufacturer: Douglas Aircraft Corporation.
- Primary Mission: Light Bomber and Attack Aircraft.
- Crew: Three.
- Power Plant: Two Pratt & Whitney R-2800-27 or -71 air-cooled radials, each rated at 2000 hp.
- Performance: Maximum Speed - 355mph at 15,000 feet, Cruising Speed - 284mph. (An altitude of 10,000 feet could be attained in 8.0 minutes).
- Service Ceiling: 22,100 feet.
- Range: Normal - 1,400 miles, Maximum - 3,200 miles.
- Dimensions: Wingspan - 70 feet, Length - 51 feet 3 inches, Height - 18 feet 6 inches, Wing Area - 540 square feet.
- Weights: Empty - 22,850lbs, Loaded - 27,600lbs, Maximum - 35,000lbs.
- Armament: Two forward-firing 0.50-inch machine guns in nose. Two 0.50-inch machine guns in a remotely-controlled dorsal turret. Two 0.50-inch machine guns in a remotely-controlled ventral turret. An internal bomb load of 4,000 pounds could be carried. Maximum total bomb load of 6,000 pounds.

NORTH AMERICAN F-86D SABRE DOG

512th FIS F-86D-50-NA (52-10110) seen on static display for the 'Armed Forces Day' at Burtonwood, Cheshire, on 19th May 1956. (photo: via Mick Sudds)

The North American F-86D evolved from the highly successful F-86A Sabre day fighter. Known as the 'Sabre Dog' or 'Dogship,' the F-86D was developed to satisfy a growing USAF requirement for a fighter capable of performing the interception mission at night and in all-weather conditions.

The origins of the interceptor radar-equipped, all-weather Sabre date back to the latter half of the 1940s when the USAAF (USAF from 1947) operated propeller-driven radar-equipped fighters such as the Northrop P-61 Black Widow and the North American P-82 Twin Mustang. The advent of the jet engine had by this time dramatically increased the operational capability and performance of fighter aircraft in general, and this coupled with the fact that more capable airborne radar systems were under development led to a requirement for an effective jet-powered, radar-equipped fighter able to operate at night and in all-weather conditions.

The necessity for this type of aircraft was further reinforced by the fact that, due to major advances in warplane technology, the continental U.S. was already under threat from air attack, either by day or night, and regardless of the prevailing weather conditions. Furthermore, the introduction of nuclear weapons made it even more essential that enemy bombers should be intercepted and totally destroyed before nearing their targets. These requirements paved the way for the development of several highly successful all-weather jet fighters such as the Northrop F-89 Scorpion, Lockheed F-94 Starfire, and the F-86D Sabre Dog.

The 28th March 1949 saw North American Aviation begin work on the F-86D (known as NA-164 by the company). The USAF, well aware of the success of the F-86A, expressed considerable interest in the project and this soon resulted in engineering work on a planned production version being undertaken from 7th April 1949.

A Letter Contract for two prototype NA-164 aircraft and 122 production NA-165 aircraft was received by NAA on 7th October 1949. The designation YF-86D was applied to the two NA-164 aircraft whilst the NA-165s became F-86Ds. A formal contract was approved on 2nd June 1950, with 31 more aircraft being added to the order bringing the total to 153 at an initial cost of $380,232 each. At the time of the formal contract the original F-86D designation had been dropped in favour of a new designation, the F-95A. This was deemed necessary as the Sabre Dog only shared some 25% commonality with the F-86A. The new designation was to be short-lived because, on 24th July, for reasons unknown, the aircraft reverted back to its original designation.

The first YF-86D (50-0577) was completed by late 1949 and, after being moved to Muroc (now Edwards Air Force Base), California, by road it took to the skies for its maiden flight on 27th December 1949 in the capable hands of NAA test pilot George Welch.

The successful flight-testing of this and the second YF-86D (50-0578) in the subsequent months confirmed the capability of this new Sabre version, although the first aircraft only approximated to the eventual production standard, flying without the planned nose radar and with some components retained from the F-86A. Contracts were subsequently placed over a period of time up to June 1953 for an overall total of 2,504 production F-86Ds, all these aircraft being contained in the production blocks between F-86D-1-NA and F-86D-60-NA.

F-86D-50-NA Sabre Dog (52-10030) of the 512th FIS/406th FIW. (photo: via Mick Sudds)

The first production aircraft, F-86D-1-NA 50-0455, was accepted by the USAF in March 1951, and represented the basic production standard for the type. The most noticeable change from the F-86A day fighter configuration was the fuselage, which was wider at the rear and longer, and also featured a prominent 30-inch dielectric nose radome, the installation of which required altering the engine air intake shape. The F-86D's radar was developed by the Hughes Aircraft Company, and at the time, was a very important step forward due to it being designed solely for single-crew operation. Other fighters intended for the same role, such as the F-89 and F-94, required a second crew member to operate the aircraft's radar systems and related avionics.

The centrepiece of the Sabre Dog's state-of-the-art equipment was the 50KW Hughes E-3 (later replaced by the E-4) fire control system which consisted of an AN/APG-36 search radar plus other associated avionics. The radar featured an 18-inch dish antenna inside the nose radome and could locate targets up to 30 miles away, but had a range of 200 plus miles for beacon and terrain search. The prototype Hughes E-3 fire control system was received at NAA on 26th May 1950 and was installed in the second YF-86D (50-0578) and tested during September. On 17th October 1950, 50-0578 went to Hughes for two years of development testing.

In order to enhance its interception mission the F-86D carried a ventral extending tray in which were installed 24 2.75-inch Mighty Mouse unguided folding fin aircraft rockets (FFAR). These weapons could be fired as a single salvo or in several other combinations. The entire complement of 24 rockets could be fired in one-fifth of a second. The 2.75-inch rocket had a 7.5lb explosive warhead, a velocity of 2,500 feet per second at burnout and a range of 4500 yards. Initial trials of the Mighty Mouse rockets commenced in February of 1951.

The Sabre Dog's power plant was the General Electric J47-GE-17, rated for production aircraft at some 7,200 lbs static thrust with afterburner. This engine provided the necessary power required for the 'D' which was heavier than its day fighter stablemate. The F-86D featured an upwards-opening cockpit canopy hinged at its rear end, instead of the F-86A's rearwards-sliding canopy. Other features standardised for the production F-86D included increased vertical tail surfaces and an 'all-flying,' powered horizontal tail with zero dihedral.

The pressure of the Korean War led to increased speculation that a Soviet attack on the continental U.S. could happen at any time. This had the effect of stepping up orders for the F-86D. An order for 188 F-86D-20-NAs was approved on 11th April 1951. Another contract for 638 F-86Ds (Block 25 through to Block 35) was approved on 18th July 1951. A total of 979 production F-86Ds were now on order.

By the time the last F-86D (Block 60) had rolled off the production line in 1955, a number of modifications had been incorporated. These included avionics and fuel system alterations, while Block 10 examples introduced a power-operated rudder without trim-tab, although the Block 30 aircraft reverted back to the standard manually-operated rudder with trim-tab. The use of 120 U.S. gallon external fuel tanks for extended operational missions as well as for ferry flights was introduced from Block 25 onwards and a braking parachute was installed from Block 45 onwards. The use of this parachute reduced the F-86D's landing roll from 2,500ft to 1,600ft.

An up-rated J47-GE-17B engine, capable of producing 7,500lbs static thrust with afterburner, was introduced from Block 40 but this was later changed to the J47-GE-33 engine from Block 45. The J47-GE-33 offered an improvement of 150lbs static thrust over its predecessor.

In fulfilling its role of interception in defence of the continental United States, the F-86D operated within the USAF command specifically tasked with this role, namely Air (later Aerospace) Defense Command (ADC). Before the Sabre Dog was able to enter operational service it was necessary to train a new breed of pilot to fly the aircraft. The single-crew design of the type required a pilot capable of operating the sophisticated avionics in addition to being able to fly the aircraft. An all-weather school was therefore established at Perrin AFB, Texas, to conduct the lengthy and detailed training of F-86D pilots.

On 18th November 1952, Captain J. Slade Nash, flying F-86D-20-NA, 51-2945, established a new world air speed record of 698.505 mph. Achieved at a height of 125 feet over a 3 km course at Salton Sea, California, this record beat a previous best held by an F-86A. The record was further extended on 16 July 1953, when Air Materiel Command test pilot, Lieutenant Colonel William F. Barnes established a new record speed of 715.697 mph in the first F-86D-35-NA (51-6145) at the same venue. The impressive performance of the F-86D resulted in two more contracts. The first of these new contracts was approved on 6th March 1952 and covered 901 F-86Ds from production blocks 40 through to 50. The last order was placed on 12th June 1953 for 624 F-86Ds from Blocks 55 and 60.

The Sabre Dog's service entry was agonisingly slow and by June 1953 only a handful of operational squadrons were flying the type. The major reason for this delay was attributed to problems with the sophisticated E-3 fire control system. This resulted in many new aircraft being stranded at NAA's Inglewood facility awaiting the installation of a fully functional radar or other associated avionics. The E-3 system was replaced by the more powerful and capable 250KW E-4 system and this was introduced from Block 5 F-86Ds (the first of which was 50-0492) onwards. The initial problems with the E-4, such as wiring deficiencies and incorrect cathode ray tubes, were ironed out and the system was eventually proven to be very reliable.

A further problem soon became apparent. Due to the large number of modifications introduced during the type's production run, the USAF was operating F-86Ds of differing capability and equipment installation. This lack of commonality required different stocks of spare parts, different instruction manuals as well as different maintenance procedures and earned the Sabre Dog the reputation of being a 'maintenance nightmare.' In late 1953 it was therefore decided to initiate 'Project Pull-Out,' the phased withdrawal of all F-86Ds from operational units for despatch to either the Sacramento Air Materiel Area or NAA's Fresno facility for modification to bring the entire fleet up the same standard. The first re-worked aircraft was completed in July 1954, and all work had been concluded by September 1955.

The last F-86D-60-NA, 53-4090, was accepted in September 1955 and by that time Air Defense Command had no less than twenty operational F-86D wings.

The continuing development of the overall U.S. air defence network, stimulated by the realities of the 'Cold War' and the increasing developments in Soviet bombers and their weapons, was a major factor behind a significant update in the Sabre Dog fleet. This led to the birth of a new version, the F-86L, which consisted of the modernising and partial modification of the F-86D-10 to F-86D-60 Sabre Dogs. In total, some 981 F-86Ds were converted to 'L' standard, the first of these being flown in October 1956. The Sabre's service within ADC was generally lengthened by these various modifications, although some of the F-86D squadrons did not go on to fly the 'L' version, instead converting directly onto the newer and more capable interceptors such as the Convair F-102A Delta Dagger.

Bentwaters-based F-86D Sabre Dog (52-10030) of the 512th FIS/406th FIW. (photo: via Mick Sudds)

In addition to service within ADC, Sabre Dogs also served in Europe and the Far East. In the latter area the first F-86Ds began to arrive during 1953-54, the generally smaller airfields there necessitating the rapid adoption of the tail-mounted braking parachute. The Sabre Dog was replaced in this area by interceptors such as the F-102A; the 16th FIS, for example, converting to this type in early 1959.

In Europe, the 406th FIW, based at RAF Manston, England, contributed to the air defence network in Great Britain during the 1950s. This Wing's 512th, 513th and 514th FISs all flew the Sabre Dog from the mid 1950s onwards. The 512th FIS transferred from its parent base to operate from RAF Bentwaters for the duration of its stay in England. In the first half of 1958, however, the Wing was deactivated and its three squadrons assigned to the 86th FIW at Ramstein AB, West Germany. On assignment the 512th, 513th and 514th FISs moved to Sembach AB, Phalsbourg (France), and Ramstein AB respectively. Prior to this the 86th FIW had already been assigned the 525th, 526th and 527th FISs with F-86Ds, and also received two further squadrons - the 440th and 496th FISs - whose aircraft were ferried to Europe aboard USS Tripoli in mid 1954.

The considerable combat capabilities of the F-86D attracted the attention of several potential overseas customers, and in the event a large number of Sabre Dogs operated with overseas air arms, some U.S.-supplied under the Mutual Defence Assistance Programme (MDAP). Further, in order to meet the requirements of several NATO countries for a capable all-weather interceptor, a new Sabre Dog version was created - the F-86K. The 'K' was based on the F-86D but the E-4 fire control system was replaced by a simpler, new MG-4 system. The Mighty Mouse rocket armament was replaced by four Ford-Pontiac M-24-1 20-mm cannons, two on each side of the engine air intake which necessitated a slight increase in the length of the nose.

In addition to these dedicated export F-86Ks, many F-86Ds and F-86Ls were also operated by overseas countries. A major user of the F-86D was Japan, the Japanese Air Self Defence Force receiving 114 examples in the late 1950s. Yugoslavia was also a major operator of the F-86D, receiving 130 (this total also included some 'K's and 'L's as well) in the early 1960s. The Turk Hava Kuvvetleri (Turkish Air Force) received 50 F-86Ds in 1959, supplemented by some 30 ex-Dutch F-86Ks in 1964. Similarly, the Elliniki Aeroporia (Greek Air Force) obtained 50 F-86Ds in the late 1950s, these serving mainly with No.335 Mire and No.336 Mire until replaced by the F-104G Starfighter in the mid 1960s. Another major European operator was Denmark which received more than 50 F-86Ds in the late 1950s. These were eventually replaced by F-104Gs in the mid 1960s. Other operators included Taiwan, the Philippines, Thailand, and South Korea.

Some time before the extended service of these export aircraft, the Sabre Dog had become operational with one other major organisation in the continental United States, namely the Air National Guard (ANG). Commencing with the 159th FIS, Florida ANG, the F-86D and later the F-86L eventually equipped 27 squadrons from 22 States. The Sabre Dog remained in ANG service until it was finally retired in the mid 1960s.

Despite the difficulties that the F-86D project encountered in the early years, it provided a solid foundation for future development of the all-weather interceptor aircraft and was pioneering by way of the introduction of the single-crew concept in this role. In addition to this, the Sabre Dog played a significant part in the development of many foreign air forces by virtue of the fact that it introduced them to a 'modern,' sophisticated aircraft.

F-86D-40-NA Specifications

- Manufacturer: North American Aviation Corp.
- Primary Mission: Night and all-weather interceptor.
- Power Plant: One General Electric J47-GE-33, rated at 5,500lbs static thrust dry and 7,650lbs static thrust with afterburner.
- Performance: Maximum Speed - 693mph at sea level, 616mph at 40,000 feet, Initial Climb Rate - 12,000 feet per minute (An altitude of 40,000 feet could be reached in 7.2 minutes).
- Dimensions: Wingspan - 37 feet 1 1/2 inches, Length - 40 feet 3 1/4 inches, Height - 15 feet, Wing Area - 287.9 square feet.
- Tactical Radius: 270 miles at 550mph.
- Ferry Range: 769 miles (with two 120 U.S. gallon underwing tanks).
- Service Ceiling: 49,600 feet.
- Weights: Empty - 13,498lbs, Loaded - 18,160lbs, Maximum - 19,952lbs.
- Armament: 24 2.75-inch Mighty Mouse unguided folding fin aircraft rockets (FFAR) carried in a ventral extending tray.

*512th FIS F-86D-50-NA (52-10035) photographed on static display for the 'Armed Forces Day' at Burtonwood on 17th May 1958.
(photo: via Mick Sudds)*

*Line-up of 512th FIS F-86Ds photographed at Wheelus AB, Tripoli, during an Armament Practice Camp in 1956.
(photo: late Peter Hutting (USAF retd) via George Pennick)*

REPUBLIC F-84F THUNDERSTREAK

F-84F-45-RE Thunderstreak (52-7105) of the 91st FBS/81st FBW. (photo: Harry Eckes)

As has been mentioned elsewhere in this work, the arrival of the first Republic F-84F Thunderstreaks at Bentwaters in October 1954 heralded a very different role for the Suffolk base. The 81st Wing's air defence role was changed to one of tactical nuclear strike as a counter to the increased nuclear threat from the Soviet Union.

Although the F-84F is now consigned to the history books, it was, in its day, as important an aircraft as the Panavia Tornado or Lockheed Martin F-16 are today. Even though its offensive capabilities, as compared to the F-16, were mediocre in terms of armament and navigational accuracy, the Thunderstreak was an aircraft with which NATO would have fought any conventional or nuclear war in the sixties. It was also the penultimate example of a famous line of U.S. fighters from the Republic stable at Farmingdale that incorporated the word 'Thunder' in their titles and, as such, it carried on a tradition that started in World War II with the introduction of the P-47 Thunderbolt.

The F-84F had a surprisingly difficult start to its operational career due to numerous engine problems, as well as shortcomings relating to the basic airframe and associated sub-systems. It was developed as a follow-on to the venerable F-84E Thunderjet which had been the mainstay of fighter-bomber squadrons in both the USAF and NATO and which had, like the contemporary F-86 Sabre, been blooded in the Korean War. Eventually, though, a requirement for a new, more powerful aircraft was established and it was felt that the easiest way to do this was to apply the lessons learned on supersonic jet aircraft at that time and produce the next generation fighter-bomber from its immediate predecessor.

The Republic design team began work in November 1949 on what would initially be known as the F-96. The team came up with a design that incorporated a new wing with nearly 40 degrees of sweep at the quarter-chord point, used many press forgings in the wing structure instead of built-up components and featured wings fitted with leading edge slats. The engine specified was the Allison J35-A-25 of 5,200lbs static thrust and although the new design had the capability of carrying heavier weapons loads than the Thunderjet, it was the engine that caused problems as soon as the prototype found its way to the flight line.

Republic were keen to emphasise to the USAF the fact that their new design used 55% of the tooling of the F-84E Thunderjet which, at the time, was just entering service. The Air Force approved the Farmingdale proposals and allocated one F-84E (49-2430) from the production line for conversion to the XF-96A prototype. The fuselage of the XF-96A was virtually identical to that of the F-84E, even the pilot's rearward-sliding canopy and under-fuselage air brake were retained. A sweptback tail unit was fitted as well as an entirely new wing with a sweep angle of 38.5 degrees. After 167 days, construction of the prototype was completed. The XF-96A was then dismantled and flown from Farmingdale by cargo aircraft to Muroc Dry Lake (now Edwards AFB). On arrival it was reassembled and made its maiden flight on 3rd June 1950, in the capable hands of Republic's Director of Flight Otto P. Haas. This maiden flight proved to be a big disappointment for Republic. It was very soon apparent that there was little, if any, performance improvement over the F-84E. Due to this the XF-96A project continued with low priority status.

The project was given a lifeline with the onset of the Korean War. The USAF made available more funds for continued development and a letter contract for F-96A production was received in July of 1950. On 9th August 1950 the XF-96A was redesignated as the XF-84F, and the name 'Thunderstreak' was chosen, the result of a naming contest amongst Republic employees.

Although the low-level performance of the XF-84F was good, the USAF felt that a more powerful engine was required to improve the aircraft's poor takeoff, climb, and high-altitude performance. The engine selected was the British-designed Armstrong-Siddeley Sapphire axial-flow turbojet. The Sapphire was a vast improvement over the J35 producing 7,200 lbs static thrust. Arrangements were made to have the Sapphire engine produced under licence in the USA by Curtiss-Wright as the J65. The Sapphire engine was considerably larger than the J35 and as a consequence the fuselage underwent a major redesign to accommodate it. The depth of the fuselage was increased by seven inches, and the nose intake was enlarged to an elliptical shape. The first prototype XF-84F (49-2430) was re-engined with an imported Sapphire, and flew for the first time with this engine on 14th February 1951. The performance was impressive but another problem was encountered.

The aircraft itself was found to be very difficult and somewhat unsafe to handle and further development flying was restricted to Muroc whilst a number of structural problems were sorted out.

The USAF issued production contract AF33(038)1438, this covering 274 F-84Fs at a unit cost of some $215,035.27 or about one third of the eventual unit cost of each airframe as it entered service. Within a year, this contract was amended with the procurement increasing to 719. Two pre-production YF-84F aircraft (51-1344 and 51-1345) with Sapphire engines were built by Republic in 1951. The second example (51-1345) was completed with air intakes set into each wing root, leaving the nose with a solid cover. The wing root intakes resulted in thrust losses when compared to the nose intake version, and were not adopted for production fighters.

The original production schedule for the Thunderstreak that was prepared in August of 1950 called for the first deliveries to be made by the autumn of 1951. The production F-84Fs were to use heavy press forgings in the construction of the wing structure but the only forge press in the U.S. suitable for the job was tied up in the B-47 programme. The situation continued a downward spiral when the press suffered a mechanical breakdown which caused further delays. To make matters worse, serious delays were encountered in the production of the J65 licence-built Sapphire engines. Added to this list was a shortage of aluminium alloy in the U.S., which compounded the situation even more. In July of 1951, Republic was finally forced to admit to the USAF that the original schedule could not be met.

F-84F-40-RE Thunderstreak (52-6535) of the 91st FBS/81st FBW, circa 1955. (photo: via Mick Sudds)

Republic's problems grew steadily worse when they discovered that their prediction of 55% of the tooling used in manufacturing the F-84E could be used to build the F-84F was wildly optimistic. In the end only 15% proved to be adaptable to the new aircraft. In order to get the program back on track, it was decided to redesign the wings so that they could be manufactured with existing tools and facilities. Although this would cure the press forgings problem, the subsequent redesign work would add many months to the delivery schedule. In order to fill in the production gap until the F-84F could be available, the USAF decided to purchase an improved version of the straight-winged Thunderjet, the F-84G, as a stopgap measure. The delays in the Thunderstreak program took so long to overcome that the F-84G actually became the most widely produced F-84 version with some 3025 examples being built before the last one rolled off the production lines on 27th July 1953.

The first production F-84F-1-RE (51-1346) made its maiden flight on 22nd November 1952 and the USAF eventually accepted the first two F-84Fs on 3rd December, some 11 months after the scheduled date. The production F-84F was different in many respects to the earlier development models. The cockpit canopy, previously a sliding bubble type similar to that fitted to the Thunderjet, was now of a hinged arm, upward-swinging type that raised part of the enclosure upward above the pilot before it swung backwards. For normal exits, the canopy was pushed upward, but for emergencies the canopy could be completely released from the aircraft to permit pilot ejection. This canopy was stronger, easier to install, and better sealed than the sliding version. The production F-84F also introduced a raised 'turtle deck' aft of the cockpit, which replaced the rear fuselage deck of the previous bubble-canopied versions. Development Thunderstreak models had a single speed brake under the fuselage, again, similar to that of the Thunderjet. The production F-84F replaced this with two perforated speed brakes, one on each side of the fuselage just aft of the wing trailing edge. The speed brakes could be opened at any speed up to the maximum dive speed without large trim changes or excessive buffeting. Leading edge wing slats were added to improve airflow characteristics. Control tabs were removed from the ailerons in favour of an irreversible power-boosted control system.

Having eventually made it through its traumatic development and into production the Thunderstreak's problems were far from over. Whilst Republic's Farmingdale plant was soon turning out three airframes a day, there were no engines available to power them. The airframes were placed in temporary storage pending the delivery of a satisfactory power plant. In 1952, General Motors were awarded a contract by Republic to build the Thunderstreak at their plant in Kansas City. With two factories now building the F-84F, production could be increased. General Motors-built Thunderstreaks were known as F-84F-GK (rather than RE), and could only be distinguished from Republic-built Thunderstreaks by their serial numbers.

Ten examples of the F-84F-1-RE were built. They were powered with the early U.S.-built Wright J65-W-1 turbojet. The F-84F-5-RE had the 7,330lbs static thrust J65-W-3 (or the equivalent Buick-built J65-B-3), with deliveries of this version beginning in the latter part of 1953. These early production aircraft were plagued by handling problems that were centered around the tail unit. This resulted in the aircraft having a tendency to suffer a high-g stall pitch-up tendency that was often severe enough to rip the wings off. It is hardly surprising that the USAF considered it unsafe to use the F-84F for any kind of tactical operations.

After more than a year of corrective effort, longitudinal and lateral control of the aircraft was still considered unsatisfactory at high speeds and it was only when an 'all-flying' tailplane was introduced that these difficulties were overcome. The first F-84F-25-RE (51-1621), incorporating the all-flying tailplane, appeared at the end of 1953, although the F-84F continued to operate under manoeuvrability restrictions throughout much of its service life. Further problems were experienced with spent cartridges hitting the air brakes when the guns were fired while certain elements of the undercarriage had to be redesigned as the hydraulic system proved over-sensitive. With regard to the equipment fit, the F-5 autopilot had to be installed and its predecessor removed as it was not sufficiently good for accurate flight at high speeds. The estimated cost of this item alone increased the bill by a further $3 million.

The first operational deployment occurred in January 1954, Strategic Air Command's 506th Strategic Fighter Wing at Dow AFB, Maine being the first unit to take delivery although their operations were limited because of the inefficiency of the engine. By May 1954 SAC had received 125 of the 400 F-84Fs having the then obsolescent J65-W-1 engine and 20 similarly configured aircraft had been delivered to Air Training Command at Luke AFB, Arizona. Tactical Air Command's 405th Fighter-Bomber Wing at Langley AFB, Virginia was next in line and this had received 36 out of its allotted 75 by the end of June. They were followed by SAC's 27th Strategic Fighter Wing at Bergstrom AFB, Texas in mid-June, these aircraft being the first to be delivered with the production J65-W-3 engine although they were six months later than the projected delivery date. Deficiencies with the J65 engine caused the USAF to ground a number of Thunderstreaks and to suspend deliveries from the factory to operational units. As part of the efforts to overcome the difficulties, the USAF initiated a new series of operational suitability tests collectively as Project Run-In. On completion in November 1954, the report stated that the F-84F was satisfactory as a fighter-bomber and considerably better than the Thunderjet in this role. Republic reorganised its quality control group, increased factory staff and the USAF asked that delivery dates be accelerated in order to make up some of the time lost.

The Thunderstreak's problems were thought to be close to final resolution but even more difficulties struck early in 1955 when TAC units began to experience difficulties in the aircraft's braking system. Meanwhile, the Wright J65 engine continued to suffer malfunctions which resulted in complete flame-outs when flying through heavy precipitation and several accidents occurred which were attributed to defective compressor shrouds. The entire fleet was grounded for a short period early in 1955 for inspection with flying eventually being resumed subject to restrictions. In addition, workers at Republic's Farmingdale factory went on strike for four months early in 1956 which further delayed the effective use of the Thunderstreak by another six months. Consideration was given to re-engining the aircraft with the General Electric J73, as used by the F-86H, but these were also in short supply and the proposal was shelved.

The F-84F-50-RE appeared in March of 1955. It had the more powerful J65-W-7 (or J65-B-7), rated at 7,800lbs static thrust. Airframe limitations prevented any improvements in low-altitude speed, but the added power increased the initial climb rate and the combat ceiling. The F-84F-75-RE was the last version of the Thunderstreak to be built at Farmingdale. It introduced a new fairing under the fuselage for the braking parachute, a feature that was later retrofitted to earlier models. The USAF had the F-84F in service with twelve Wings by June of 1955, six with TAC and six with SAC. The F-84Fs serving with TAC were equipped for the delivery of nuclear weapons. The nuclear bomb-toting Thunderstreaks were equipped with the Low Altitude Bombing System (LABS). When using the LABS to deliver a nuclear bomb, the strategy was for the F-84F to approach the target at low-level and high speed. When nearing the target, the F-84F would execute a half loop upward, release its bomb, and then escape the nuclear blast by completing a high-speed 'Immelmann Turn' to head back in the direction it came from.

Fortunately, the Thunderstreak was never called upon to carry out such missions in real combat. The Thunderstreak-equipped USAF wings attached to SAC served as fighter escorts for B-29, B-50, and B-36 long-range strategic bombers but, as these bombers were replaced by jets, SAC relinquished its F-84Fs and turned them over to TAC. By mid 1957, all the USAF Thunderstreaks had been transferred to TAC.

The last Thunderstreak rolled off the production line at Farmingdale in August of 1957. A total of 2112 examples had been built whilst an additional 599 had been built by General Motors.

F-84F-45-RE Thunderstreak (52-6777) of the 91st FBS/81st FBW. (photo: H Lee via Mick Sudds)

Gradually, the F-84F was replaced in front-line service by the North American F-100 Super Sabre. Numerous F-84Fs were turned over to Air National Guard units as they were withdrawn from USAF units. However, the Berlin Crisis of 1961 saw the recall of four F-84F Wings to active duty. The F-84F remained with TAC until the mid 1960s, when it was replaced by McDonnell Douglas F-4C Phantom. USAF Thunderstreaks remained in Europe with the new 366th TFW after the withdrawal of the ANG units sent to bolster USAFE. But, as more modern fighters became available, the F-84Fs were returned to ANG units and the beginning of the end came in June 1964 when 13 years of Mutual Defense Assistance Programme (MDAP) F-84B/C/F training ended at Luke AFB. In July 1964 TAC handed over its last F-84F to the ANG.

Surprisingly, the aircraft was to last a long time in Guard squadrons, the last unit to use this type being the 183rd Tactical Fighter Group at Springfield, Illinois. Following a tragic accident caused by structural corrosion in November 1971, the remaining aircraft were grounded for inspection and it was found that 90% showed similar signs of wear. However, the damage was so extensive that it was decided not to make repairs as the 183rd was due to replace its F-84Fs with the F-4C Phantom in the immediate future.

The career of one of the least popular USAF post-war aircraft had finally drawn to an end although TAC and ANG squadrons had used them very effectively once the numerous problems were overcome. In Europe, it was a different story for the F-84F was accepted with great enthusiasm irrespective of all the problems that had gone before. The Thunderstreak saw service with the air forces of West Germany, Holland, Belgium, France, Italy, Greece and Turkey.

West Germany was the main overseas recipient of the Thunderstreak and it became the first front-fine fighter-bomber aircraft of their reborn air force. Due to the inexperience of both Luftwaffe ground and air crews, the F-84F suffered a higher attrition rate than the Lockheed F-104G Starfighter which followed, a fact that is not widely known. A total of 29%, some 162 aircraft out of the 450 delivered, crashed during the eight years that the Thunderstreak was in service. This works out at an average of around 20 Thunderstreaks lost for each year of operation. Nevertheless, the Thunderstreak became an important part in the reformation of West Germany's offensive capabilities. The first 20 aircraft were shipped across the Atlantic as deck cargo in plastic cocoons before being handed over at Fürstenfeldbruck AB on 13th November 1956. The Luftwaffe Thunderstreaks had only been in service for five years before the question of finding a replacement was considered. Lockheed's F-104G Starfighter was eventually selected as the successor with the first of the new type delivered to JbG 31 in 1961. The entire F-84F fleet had been phased out by 1968. Many of the redundant F-84Fs were transferred to other NATO countries such as Greece and Turkey where they saw several more years of service before they were formally retired.

Line-up of 91st FBS F-84Fs at a snow-covered Bentwaters during the winter of 1954. (photo: Harry Eckes)

France was the only country to use the F-84F in battle and was the second largest operator of the type. Approximately 175 entered service with the Armee de l'Aire, these being funded entirely by MDAP. The 3 Escadre at Reims was first to receive the new aircraft, 35 being handed over on 4th November 1955. EC1 at St Dizier came next and these two units formed the French contingent that was dispatched to Israel using hastily applied Israeli markings for the start of the Suez campaign in 1956. A total of 36 Thunderstreaks of EC1 arrived at Lydda on 25th October while EC3 moved to Akrotiri, Cyprus in support. The most memorable action that these aircraft took part in was the attack on Luxor on 5th November when eight Thunderstreaks with long range tanks shot up the entire force of Egyptian Il-28 bombers. Only one Thunderstreak was lost during the operations conducted by the French. A further two Wings - EC4 and EC9 were also formed at Metz, these being committed to NATO duties. EC4 eventually moved to Bremgarten in West Germany and became the last French unit to use the Thunderstreak, replacing it with the Mirage IIIE in 1966.

The Belgische Luchtmacht (Belgian Air Force) operated 197 Thunderstreaks which were split between two Wings - 2 Wing at Florennes and 10 Wing at Kleine Brogel. Delivery of the initial batch of 180 began on 4th June 1955 and was completed on 29th January 1958. A further 17 surplus USAFE examples were received in April 1958. No less than 105 F-84Fs were written off in accidents whilst in Belgian service so the attrition rate was no better than any other NATO country in spite of the extra experience that Belgian aircrew may have had. Both Wings re-equipped during the sixties with either the F-104G Starfighter or Mirage 5B and the remaining 74 F-84Fs were put into storage at Koksijde.

The Netherlands' experiences with the Thunderstreak were similar, this nation receiving 180 MDAP-funded aircraft. The attrition rate was slightly less than that of the Belgians, 76 being written off in accidents. Six Koninklijke Luchtmacht (Royal Netherlands Air Force) squadrons eventually received the F-84F, all having previously flown the F-84G Thunderjet. During its Dutch service the Thunderstreak equipped aerobatic teams such as the Skybirds, Sandbag Diamond Team and Whisky Four. The latter's colour scheme was red, white and blue in an attractive pattern but sadly the team was forced to disband before its first public display after an accident in which one of the aircraft went out of control and crashed.

The Aeronautica Militare Italiana (Italian Air Force) took delivery of around 150 Thunderstreaks commencing in the spring of 1956. In common with the Belgian and Dutch Air Forces, the Italians also used some F-84Fs to form an aerobatic team. The team was named the Diavoli Rossi and made its first appearance in 1958. In 1960 the Italian Air Force replaced the Diavoli Rossi with another F-84F aerobatic team, the Getti Tonanti. The Italian Air Force had retired its last Thunderstreak by 1973.

Apart from the brief action that the French Thunderstreaks saw during the Suez campaign, the Thunderstreak was never used in anger. Nevertheless, its role in providing NATO with a powerful offensive capability helped to maintain peace during a period of world instability. Farmingdale's first swept wing fighter suffered high attrition rates in all of the air forces that operated it but, without this type the present day fighter and attack aircraft could not have been developed. The Thunderstreak should be remembered as an innovative design for without it, neither the United States nor the NATO air arms would possess the abilities they do today.

F-84F-25-RE Specifications

- Type: Tactical Fighter-Bomber.
- Crew: One.
- Power Plant: One Wright J65-W-3 turbojet rated at 7,220lbs static thrust.
- Performance: Maximum Speed (clean) - 695mph at sea level (Mach 0.91), 658mph at 20,000 feet (Mach 0.94), Initial Climb Rate (clean) - 8,200 feet per minute.
- Dimensions: Wingspan - 33 feet 7 1/4 inches, Length - 43 feet 4 3/4 inches, Height - 14 feet 4 3/4 inches, Wing Area - 325 square feet.
- Weights: Empty - 14,014lbs, Combat (clean) - 19,340lbs, Normal Loaded - 26,000lbs, Maximum Takeoff - 28,000lbs.
- Range: Tactical Radial (clean) - 450 miles at 36,000 feet, Combat Radius (with two 230 U.S. gallon drop tanks) - 790 miles, Ferry Range (with four 230 U.S. gallon drop tanks) - 2,140 miles.
- Service Ceiling: 46,000 feet.
- Armament: Six 0.50-inch M-3 machine guns, four mounted in the nose and two mounted in the wing roots. A maximum of 6,000lbs of external ordnance could be carried, a typical load being two 2,000lb bombs and eight 5-inch HVARs or four 1,000lb bombs and 24 3-inch rockets.

DE HAVILLAND CANADA L-20A BEAVER

Woodbridge-based DHC L-20A Beaver (52-6138) of the 78th FBS/81st FBW. (photo: George Pennick)

Development of the Beaver began before the end of the Second World War when de Havilland Aircraft of Canada set to work on designing an aircraft that could operate in the hostile environment of Canada's Northern Territories. The original design was similar in comparison to the DH.80A Puss Moth, a high winged, strut braced monoplane, albeit larger and of all-metal construction. DHC was a small company, being considered nothing more than an extension of the main de Havilland company in the U.K. and providing an additional manufacturing base for such types as the Mosquito, Anson and Tiger Moth. In 1945, wartime aircraft production drew to a close and as a consequence DHC were forced to make large numbers of their work force redundant. The Beaver project, now at an advanced stage, was shelved in order for the company to concentrate on producing their first in-house design, the Chipmunk.

The Beaver was brought back to life in the spring of 1946 when R D Hissocks joined DHC. Hissocks was put in charge of the project and immediately he made several changes, the main one being a completely revised wing incorporating a combined flap/aileron system. Another modification was the provision of a large freight door in the fuselage. The next item for consideration was the power plant. The original design specified a 330hp Gipsy Queen but this was changed to the 450hp Pratt and Whitney Wasp Jr. It was thought that the additional horsepower gave the Beaver a potential of short takeoff and landing (STOL) performance due to the wing and flap configuration.

Construction of the prototype (CF-FHB) started on 15th January 1947 and seven months later, on 16th August, it made its maiden flight flown by Russell Bannock.

Due to its simplistic design the Beaver went into production virtually unchanged from the prototype. The only modification deemed necessary was to alter the curvature of the windscreen in an attempt to improve airflow around the outer edges. Orders rolled in thick and fast with Beavers being exported to 62 different countries including many of the world's air forces. DHC's original concept of the Beaver was that it should be developed solely for Canadian bush fliers but to their surprise a number of air forces showed interest in the robust construction and the possible use of the aircraft as a replacement for their wartime utility aircraft for communications and various other second line duties.

The main contenders were both the United States Air Force and United States Army who saw the Beaver as being an ideal machine for their purposes. DHC were almost one step ahead of the official orders because Russell Bannock, by then head of military sales saw the opportunity of taking one of the company prototypes to Alaska and demonstrating this to the military. In June 1949 he set off on a sales tour in CF-FHS and gave several demonstrations at places like Elmendorf AFB which raised many questions about the ability of the current aircraft assigned to these commands.

Recommendations were made by senior officers and because of the need to show fairness to all competitors, particularly as procurement of the Canadian machine meant buying from another country, U.S. manufacturers were given the opportunity to present their products at a series of competitive trials held at Wright-Patterson AFB, Ohio, in December 1950. Beaver CF-GQO flown by Bannock, attended and excelled in every parameter set for an aircraft of this weight and carrying capacity. The nearest competitor was the Helio Courier and although the USAF did order a number of these aircraft at a later stage, the Beaver was obviously the choice as far as its performance was concerned. Bannock demonstrated that the Beaver could carry heavier loads further and with easier loading than any of the other aircraft present. The U.S. Army arranged to have its own competition at Fort Bragg in May 1951 - the result was the same.

Accordingly an initial order was placed with DHC for six Beavers designated YL-20s. These aircraft were taken straight from the production line and were basically civil aircraft in military markings. Production aircraft became L-20As until 1962 when, with the re-designation of USAF aircraft, they were renamed U-6As. For military purposes various changes were required including four windows installed in the cockpit roof, increased instrumentation and radio plus a seating change. The L-20A/U-6A was used for a number of roles including, courier service, passenger transport, light cargo hauling, reconnaissance, rescue, and aerial photography.

A total of 980 L-20 Beavers were produced for the U.S. armed forces before production ceased, representing some 58% of all Beaver production. These figures doubtless led to other countries seeking out DHC for their own requirements including the British Army and Royal Netherlands Air Force in Europe. The Beaver went on to do sterling service with American forces, initially in Korea, later in Vietnam and then in many other locations including Europe where its abilities were used to the full.

L-20A Specifications

- Primary Mission: Utility, Transport and Liaison.
- Manufacturer: de Havilland Aircraft of Canada.
- Crew: 1 (plus 5 passengers).
- Power Plant: One Pratt and Whitney R-895 radial engine rated at 450 horsepower.
- Performance: Maximum Speed - 163mph, Cruising Speed - 120mph.
- Dimensions: Wingspan - 48 feet, Length - 30 feet 4 inches, Height - 10 feet 5 inches.
- Weight: 5,100lbs loaded.
- Range: 455 miles.
- Service Ceiling: 20,000 feet.

DHC L-20A Beaver 52-6138 of the 81st TFW pictured on static display at Bentwaters 'Armed Forces Day' on 14th May 1961. This particular Beaver is still flying today. Currently carrying the civil registration N530BJ, it has been converted to a floatplane and operates from Lake Hood, Anchorage, Alaska. (photo: George Pennick)

LOCKHEED T-33A

A pair of Lockheed T-33As of the 81st TFW roll out after landing at Bentwaters on 11th May 1963. (photo: George Pennick)

The Lockheed T-33A served in almost all European and NATO air forces, the United States, Canada, many South American republics, Japan, Pakistan, parts of Africa and even in communist Yugoslavia. The 'T-bird' has become the best-known jet trainer that has ever been produced and comes close to equalling the popularity of such aircraft as the Harvard and the Dakota.

Ironically the T-33A was almost a non-starter, as Army Air Force planners saw no need for a jet trainer. They had had no requirement in the past for such aircraft as a two-seat P-51 Mustang or a P-47 Thunderbolt so why should their latest fighter, the P-80 Shooting Star, need one? They had to concede that a jet aircraft was very different to a piston engined one and subsequently a P-80 airframe was secured to the ground by steel frames around the wings allowing trainee pilots to 'fly' the aircraft without leaving the ground. On the other side of the Atlantic the British had led the way in realising that front-line jet fighter aircraft could not be handled by a pilot straight from training on aircraft like the Harvard and that two-seaters, such as the Meteor T.7 and the Vampire T.11, were a necessity for jet conversion training.

The Lockheed P-80 Shooting Star was the USAAF's first operational front-line jet fighter and was derived from the first jet designed and built in the U.S., namely the P-59 Airacomet. On 23rd June 1943, Lockheed were given a USAAF letter contract to build a jet fighter using the de Havilland Goblin jet engine from England and were given 180 days in which to complete it.

They achieved this after only 143 days with the prototype being ready for flight by 15th November 1943. The project suffered a set back when both air intake ducts collapsed during engine runs causing damage to the engine. The damage was such that a replacement engine needed to be sent from the U.K. The XP-80 eventually took off on its maiden flight from Muroc Dry Lake (now Edwards AFB) on 8th January 1944.

Not long after the P-80 first entered service it was found that the accident rate was higher than any other fighter then in existence. The USAF still did not take any notice of Lockheed's suggestion that they develop the P-80 into a two-seat trainer for conversion of piston engine experienced pilots.

The company, under the leadership of Mac V.F. Short, vice president in charge of military relations, took the initiative and invested $1million of its own money to develop a trainer version of the P-80. In May 1947 Lockheed set up a design team headed by Don Palmer and began work on the project, which had been given the company designation Model 580. The Air Force finally expressed some interest three months later when they authorised the modification of one P-80C airframe then under construction to become the TP-80C prototype.

Palmer's design team revised the P-80 fuselage by inserting a 38.6 inch plug forward of the wing and a 12 inch plug aft in order to accommodate the second pilot. The centre fuselage fuel tank was decreased in size from 207 to 95 U.S. gallons but they then made provision for extra fuel to be placed in wing tanks and later by adding the two distinctive wing tip tanks.

Other features were the large clamshell-type canopy, which was insisted upon by the USAF against the original Lockheed proposals of a three-piece sideways opening cockpit covering. The P-80's nose armament of six .50 calibre machine guns was reduced to two but provision could be made for the full fighter armament to be used if required. Finally, the trainer was fitted with two ejection seats and full dual controls making it the ideal jet transition aircraft. The TP-80C (48-0356) made its first flight from Van Nuys Airport, California in the hands of Lockheed test pilot Tony LeVier on 22nd March 1948. Early flights proved that the aircraft was very similar in character to the P-80 yet surprisingly its operating speeds were slightly higher at equivalent engine settings.

Shortly thereafter the USAF placed an order with Lockheed for an initial batch of 20 TP-80Cs (48-0356 to 48-0375), although this number seemed to be very small considering the importance of the task it was expected to fulfil. Orders came quickly thereafter as the TP-80C was sent out on a number of demonstration tours to USAF bases and U.S. Naval Air Stations. By now the designation of the aircraft had changed to TF-80C and later on 5th May 1949, it became the T-33A. Final production orders for the T-33A and the TV-2, which was the U.S. Navy designation, amounted to 5,691 aircraft in 28 batches involving funds from 11 successive Fiscal Years. Apart from the U.S. Navy who had 699 the U.S. Mutual Defense Assistance Program (MDAP) accounted for 1,058 of this total. The figure does not include aircraft produced under licence in Canada and Japan.

The USAF was soon to realise that the 'T-bird' was a good communications aircraft. Most Generals had their own personal T-33A for visiting various sections of their commands. Desk-bound pilots who needed to keep current for their flying pay soon found that they could build hours on the aircraft yet still maintain their office jobs in readiness to return to a flying post as soon as requirements necessitated. Air National Guard and Air Force Reserve pilots trained and kept current on the T-33A. It could do anything that the fighters of the 1950s and 1960s could though obviously at slower speeds and without the sophistication of advanced weapons systems that were then coming into service. It became a weapons trainer, navigation and instrument flying tasks came its way and it was even adapted as a target tower and as a pilotless drone aircraft for the development of weapons systems and missiles.

The T-33A remained the USAF's only jet trainer until the advent of the T-37 in 1957 and the T-38A in 1961. Even so it was not finally phased out of USAF service until 1988.

Two overseas countries, Canada and Japan, put the Lockheed T-33A into production for their own air forces and in the case of Canada also contributed to the Mutual Defence Assistance Program by providing T-33s for France, Bolivia, Greece, Portugal and Turkey.

There have been few aircraft that have exceeded 40 years in active service in the same role as when they were originally conceived. The Lockheed T-33A is one of these and the fact that so few modifications were made to it during this period is indicative of the robustness of the original design. Decades after the last P-80 flew, the T-33A, its two-seat trainer version, was still in active service. The 'T-bird' never made the headlines and, as such, is not as famous as other jet aircraft of its era but there are a large number of pilots still flying today who have the T-33A to thank for helping to develop their flying skills. It has been estimated that over 90% of all the Free World's pilots trained in the 1950s and 1960s, trained in the T-33A and that figure must surely speak for itself.

T-33A Specifications

- Manufacturer: Lockheed Aircraft Corp.
- Primary Mission: Trainer.
- Crew: Two.
- Power Plant: One Allison J33-A-4-35 turbojet engine producing 6,100lbs static thrust.
- Performance: Maximum Speed - 543mph.
- Dimensions: Length - 37 feet 9 inches, Height - 11 feet 4 inches, Wingspan - 38 feet 10 inches.
- Maximum Weight: 15,000lbs.
- Ceiling: 47,500 feet.
- Range: 970 miles.
- Armament: Two .50 calibre machine guns (seldom fitted).

81st TFW T-33A-1-LO (52-9597) at Bentwaters 'Armed Forces Day' on 24th May 1964. (photo: Mick Sudds)

T-33A-5-LO (57-0687) of the 81st TFW photographed at RAF Coltishall 'Battle of Britain Day' on 15th September 1962. (photo: Mick Sudds)

DOUGLAS C-47D SKYTRAIN

Douglas C-47D Skytrain (42-100883) of the 81st TFW seen on static display at Bentwaters 'Open House' on 11th May 1963. (photo: George Pennick)

The C-47 Skytrain is probably one of the best known and widely used aircraft that has ever been produced. Affectionately known as the 'Gooney Bird,' the C-47 was adapted from the popular DC-3 twin-engined commercial airliner that first flew on 17th December 1935. The popularity of the C-47 was largely due to its low operating and maintenance costs, ruggedness, ease of pilot training, and versatility. It served primarily in the cargo and transport roles but was adapted to carry out a wide variety of other missions. In Royal Air Force service the type was given the more familiar name of Dakota.

In 1939, with the threat of war in Europe looming, the DC-3 was utilised to assist the Allied forces. Many European commercial carriers put their DC-3s to use as military transports. In 1940 the USAAF, realising the value of the DC-3, placed orders for military versions modified for troop transport and cargo carrying duties under the designations of C-47 and C-53.

The first of these to enter production was the C-53 Skytrooper in October 1941 but only 250 were ever built. The definitive military version was, however, the C-47 Skytrain which first entered production in January 1942. This version incorporated a reinforced fuselage, stronger cabin floors for heavy loads, large doors in the rear fuselage for loading cargo and dropping paratroops, and more powerful engines. By the time production of the C-47 had ceased in the summer of 1945, some 10,368 had been built with an additional 2,000 being built under licence by the former Soviet Union as the Lisunov Li-2.

During World War II the C-47 proved to be a valuable workhorse carrying out transportation and troop carrying duties during all phases of the conflict. The type was also used for towing troop-carrying gliders and dropping U.S. and British paratroopers in North Africa, Sicily, the Normandy Invasion, the Arnhem operation, and the crossing of the Rhine. Of these operations, the most spectacular and significant took place on the eve of D-Day, 6th June 1944, when more than 1,000 C-47s were involved in dropping U.S. and British paratroopers and towing assault gliders to areas behind the beachheads. C-47s were also used to insert British and American troops behind Japanese lines in Burma by glider, and for paratroop drops on Corregidor Island in the Philippines.

In recognition of the part played by the C-47 during World War II, General Dwight D. Eisenhower cited the type as one of the most important instruments of victory over Nazi Germany.

After the war some C-47s remained in USAF service, participating in the Berlin Airlift and other peacetime activities. During the Korean War C-47s evacuated wounded troops, dropped paratroopers, transported cargo and dropped flares for night bombing attacks.

The Vietnam War saw the birth of a very different C-47. Nicknamed 'Puff the Magic Dragon,' the AC-47 gunship was armed with three side-firing 7.62mm miniguns, each firing 6,000 rounds per minute. The AC-47 flew numerous ground attack missions against the Viet Cong troops attempting to infiltrate friendly positions inside South Vietnam.

More than 13,300 C-47/DC-3s (in all its forms) were built, including those examples manufactured in Japan and the Soviet Union. In addition to the roles already mentioned, versions of the C-47 were produced for VIP transport, rescue, reconnaissance, crew training and the calibration of radar and navigational aids. The C-47D based at Bentwaters was used for the utility/transport role.

C-47D Specifications

- Manufacturer: Douglas Aircraft Corp.
- Primary Mission: Transport.
- Crew: 3 (pilot, co-pilot, flight engineer).
- Power Plant: Two Pratt and Whitney R-1830-92 Twin Wasp radial engines rated at 1,200hp each.
- Performance: Maximum Speed - 200kts (370km/h; 230mph) at 8,800ft (2,680m), Cruising Speed - 139kts (257km/h; 160mph), Climb to 10,000ft (3,050m) - 9.6 minutes.
- Dimensions: Length - 63 feet 9 inches (19.43m), Height - 17 feet (5.18m), Wingspan - 95 feet 6 inches (29.11m), Wing Area - 987 square feet (91.695m^2).
- Weights: Empty - 17,865lbs (8,103kg), Maximum Takeoff - 26,000lbs (11,793kg).
- Service Ceiling: 24,000ft (7,315m).
- Range: 1,600 miles (2575km) (with standard payload).
- Payload: 4,500kg of freight or 28 seats.
- Armament: None.
- Year in Service: 1941.

MCDONNELL F-101A/C VOODOO

F-101C-45-MC (56-0013) of the 81st TFW makes a typically spectacular departure from Bentwaters on 17th June 1962. (photo: George Pennick)

The McDonnell F-101 Voodoo was the first production fighter capable of exceeding 1,000mph in level flight and was developed to satisfy a Strategic Air Command (SAC) requirement for a long-range escort and penetration fighter. The F-101 first entered operational service some 11 years after its initial conception, which, in comparison to other U.S. fighters of the same era, was an unusually long time. Ironically, by the time that the Voodoo finally entered service, SAC had modified its operational strategies to take advantage of the new Boeing B-52 Stratofortress. Despite this, the Voodoo did enjoy a fairly lengthy operational career where it served as a tactical fighter, a reconnaissance platform and as an interceptor by Tactical Air Command and Air Defense Command with no less than 807 examples rolling off the production line during the fifties and early sixties.

Development of the F-101 began in June 1946 when McDonnell Aircraft of St Louis, Missouri, initiated design work in response to a USAF request for a strategic penetration fighter to act as an escort for the B-29, B-36 and B-50 bomber aircraft of SAC. Impressed by McDonnell's initial design, the USAF ordered two prototypes under the designation XF-88. The prototypes were to be fitted with two Westinghouse J34 turbojet engines. The first prototype (46-525) made its maiden flight on 20th October 1948, nearly six months behind schedule. The delay was due to a number of structural changes that McDonnell had to incorporate into the design. Amongst these changes was the provision of a 35-degree swept wing in place of the originally envisaged straight wing and this in turn necessitated a change to the air intake ducts.

Two years passed before the second prototype XF-88 (46-526) made its maiden flight. This aircraft was fitted with shorter afterburner units providing a dramatic increase in power. The project was dealt a major blow in August 1950 when the USAF decided to cancel it. The reasons behind this decision were cited as a shortage of funds and the role of escort fighter being performed adequately by existing types, namely the F-84E Thunderjet and the F-84F Thunderstreak.

In January 1951 the project was brought back to life. The popularity of the F-84F with SAC had deteriorated rapidly and the requirement for a strategic escort and penetration fighter had materialised again. McDonnell, along with Lockheed, North American, Northrop, and Republic all submitted proposals. Lockheed submitted both the F-90 and the F-94, North American submitted the F-93, and Northrop proposed an escort version of the F-89 Scorpion all-weather interceptor. Republic submitted three separate proposals, the F-91 Thunderceptor, the F-84F, and a turboprop powered version of the F-84F. McDonnell submitted a revised version of the F-88 and, in May 1951, this proposal was deemed the most suitable and was selected for further development. On 30th November, the designation was changed to F-101 to reflect the improvements incorporated into the 'new' Voodoo.

F-101C-40-MC Voodoo (54-1486) of the 81st TFW, pictured at Wethersfield in 1962. (photo: via Mick Sudds)

In October of 1951, the USAF released fiscal year 1952 funds previously allocated to the F-84F and F-86F programme to get McDonnell's proposal underway. The F-101 programme would follow the 'Cook-Craigie' production policy in which the prototype stage in development would be skipped and full production be initiated from the start. As the first production aircraft rolled off the line, they would be tested and any necessary changes would be introduced on the following aircraft to come off the line. It was anticipated that this policy would see the new fighter delivered to operational units in the shortest possible time.

In December 1951, the McDonnell team lead by Edward M. Flesh recommended that the F-101 be powered by a pair of afterburning Allison J71 turbojets. This nearly tripled the thrust of the pair of Westinghouse J34s that had powered the XF-88, and was twice the thrust of the Westinghouse J46s proposed for the production F-88. The USAF were not convinced that the additional power was enough and preferred the use of the more powerful Pratt & Whitney J57 afterburning engines. Unfortunately, the use of these engines necessitated some major design changes to the airframe. Although the location for the engines was to remain the same as it was for the XF-88, the air intakes located in the wing roots had to be extensively redesigned and enlarged to accommodate the increased airflow requirements of the J57. The use of the J57 also required the need for a greater internal fuel capacity. This was achieved by lengthening and widening the fuselage which increased the internal fuel capacity from 734 U.S. gallons to 2,341 U.S. gallons. In addition to this provision was also made for the fitting of a pair of 450 U.S. gallon external tanks underneath the fuselage.

Other modifications included a pressurised cockpit (complete with an ejection seat) enclosed by a clamshell-type canopy, the addition of rear fuselage airbrakes and a braking parachute. The latter enabled the Voodoo to land on shorter runways. Provision was also made for the Voodoo to be compatible with both USAF in-flight refuelling systems that were in use at the time. A retractable fuelling probe was installed forward of the cockpit and a refuelling boom receptacle was installed on top of the fuselage.

Sign outside the 81st TFW complex at Wheelus AB, Libya in 1961. The names on the sign read: Col Eugene L. Strickland (81st TFW commander); Lt Col Peter Stuyvesant (78th TFS commander); Lt Col Brian J. Lincoln (91st TFS commander); Lt Col John J. Burns (92nd TFS commander). (photo: via Mick Sudds)

On 28th May 1953 the USAF placed an order for 29 pre-production F-101As, all destined to be used in the flight-test programme. The ending of the Korean War allowed the USAF to treat procurement plans with far less urgency. This in turn resulted in another setback for the project in May 1954 when the USAF decided that Fiscal Year 1954 funds would not be released until Category II flight-testing was completed in March 1955.

81st TFW F-101A-30-MC (54-1464) photographed on static display at RAF Waddington in 1965. (photo: Mick Sudds)

Worse was to come when, during 1954, SAC decided to cancel the original requirement altogether. The reason behind this decision was that the range of the F-101A, although impressive in its own right, was not nearly great enough to be able to carry out escort missions for SAC's bombers all the way to the targets in the Soviet Union. Consequently, SAC no longer believed in the viability of the F-101 and lost any interest in the aircraft as an escort fighter. This probably would have spelled the end for the Voodoo had it not been for Tactical Air Command providing a lifeline when it expressed an interest in the aircraft as a nuclear-capable fighter-bomber.

The F-101A that was eventually to roll off the production line would be a dual-role aircraft, fitted with an APS-54 radar and a MA-7 fire-control system for the air-to-air role, and a LABS (Low-Altitude Bombing System) for the 'toss-release' delivery of a single nuclear weapon.

Continued development work under the designation of 'Weapon System WS-105A' culminated in the successful maiden flight of the first F-101A (53-2418) at Edwards AFB on 29th September 1954. McDonnell test pilot Robert C. Little was at the controls during this first flight and he achieved a maximum speed of Mach 0.9 at 35,000 feet. Less than a month later, the F-101A's maximum speed had been pushed to Mach 1.4. By the end of 1954 another three F-101As had joined the flight-test programme.

Once flight-testing had begun it was soon found that the Voodoo had a number of inherent deficiencies including persistent compressor stalls and a tendency to 'pitch-up' into a nose high attitude without warning. The latter was due to the way in which air flowed over the wings and under the high tail. Repeated attempts to eradicate the problems had not succeeded by May 1956 resulting in the USAF calling a brief halt to production. When the hold order was lifted, production was limited to eight aircraft per month for the rest of 1956. The limit was to allow McDonnell the time to implement 300 USAF-recommended changes (in addition to around 2,000 of its own), to existing F-101As instead of building new examples. Included amongst the improvements was the installation of an active inhibitor system, intended to counter the 'pitch-up' problem. This improvement did go some way to providing a cure for the problem but it did not completely eliminate it. The 'pitch-up' problem was to remain a factor throughout the Voodoo's operational career.

In addition to the 29 F-101As involved in the flight-test programme, a further 48 production F-101As were delivered to the 27th Strategic Fighter Wing at Bergstrom AFB, Texas from 2nd May 1957. At the time, the 27th was a SAC unit but on 1st July 1957 it was transferred to TAC, redesignated as the 27th Fighter-Bomber Wing and assigned the mission of nuclear strike. The last of 77 F-101As (including those involved in flight-testing) was delivered to the 27th FBW on 21st November 1957.

The F-101A was not suited to low-altitude tactical strike operations as its airframe could only accept a maximum G-loading of 6.33. This limitation was addressed in the F-101C, an improved version of the F-101A, which had a strengthened airframe capable of withstanding a G-loading of up to 7.33 G. The F-101C was virtually identical to the F-101A and had similar internal equipment and armament but, due to it's stronger airframe, the 'C' was 500lbs heavier than the 'A.' The only means of distinguishing the two versions externally (other than by their serial numbers), was by the small fairing on the leading edge of the fin (approximately in line with the horizontal tail), which was only present on the 'C.'

The first F-101C made its maiden flight on 21st August 1957, and the last of 47 examples was delivered to the 27th FBW at Bergstrom AFB in June 1958. Ninety-six aircraft (56-0049/56-0135) originally ordered as F-101Cs were completed as RF-101Cs after a USAF decision not to acquire any more Voodoo single-seat strike fighters. The F-101C first served alongside the F-101A with the 27th Fighter Bomber Wing based at Bergstrom AFB. On 7th July 1958 the 27th FBW was redesignated as the 27th Tactical Fighter Wing.

In 1958 the USAF decided to move its operational F-101A/Cs closer to their designated targets in the Soviet Union. Before the last of 47 F-101Cs could be delivered, the USAF transferred all of TAC's single-seat Voodoo fighters to USAFE (USAF in Europe), where they were assigned to the 81st Tactical Fighter Wing at RAF Bentwaters and RAF Woodbridge. The first five F-101s for the 81st TFW, all 'A' models, arrived at Bentwaters on 4th December 1958. This followed a preliminary visit by seven 27th TFW examples on 10th August. The 81st TFW operated three squadrons, the 78th TFS at Woodbridge and the 91st and 92nd TFS, both at Bentwaters. In the event of war, the mission of each of the 81st's Voodoos was to deliver a single nuclear weapon onto a target in the Soviet Union.

The F-101A/C remained in service with the 81st TFW until 1965-66 when it was replaced by the McDonnell Douglas F-4C Phantom II. The ex-81st TFW Voodoos had not yet reached the end of their career because on their return to the U.S. they were modified by Lockheed Aircraft Service Company of Ontario, California, to serve with the Air National Guard as unarmed reconnaissance aircraft. The modified F-101As were redesignated as RF-101Gs and the F-101Cs became RF-101Hs. These aircraft were assigned to the 154th Tactical Reconnaissance Squadron of the Arkansas ANG, the 165th TRS of the Kentucky ANG and the 192nd TRS of the Nevada ANG. The last reconnaissance Voodoos were finally withdrawn from ANG service in 1979.

From an operational perspective the F-101A/Cs were of limited use due to the fact that, in the early days at least, they lacked the ability to carry conventional bombs. Although they were fitted with four 20mm cannons in the forward fuselage their principal armament was a single one-megaton tactical nuclear weapon.

Although the fighter-bomber variants of the Voodoo spent only a short time with SAC and TAC, they did become a USAFE stalwart, serving solely with the 81st TFW at Bentwaters and Woodbridge. For those people lucky enough to have witnessed all or part of its six-year life at the 'Twin Bases,' the Voodoo was undoubtedly an impressive and noisy aircraft. Consequently there were a lot of people who were sad to see it go, but all was not lost with the departure of the 'One-O-Wonder' from Bentwaters and Woodbridge because it was replaced by an even more impressive aircraft - the McDonnell Douglas F-4 Phantom II.

F-101A/C Specifications

- Manufacturer: McDonnell Aircraft Corporation (McAir).
- Crew: One.
- Power Plant: Two Pratt & Whitney J57-P-13 turbojets rated at 10,200lbs static thrust dry and 15,000lbs static thrust with afterburner.
- Performance: Maximum Speed - 1,012mph at 35,000 feet, Initial Climb Rate - 45,000 feet per minute.
- Dimensions: Length - 67 feet 6 inches, Height - 18 feet 0 inches, Wingspan - 39 feet 8 inches, Wing Area - 368 square feet.
- Ceiling: Service - 55,100 feet, Combat - 51,540 feet.
- Range: Normal - 1,315 miles, Maximum - 2,125 miles.
- Weights: Empty - 26,277lbs, Gross - 48,908lbs, Combat - 39,495lbs, Maximum Takeoff - 51,000lbs.
- Internal Fuel Capacity: 2,250 U.S. gallons. A total of two 450 U.S. gallon under-fuselage drop tanks could be carried, increasing maximum fuel load to 3,150 U.S. gallons.
- Armament: Four 20mm Colt-Browning M38 cannon. A single Mk.7 nuclear weapon could be carried on the centreline station. This device weighed in at 3,271 lbs and had an explosive yield of 1 megaton. A baggage pod, training shape or SUU-21 practice bomb dispenser could be carried on the centreline station in place of the nuclear weapon.

A pair of 81st TFW F-101 Voodoos during a visit to RAF St. Mawgan, Cornwall in 1965. (photo: Ashley Annis)

F-101C-45-MC Voodoo (56-0019) of the 91st TFS/81st TFW photographed on static display at RAF Gaydon on 17th September 1960. (photo: via Mick Sudds)

81st TFW F-101 Voodoo Colours & Markings

The 81st's F-101A/C Voodoos first entered operational service with the 27th FBW at Bergstrom AFB, Texas in 1957. The 27th FBW consisted of four squadrons - the 481st FBS, 522nd FBS, 523rd FBS and the 524th FBS. Each squadron had its own markings in the form of a solid colour tail adorned with stars. Squadron colours were green for the 481st, red for the 522nd, blue for the 523rd and yellow for the 524th, with each side of the tail carrying at least twenty-seven white stars (black in the case of the 524th).

Unit badges were carried below the cockpit; wing on the starboard side and squadron on the port. These markings were later changed, with the number of tail stars being reduced from twenty-seven to thirteen and Tactical Air Command badges replacing the wing and squadron badges. The 27th FBW was redesignated as a Tactical Fighter Wing on 7th July 1958.

Late 1958 saw the 27th TFW transfer the first of its Voodoos to the 81st TFW. The majority of the 27th's personnel transferred to the 81st along with the aircraft but prior to this a number of 81st TFW personnel had been sent to Bergstrom to transition to the new type. On arrival in the U.K., both personnel and aircraft from the 27th's component squadrons were allocated to separate squadrons within the 81st. The 522nd was absorbed by the 78th TFS at Woodbridge whilst the 523rd and 524th were taken over by the Bentwaters-based 91st TFS and 92nd TFS respectively. Aircraft and personnel of the 27th's remaining squadron (the 481st TFS) were divided up amongst all three squadrons.

After removal of the 27th TFW markings the 81st's 'new' Voodoos remained completely anonymous for a time whilst a decision was made regarding the style of unit markings. A decision was reached in early 1959 and the first of an eventual three styles of unit markings were applied.

The first style consisted of two squadron-coloured sunray streaks on the tail complete with the squadron badge above. The squadron colours were as follows: red for the 78th, blue for the 91st and yellow for the 92nd. These colours were also reproduced on wingtips, tailplanes, wing fences, crew name blocks and main undercarriage doors, the latter taking the form of a smaller version of the tail markings. The 81st TFW badge was applied on both sides of the forward fuselage, below and to the rear of the cockpit canopy. In an attempt to enhance its yellow tail markings, a number of 92nd TFS Voodoos later appeared with black outlines to the yellow sunray streaks - an example being F-101A-35-MC s/n 54-1468. One exception to the single-colour sunray markings was applied to F-101C-40-MC s/n 54-1491. This aircraft was assigned to the 81st TFW commander, Col James R. DuBose Jr. and carried all three squadron colours and badges.

Early 1961 saw the introduction of the second style of markings. Bearing an obvious similarity to those that adorned the aircraft when they were operated by the 27th TFW, the markings consisted of a solid-colour tail and thirteen stars of differing sizes. Additional colouring remained the same as that of the previous style with wing fences, crew name blocks and wingtip markings painted in squadron colours. The main undercarriage doors differed in that the bottom half was painted in the squadron colour complete with a centrally placed white star (black in the case of the 92nd TFS). Exceptions to this were the three aircraft assigned to the respective squadron commanders. These were painted with four stars on the undercarriage doors instead of one.

In May 1962 a new directive was issued to all USAF wings which stated that aircraft were to be assigned at wing level and not squadron level. The outcome of this, as far as the 81st TFW was concerned, was the removal of all individual squadron colouring and badges and the introduction of the third and final style of markings. Individual squadron markings were replaced by the three combined colours (complete with thirteen stars) on the tails of all aircraft assigned to the wing. No other colouring or markings were applied except for a wing badge applied to both sides of the forward fuselage below and aft of the cockpit canopy although this was not always carried. Not long after the introduction of the new markings the Voodoo lost its natural metal finish in favour of one of overall sprayed aluminium paint. Some parts of the airframe were also sprayed with a light grey anti-corrosion paint. As was the case with the two previous styles, there were exceptions to this. Aircraft s/n 54-1457 and s/n 56-0036 were painted in an overall gloss light grey paint with no other colouring or markings except for 81st TFW badges on the forward fuselage. This scheme was similar to that worn by F-101Bs assigned to U.S.-based fighter wings.

Third and final style of markings incorporating all three squadron colours, seen applied to the tail of F-101A-25-MC 54-1452. (photo: David Baker)

81st TFW F-101A/C Voodoo Accidents

Date of Accident	Serial Number	Location	Additional Info
08 Dec 1958	54-1467	Lajes Field, Azores	On delivery to the 81st TFW. Fuel exhaustion caused by the failure of the refuelling probe during hook up, and pilot's failure to declare an emergency. Aircraft flamed out and landed gear up, at night and sustained light damage. Pilot Lt Paul Baker. Aircraft transferred to 1605th ABW charge at Lajes two days after the incident and then dispatched to Ogden AMA (Hill AFB, Utah) for repairs in Feb 1959. 54-1467 was eventually delivered to Bentwaters in Dec 1959.
20 Dec 1958	54-1480	RAF Bentwaters, Suffolk	Crashed on landing, aircraft written off. Pilot R. E. Minter escaped uninjured. Below is a brief account of the mishap by Col George Berke, a former 92nd TFS Voodoo pilot: "Bud Minter thought he blew a tire. After all, what pilot expects his right landing gear to retract just after touchdown? Somehow the squat switch in the strut that protects the gear from being retracted on the ground did the opposite. As the right side came down on the drop tank, the fumes in the empty tank blew, contributing to the impression that

			a tire had blown. As the right wingtip dug in, the plane took off into the grass, collapsing the other gear and the intakes scooped up dirt into both engines. The plane was a write-off."
12 Feb 1959	56-0024	Iken, Suffolk	Believed 91st TFS aircraft. Crashed in mudflats shortly before 2100 hrs whilst on GCA approach to Bentwaters. Pilot Capt L. Ervin ejected successfully. Dick Mael, an Iken resident, awarded USAF's "Exceptional Service Award" for helping rescue pilot from mudflats.
02 Mar 1959	54-1487	Wheelus AB, Libya	Crashed following severe pitch-up, aircraft rebuilt. Pilot 1st Lt William O. Roberts. Below is a brief account of the mishap by Col George Berke, a former 92nd TFS Voodoo pilot: "The pitch up occurred pulling out from a dive bombing pass, at about 500 knots airspeed. The resulting G blacked out the pilot, pulled the landing gear out of its up locks and ruptured the utility hydraulic system (flaps, speed brakes, wheel brakes, nose wheel steering). When Bill recovered his senses he deployed the drag chute, standard procedure to correct pitch up. Landing without flaps, brakes or drag chute was hazardous, resulting in further damage. There was never any official finding of cause, since the accident was not considered possible (McDonnell's reaction). As deputy investigator, I concluded, but could not prove, that the control feedback system had a transient failure which we could not duplicate on the ground. No one likes "unexplained," least of all the pilot, who always wonders if it was something he did." Following the incident, the aircraft was transferred to 7272nd ABW charge at Wheelus on 24 Mar 1959 and then shipped to Ogden AMA in Aug 1959 for repairs. 54-1487 returned to Bentwaters in Aug 1960.
01 Apr 1959	54-1448	North Sea off Orfordness, Suffolk	Crashed into sea following an engine fire on take-off from Bentwaters. This was 1st Lt William O. Roberts' first flight since his accident at Wheelus less than a month earlier. Unfortunately fate wasn't on his side this time. His initial ejection attempt failed when the canopy didn't jettison. The second attempt resulted in a successful ejection into the sea, five miles from shore. Two attempts to recover the pilot by two RAF SAR helicopters failed. 1st Lt Roberts was not able to detach himself from his parachute and the pull of the tide on the 'chute had caused the winch cables on both helicopters to be severed. The pilot was finally taken aboard an RAF rescue launch from Felixstowe but, due to the length of time he had spent in the sea, he died shortly afterwards. Of all the 81st TFW Voodoo accidents, this one has to be the most tragic.
20 Jun 1959	56-0022	Not Known	78th TFS a/c. Major accident, aircraft rebuilt. Pilot C. W. McKenzie. Aircraft shipped to Mobile AMA (Brookley AFB, Alabama) in Oct 1959 and then to Ogden AMA in Apr 1960 for repairs. 56-0022 returned to Woodbridge in Jan 1961.
14 Aug 1959	54-1465	RAF Woodbridge, Suffolk	91st TFS a/c. Crash occurred at east end of runway during an attempted emergency landing. Aircraft had taken off from Bentwaters shortly before. Pilot, 1st Lt Sterling H. Lee, ejected when down to an estimated 100ft, but did not survive. At least one report suggested a 'chute failure. Aircraft totally destroyed.
26 Nov 1959	56-0021	Atlantic Ocean	On "Hi-flight" delivery back to the 81st following maintenance at Mobile AMA. Flown by 78th TFS pilot Capt James Stevenson - his 13th Atlantic crossing!! He was flying in company with Lt John T. Clark of the 92nd TFS. Having ejected safely, Stevenson was located by a 57th ARS SC-54D (from Lajes Field, Azores) which dropped a survival pack to him. He was adrift for around four hours before being picked up by the Norwegian freighter, "Sungran." He was eventually re-united with his wife on docking at Avonmouth. The point of departure for this unsuccessful crossing has been cited as either Langley AFB or Shaw AFB. The cause of the crash was attributed to a clamp failure resulting in loss of fuel.
23 Jan 1960	56-0008	Not Known	78th TFS a/c. Pilot E. M. Dobson.
24 Jan 1960	54-1492	Not Known	Pilot H. N. Wills.
15 Dec 1960	56-0028	Ten miles west of Ramsey, Isle of Man	Crashed into wooded area following loss of fuel due to clamp failure. Pilot Lt Roger H. Bye of the 78th TFS ejected safely. Bye's wingman on the mission to Jurby range, IoM, was Lt Clyde L. Brothers.

Date	Serial	Location	Details
03 Feb 1961	54-1456	Solway Firth, Dumfries, Scotland	78th TFS a/c. Autopilot error pitched aircraft down at low altitude. Wreckage was found three days later under about three feet of tidal water. Pilot R. S. Nishibayashi killed.
06 Mar 1961	54-1457	RAF Bentwaters, Suffolk	Caught fire during start-up. Aircraft shipped back to Ogden AMA in Apr 1961 for repairs and returned to Bentwaters in Feb 1963. Pilot J. J. Burns.
05 Apr 1961	54-1489	Wheelus AB, Libya	Pilot J. M. Counce.
21 Apr 1961	54-1450	Not Known	Second accident for Lt Roger H. Bye in less than four months - fatal this time.
15 Aug 1961	56-0017	RAF Bentwaters, Suffolk	Aircraft had departed Bentwaters on cross-country flight at approx. 0915 hrs, and was landing on return just prior to 1130 hrs. 56-0017 left the runway and crashed into a hangar. Pilot, Capt J. P. Hampton, was killed.
30 Aug 1961	54-1458	North Sea off Thorpeness, Suffolk	Crashed into sea due to hydraulic leak in the rear of the aircraft and a subsequent fire. Having ejected safely, Capt Philip C. Gast of the 91st TFS was saved by the prompt action of four men who witnessed the event from Sizewell beach. The men used a nearby boat to successfully bring Capt Gast ashore.
20 Nov 1961	54-1467	Boyton, Suffolk	Starboard engine fire shortly after takeoff from Bentwaters led to accident. Pilot, Capt R. T. Campbell, ejected safely from 3000ft.
29 Nov 1961	56-0019	Not Known	Major accident, aircraft rebuilt. Pilot J. R. Hopkins.
02 Apr 1962	56-0022	Not Known	Pilot D.J. Foster.
11 Apr 1962	54-1491	RAF Tangmere, West Sussex	Badly damaged in gear-up landing. Pilot R. C. Tarver. Returned to Bentwaters by road on 25 Apr 1962. Shipped to Chateauroux in May 1962 and then to Ogden AMA in Aug 1962. 54-1491 was repaired and later served with 165th TRS as RF-101H.
09 May 1962	56-0005	Not Known	78th TFS a/c. Pilot D. L. Culver.
28 Nov 1962	56-0015	Not Known	78th TFS a/c. Major accident, aircraft rebuilt. Pilot O. W. Ainaire.
19 Dec 1962	54-1474	Not Known	Major accident, aircraft rebuilt. Pilot G. S. Guinn.
19 Dec 1963	56-0007	RAF Bentwaters, Suffolk	Swerved off runway after landing and heavily damaged. Two airman, running away from one of several threatened stationary vehicles waiting to cross runway, were overtaken by runaway jet and killed. Pilot C. H. Powers of the 92nd TFS, stayed with the aircraft and only suffered superficial back and facial injuries.
22 Feb 1964	56-0015	Lampard Brook nr. Framlingham, Suffolk	Second accident involving 56-0015. Crashed following a mid-air explosion during a post-maintenance test flight from Woodbridge. Pilot, Maj Ross W. Watt of the 78th TFS ejected safely.
07 May 1964	56-0013	Maol Odhar, Kinlochleven, Scotland	Crashed into mountains during a three-ship low-level navigation mission. Wreckage found by the crew of an 81st TFW C-47D after a nine-day search. Pilot, Capt Morris H. Reed was killed.
01 Jun 1964	54-1474	Wheelus AB, Libya	Written off following an accident during a weapons training detachment. Pilot W. R. Wilson.
05 Aug 1964	54-1446	North Sea, The Wash	Crashed into sea five miles off Holbeach during a practice bombing mission, flying out of Bentwaters. Believed to be on fire at the time of its loss. Pilot Maj D. McCartyer killed.

The author wishes to acknowledge the help received from George Pennick, Paul Stevens, Mick Sudds, David Baker, Andrew Horrex and Col George Berke during the preparation of this list.

F-101C-40-MC 54-1491 of the 81st TFW pictured at Bentwaters 'Armed Forces Day' on 14th May 1960. This aircraft was badly damaged in a gear-up landing at RAF Tangmere, West Sussex on 11th April 1962. (photo: Mick Sudds)

F-101C-45-MC Voodoo 56-0015 pictured on its landing roll at Bentwaters on 11th May 1963. 56-0015 was written off in a crash at Lampard Brook near Framlingham, Suffolk, on 22nd February 1964, during a post-maintenance test flight. The pilot, Maj Ross W. Watt of the 78th TFS ejected safely. (photo: George Pennick)

NORTH AMERICAN T-39A SABRELINER

81st TFW T-39A-1-NO (62-4469) pictured on static display at the Bentwaters 'Armed Forces Day' on 6th May 1967. 62-4469 arrived at Bentwaters in June 1963. (photo: Ashley Annis)

The development of the T-39A Sabreliner began as a response to a United States Air Force specification for a Utility Trainer Experimental (UTX) promulgated in August 1956. A clause in this specification stated that the manufacturer was required to design and fly a prototype at its own expense as a private venture with no guarantee of a production order.

North American were at a distinct advantage as they already had a design for a small jet transport aircraft (known as the NA-246) on the drawing board. This design was more than suitable for the UTX requirement and the company realised that their project stood a good chance of success. If they were successful they would also have a firm footing for marketing a jet executive aircraft that was almost unheard of at that stage in corporate use of jet aircraft. North American took the gamble and agreed to build a prototype.

The first airframe, civil registered as N4060K, was readied for its maiden flight by May 1958 but this had to be postponed due to a delay in the supply of suitable engines. This delay was due to the fact that the engine units required for the NA-246 needed to be considerably smaller than those that were currently in production for front-line fighters and bombers.

With this problem overcome, the prototype took to the air for its maiden flight on 16th September 1958 after being fitted with two General Electric J85 turbojets.

Although a totally different aircraft, many people have associated the F-86 Sabre and F-100 Super Sabre with the T-39 Sabreliner design. There can be no doubt that its leading edge slats, swept-back wing, and tail gave it a strong resemblance to the F-86 and the F-100, but all three were entirely separate designs.

The Sabreliner had an impressive performance with a maximum speed in military guise of 595 mph at 36,000 ft. It could also cruise at 452 mph at 40,000 ft and had a range of 1,725 miles. The aircraft required a crew consisting of two pilots and was capable of carrying four to six passengers. As a cargo carrier, the T-39A could transport items weighing up to 2,300 pounds with a length of 16 feet. Seat tie-down fittings were also suitable for use as cargo rings when lashing down equipment.

The first production T-39A flew on 30th June 1960 and was delivered to the USAF in October of the same year. Prior to this, N4060K had completed military evaluation at Edwards AFB in December 1958 and the USAF, under the development specification of Weapon System SS452L, had placed an initial order for seven examples serialled 59-2868 to 59-2874.

The power plant had also undergone a change whilst these tests were being carried out and production aircraft were fitted with two Pratt & Whitney J60-P-3s, each producing 3,000lbs static thrust. Internal changes were made to suit the aircraft for either the utility role as a fast jet transport or as a navigational trainer.

The USAF was more than satisfied with the T-39A and, by the end of 1960, a further 94 had been ordered followed by yet another order for an additional 55 by the end of 1961. Initial deliveries were to Randolph AFB for Air Training Command and very soon afterwards the T-39A found its way onto the fleet of aircraft operated by the other USAF Headquarters such as Strategic Air Command and U.S. Air Forces in Europe.

The USAF's use of the T-39A Sabreliner as a trainer and fast jet transport soon attracted the interest of the U.S. Navy. They also had a requirement for an aircraft of this type for training their own aircrews and accordingly an order was placed with North American in 1962 for a maritime radar operator trainer under the initial designation of T3J-1. This designation was subsequently changed to T-39D. Two squadrons were formed for training purposes at NAS Miramar, namely VT-10 and VT-86. The T-39 Sabreliner also found an additional U.S. Navy task in a similar vein to its USAF equivalent. Designated CT-39E and starting in 1969 the U.S. Navy and Marine Corps bought off-the-shelf civil versions of the Sabreliner for rapid response airlift of high priority passengers and freight.

With North American's original ideas fully satisfied by the orders placed by both the USAF and U.S. Navy, the company pressed on with their plans for an executive jet for sale on the civil market. The Sabreliner rewarded North American's initial gamble by becoming one of the most successful executive jets of its era.

T-39A Sabreliner Specifications:

- Primary Mission: Military Trainer/Executive Transport.
- Manufacturer: North American Aviation Corp.
- Crew: 2 plus 4-8 passengers depending on role.
- Power Plant: Two Pratt & Whitney J60-P-3A of 3,000lbs static thrust each.
- Performance: Maximum Speed - 540mph, Cruising Speed - 502mph.
- Dimensions: Length - 44 feet, Height - 16 feet, Wingspan - 44.5 feet, Wing Area - 342.1 square feet, Tail Span - 17.5 feet.
- Weight: Empty - 9,265lbs, Maximum Takeoff Weight - 17,760lbs.
- Fuel Capacity: 6,864lbs (1,056 U.S. gallons).
- Ferry Range: 1,950 miles.
- Service Ceiling: 45,275 feet.

MCDONNELL DOUGLAS F-4C/D PHANTOM II

F-4D-29-MC 66-7620/WR of the 81st TFW taxies for takeoff at Bentwaters in July 1978. (photo: Ashley Annis)

The 81st TFW's first McDonnell Douglas F-4 Phantom II arrived at Bentwaters on the 4th October 1965. Initially equipped with the 'C' model, the 81st TFW were destined to operate the Phantom for some 13 years and as such the type became a familiar sight in the skies around the 'Twin Bases.'

The USAF's association with the Phantom began in April 1962 when an order was placed for 280 F-110As. This Air Force specific designation was short-lived because in September of that year it was changed to F-4C in order to achieve some commonality with the U.S. Navy's designation for the type. For three months the Air Force had been flying a pair of loaned F-4B fleet defence fighters (BuNos 149405 and 149406), which had been delivered to Langley AFB, Virginia, for evaluation purposes. The USAF were suitably impressed with the big, smoky Phantom and saw it as a good, all-round prospect for the attack mission. In February 1963, thirty U.S. Navy F-4Bs were temporarily assigned to the 4453rd Combat Crew Training Wing at MacDill AFB, Florida. These aircraft were immediately pressed into use in an effort to train a large number of pilots as instructors on the new type prior to the delivery of the Air Force's own F-4Cs.

The F-4C incorporated a number of changes from the Navy model, as laid down in Specific Operational Requirement (SOR) 200, submitted in August 1962. The most significant of these was the adoption of Westinghouse AN/APQ-100 radar with ground mapping capability, an AN/APA-157 CW illuminator for the AIM-7 Sparrow family of air-to-air missiles, an AN/AJB-7 all-altitude nuclear bomb control system with low-altitude release capability and option for Bullpup release, a Litton AN/ASN-48 (LN12A/B) inertial navigation system, and an AN/ASN-46 navigation computer. The F-4C was to be equipped with dual controls to satisfy a USAF policy stating that the Phantom was to be crewed exclusively by two rated pilots. This was in marked contrast to the U.S. Navy's policy of having the rear seat occupied by a mission specialist/navigator. Further refinements included a dorsal in-flight refuelling receptacle compatible with the USAF's boom-equipped tanker aircraft and the fitting of two General Electric J79-GE-15 afterburning turbojets rated at 17,000lbs static thrust.

As the F-4C would be operating solely from airfields and not aircraft carriers like the 'B' version, wider, lower pressure wheels and tyres were fitted, resulting in a thicker wing root at the main undercarriage bays. Four AIM-7D or AIM-7E Sparrow missiles could be mounted in recesses underneath the fuselage whilst four AIM-4D Falcon or AIM-9B or AIM-9D Sidewinder infrared homing air-to-air missiles could be carried externally on the inboard underwing pylons. Air-to-ground missiles such as the AGM-12 Bullpup, the AGM-45 Shrike, and the AGM-65 Maverick could also be carried as well as unguided rocket launchers and both retarded and unretarded bombs. The Mk.28 'special store' could also be carried, although as far as the F-4C was concerned, the nuclear strike mission was of secondary importance.

Despite these changes, the F-4C remained identical to the F-4B when it came to ground attack missions with rockets or 'iron' bombs. This was due to the fact that the F-4C had only a fixed gunsight reticle, depressed prior to an attack run by the pilot to compensate for ordnance ballistics at the planned dive angle. Each dive angle had its optimum weapons release height above ground level, forcing crews into predetermined attack runs. The predictable attack profile together with the smoky J79 power plant made the F-4C vulnerable to anti-aircraft fire. SST-181X 'Combat Skyspot' equipment was later added to enable the aircraft to bomb from high altitude in level flight. Altitude work also had the added benefit that the aircraft would be best prepared to engage enemy fighters with its four heat seeking AIM-9 Sidewinders and four AIM-7 Sparrow semi-active radar-homing missiles.

The first of an eventual 583 production F-4Cs (62-12199) made its maiden flight on 27th May 1963 under the company designation of Model 98DE. The first aircraft off the production line went to the Air Force Flight Test Center (AFFTC) at Edwards AFB, California, for follow-on 'Category' avionics and aerodynamic trials in order to write the manuals on the aircraft type. F-4Cs for operational units soon followed, with the first being delivered to the 4453rd CCTW at MacDill AFB followed by the 12th and 15th TFWs, also at MacDill. The 4453rd CCTW transferred to Davis Monthan AFB, Arizona, where trainees could take advantage of the near perfect weather conditions in order to get to grips with the new aircraft.

The beginning of the conflict in South East Asia (SEA) saw the Phantom quickly assigned to that theatre. MacDill's two combat-ready wings were the first choice and, in December 1964, four F-4Cs from the 12th TFW flew an 18-hour 10,000-mile mission, proving they were capable of long, arduous deployment. The aircraft set an unofficial endurance record for jet fighters.

The 15th TFW was the first to see action in SEA after one of its component squadrons, the 45th TFS, arrived for TDY at Ubon, Thailand in July 1965. On the 10th of the month the squadron claimed the first Phantom aerial victory in the conflict when Captains Kenneth Holcombe and Arthur Clark, and Thomas Roberts and Ron Anderson destroyed a pair of MiG-17s with AIM-9 Sidewinders. Eventually, the F-4C carried out the majority of the heavy fighting over North and South Vietnam. On a typical mission over the North, an F-4C would carry four Sparrows, four Sidewinders and eight 750lb bombs.

The 45th TFS suffered its first loss on 24th July when an F-4C (63-7599) was downed by a North Vietnamese SA-2 surface-to-air missile (SAM). Three other aircraft suffered shrapnel damage but managed to return to base. The USAF issued Quick Reaction Contracts to U.S. companies to provide electronic countermeasures (ECM) pods and RHAWS radar detectors in order to counter this Soviet-backed North Vietnamese threat. The ECM pods and RHAWS system were gradually retrofitted to the F-4C's nose fairing and fin cap from early 1966.

Permanent F-4 bases soon became established throughout South Vietnam (SVN). The 12th TFW moved from MacDill to Cam Ranh Bay in November 1965 and provided the majority of the close air support that was carried out by Phantoms for the Marines and Army troops during the ground war in the South.

The following October saw the number of F-4Cs in theatre increased to form an air defence and MiG combat air patrol (MIGCAP) Organisation at DaNang, under the control of the 366th TFW. The 366th TFW were the first unit to employ the General Electric ram air turbine-driven SUU-16/A 20mm Gatling gun pod. The F-4C could carry as many as three SUU-16/A pods, each housing an M61A1 cannon and 1,200 rounds of ammunition. The SUU-16/A went some way to overcoming the F-4Cs (and the later F-4Ds) inherent deficiency of the lack of an internal gun, a problem that would dog both variants throughout their operational careers.

F-4C-24-MC 64-0865 wearing the original US Navy-style camouflage scheme, pictured at Bentwaters in 1966. (photo: Ashley Annis)

In the first two years of combat in SEA, the attrition rate among the first F-4C squadrons had reached almost 40%, for a total of 54 aircraft. Most of these were lost to AAA, but a few were lost in stall/spin accidents at low altitude. During close-in dogfights, when pulling high-g's or when at steep angles of attack, it was very easy to lose control of an F-4C, especially if it was carrying a SUU-16/A or other centreline store. Recovery from a spin at an altitude below 10,000 feet was impossible with ejection being the only option available to the crew.

In 1969 the USAF decided that the two-pilot policy for the F-4C was a mistake. As a result, flight controls were removed from the rear cockpit and the backseat crew member became a weapons system officer (WSO).

Production of the F-4C ceased on 4th May 1966 but the type remained a stalwart of the SEA campaign until the spring of 1967, when the first examples of the F-4D filtered through to the wings.

The only F-4Cs exported to overseas customers were ex-USAF machines (mainly from the 81st TFW at Bentwaters and Woodbridge), which were shipped to Spain's Ejercito del Aire in 1971-72.

First flown on 7th December 1965, the F-4D was externally similar to the F-4C. Internally the changes were in abundance; among these were a new AN/APQ-109A radar, a GE ASG-22 lead computing optical sight (LCOS) and an AJB-7 all-altitude bomb delivery system which was linked to an ASQ-91 weapons release computer system (WRCS), the latter being for the delivery of laser guided 'Smart' bombs. The Litton ASN-48 inertial navigation system of the F-4C was replaced by an ASN-63 system, which was improved and reduced in weight.

AIM-9B Sidewinders were replaced by Hughes AIM-4D Falcons starting with F-4D No.42 (64-970), while provisions were made for the fitting of 'strap-on' electronic countermeasure (ECM) pods. These included the Hughes ALQ-71 and ALQ-72, General Electric ALQ-87, and the Westinghouse ALQ-101 and ALQ-119 noise/deception jammers.

Some 793 F-4Ds were delivered to the USAF, initial production aircraft being assigned to the 36th TFW at Bitburg AB, West Germany, followed by the 4th TFW at Seymour Johnson AFB in North Carolina. Although it still lacked an internal gun, the 'D' was a far more capable aircraft than the 'C' due to a completely new avionics suite making this version better suited to the initial requirements of the USAF. In order to redress that fact that the Phantom still lacked an internal gun, the F-4D introduced the gas-powered SUU-23/A gun pod. Although far from ideal, this was an improvement over the previous SUU-16/A. The 'D' also featured a zero-zero ejection seat, the Martin-Baker Mk.H7. This replaced the Mk.H5 seat in the 'C', which required a minimum 130 knots airspeed at ground level to permit a safe escape.

The 'D' initially appeared over Vietnam in the spring of 1967 with the 8th TFW 'Wolfpack,' led by Col Robin Olds, a former commander of the 81st TFW at Bentwaters and Woodbridge. The WRCS, LCOS and ECM systems met with great approval, but the same could not be said for the AIM-4D Falcon. Despite numerous clashes with MiGs, the Falcon claimed only four MiG-17s and one MiG-21 between 26th October 1967 and 5th February 1968 and as a result were taken out of service. The F-4Ds were modified 'in the field' to restore the AIM-9 Sidewinder capability on the inboard pylons. The first F-4D MiG 'kill' with an AIM-9 took place on 5th June 1967, when Maj Everett T. Raspberry and Capt Francis Gullick shot down a MiG-17 near Hanoi. The F-4D eventually destroyed 45 enemy aircraft, and the USAF's 3 Vietnam-era aces got their fifth kills in F-4Ds during the Linebacker campaign of 1972. Captain Steve Ritchie of the 432nd TFW got his fifth kill in F-4D 66-0167 on 18th August 1972.

F-4C-24-MC (64-0829/WS) of the 91st TFS pictured at its dispersal at Bentwaters. This aircraft was flown by Col Robin Olds during the South East Asia conflict and is currently preserved at the USAF Museum, Wright Patterson AFB, Ohio. (photo: George Pennick)

F-4C-23-MC 64-0765/WR of the 81st TFW at Bentwaters on 26th May 1973. (photo: George Pennick)

For Robin Olds and his colleagues, the F-4's problem was still the lack of an internal gun. The new SUU-23/A still suffered from excessive vibration and 'scatter', making it more of an air-to-ground weapon. From the outset McDonnell Douglas had been drawing up revisions to the basic Model 98 design, adapting it to carry an integral gun and this culminated in the introduction of the F-4E.

As the active forces started trading in their F-4Ds for the new Fairchild A-10 Thunderbolt, McDonnell Douglas F-15 and General Dynamics F-16 under Operation 'Ready Team' and 'Ready Switch', so the older machines were passed on to the Air National Guard (ANG) and Air Force Reserve (AFRes), who in turn scrapped their old but well-loved 'Century Series' fighters.

F-4C/Ds went on to form the bulk of ANG and AFRes close air support, battlefield area interdiction and maritime strike aircraft, equipping some 15 ANG and five AFRes units at peak Phantom strength. First to transition was the 170th TFS, 183rd TFG at Springfield, Illinois, who on 31st January 1972 started to retire its old F-84F Thunderstreaks when F-4Cs began to fly in from George AFB. F-4Ds joined the AFRes in 1978 and in 1985 the first of the gun-equipped F-4Es were integrated into the part-time forces, starting with the 131st TFW 'Lindbergh's Own' at Lambert Field, adjacent to the birthplace of all USAF Phantoms, the McDonnell Douglas plant in Missouri.

The F-4D also saw service with the Imperial Iranian Air Force and the Republic of Korea Air Force.

All versions of the Phantom have since been retired from U.S. military service except for a small number that have been converted to unmanned target drones. The type does, however, remain in service with the air forces of countries such as Germany, Greece, Turkey and Israel.

F-4C Specifications

- Manufacturer: McDonnell Douglas Aircraft Corp.
- Power Plant: Two General Electric J79-GE-15 turbojets, 10,900lbs static thrust dry, 17,000lbs static thrust with afterburner.
- Performance: Maximum Speed - 1,433mph at 48,000 feet and 826mph at sea level, Landing Speed - 165mph, Initial Climb Rate - 40,550 feet per minute.
- Dimensions: Wingspan - 38 feet 5 inches, Wing Area - 530 square feet, Length - 58 feet 3 3/4 inches, Height - 16 feet 3 inches.
- Weights: Empty - 28,496 lbs, Gross - 51,441lbs, Combat - 38,352lbs, Maximum Takeoff - 58,000lbs
- Ceiling: Service - 56,100 feet, Combat - 55,600 feet.
- Range: Combat - 538 miles, Maximum - 1,926 miles with maximum external fuel.
- Maximum Internal Fuel: 1,986 U.S. gallons (1,343 U.S. gallons in fuselage, 630 U.S. gallons in wings).
- Maximum External Fuel: 600 U.S. gallons in centerline tank underneath the fuselage and 740 U.S. gallons in two underwing tanks, bringing total fuel to 3,326 U.S. gallons.
- Armament: Four AIM-7 Sparrow semi-active radar homing missiles in underfuselage recesses. Inner underwing pylons could each accommodate a pair of AIM-9 Sidewinder infrared homing missiles. For ground attack missions, could carry as much as 16,000 lbs of ordnance on centerline pylon underneath the fuselage and on four underwing hardpoints.

81st TFW F-4C/D Phantom II Accidents

Date of Accident	Model	Serial Number	Location	Additional Info
06 May 1966	F-4C-25-MC	64-0885	North Sea off Winterton, Norfolk	92nd TFS a/c. Crashed into North Sea three miles east of Winterton at about 0915 hrs, whilst on a routine training flight. Eye-witness reported two aircraft together, rising vertically and appearing to collide: one aircraft, in flames, was then seen plunging into the sea. The fate of the crew is not known but it is assumed that they were lost in the accident.
13 Sept 1967	F-4C-25-MC	64-0921	RAF Woodbridge, Suffolk	78th TFS a/c. Crashed one mile south of Woodbridge runway whilst on approach to land. One of two Phantoms flying in formation, '921 turned on its back and crashed to the ground, exploding on impact. The crew, Capt Joseph T. Kirby and 1st Lt James B. Pierce, ejected safely.
15 Aug 1968	F-4C-25-MC	64-0901	RAF Bentwaters, Suffolk	92nd TFS a/c. Overran runway on landing. Written off.
05 Feb 1969	F-4C-24-MC	64-0873	Nr. Doncaster, Yorkshire	92nd TFS a/c. Collided with 64-0874. Routine training flight out of Bentwaters when accident occurred, both aircraft reportedly crashing in unpopulated, open countryside near Lindholme, Yorkshire. Both crews ejected, all sustaining minor injuries. The four airmen were: Lt Col Ronald Lynch (92nd TFS commander); Capt Anthony Sultan (91st TFS); Capt Dennis Petty (91st TFS); Maj Max Ownes (91st TFS).
05 Feb 1969	F-4C-24-MC	64-0874	Nr. Doncaster, Yorkshire	92nd TFS a/c. Collided with 64-0873.
25 Mar 1969	F-4C-25-MC	64-0898	Nr. East Dereham, Norfolk	78th TFS a/c. One of two aircraft out of Woodbridge on training flight. Crew ejected after aircraft entered a spin following a loss of control, both receiving injuries. Pilot - Capt Kristian Mineau, WSO - Capt Michael L. Hinnebusch.
11 Nov 1970	F-4C-24-MC	64-0863	Gedgrave Marshes Nr. Orford, Suffolk	91st TFS a/c. Routine training flight, on radar approach to Bentwaters, when aircraft was seen spiralling out of the clouds. Two reports (one from the pilot), indicated that the rear of the plane was on fire. Crew ejected to safety, landing in the North Sea. They were picked up unhurt by a Woodbridge-based rescue helicopter.
18 Jan 1971	F-4C-25-MC	64-0916	Nr. Furstenfeldbruck, Germany	92nd TFS a/c.
01 Feb 1972	F-4C-17-MC	63-7450	Nr. Aviano Gunnery Range, Italy	92nd TFS a/c.
09 May 1972	F-4D-28-MC	65-0673	North of Madrid, Spain	78th TFS a/c.

| 21 Aug 1972 | F-4C-24-MC | 64-0824 | North Sea off Lowestoft, Suffolk | Collided with 64-0812 shortly after 1400 hrs at an estimated 7 miles offshore from Lowestoft. Prior to crashing into the North Sea, both crew members ejected, but sadly did not survive. Pilot was Maj Earl E. Chapman Jnr. and his WSO was Capt John S. Davis. The other Phantom involved in the accident (64-0812), suffered considerable damage to its tail but was successfully flown back to Bentwaters by its crew, pilot Capt Ronald Scheck and WSO Maj Robert Chittenden. |
| 09 July 1974 | F-4D-29-MC | 65-0776 | Grafenwohr, Germany | 91st TFS a/c. Crashed during a weapons training mission out of Bentwaters. Capt Steve Berta (pilot) and Major Joe Wilson Jnr. (WSO) killed. |

The author wishes to acknowledge the help of Alan Howarth and David Baker during the preparation of this list.

F-4C-24-MC 64-0863 seen at its dispersal at Bentwaters, shortly after delivery to the 81st TFW in October 1966. 64-0863 was written off in a crash at Gedgrave Marshes near Orford, Suffolk on 11th November 1970. (photo: Ashley Annis)

FAIRCHILD REPUBLIC A-10A THUNDERBOLT II

A-10A 82-0655/WR of the 81st TFW pictured at Bentwaters in September 1992. This particular jet was assigned to the 81st TFW commander, Col Roger R. Radcliff. (photo: Trevor Rose)

For many people the arrival of the Fairchild Republic A-10A Thunderbolt II at Bentwaters in late 1978 may have seemed strange; after all the A-10 was at the opposite end of the performance scale when compared to the aircraft it replaced - the F-4D Phantom. The Phantom was a very good all-round fighter but the A-10 was dedicated to the role of close air support and, as was proved in Desert Storm, the 'Warthog' can pack an impressive punch. 144 A-10s flew 8,624 missions during the conflict for the loss of only 5 aircraft, destroying 25% of Iraq's military arsenal. This figure comprised 967 tanks, 1,026 artillery pieces, 1,306 trucks, 281 military buildings, 53 Scud missiles, 10 aircraft on the ground and 2 aircraft in the air. The A-10's stay at Bentwaters and Woodbridge spanned some 15 years and the type has the honour of being the last military type to operate at both bases before the USAF withdrawal in 1993.

Although the A-10's development began in May 1970, the USAF requirement for a dedicated close air support aircraft can be traced back 10-years earlier to March 1960. This original requirement (known as AX) specified a low-cost, low-maintenance, highly manoeuvrable aircraft capable of STOL (short takeoff and landing) performance and with a large combat radius. The AX also had to be able to carry a heavy armament payload and operate from unprepared airstrips. Twenty-one companies were invited to submit proposals resulting in preliminary design contracts being awarded to General Dynamics, Grumman, Northrop and McDonnell.

Nothing further happened until May 1970 when twelve companies were requested to submit proposals for the resurrected AX project. By August 1970, six of these companies (Boeing, Cessna, Fairchild Republic, General Dynamics, Lockheed and Northrop) had submitted design proposals and, on 18th December, Fairchild Republic and Northrop were each awarded contracts for the manufacture of two prototypes. The two designs became known as the Northrop YA-9A and the Fairchild Republic YA-10A.

Of the two designs, the first to take to the skies was the YA-10A, which made its maiden flight from Edwards AFB on 10th May 1972. A little under three weeks later, on 30th May, the YA-9A made its maiden flight also from Edwards AFB. Following the completion of their respective manufacturer's flight trials, the two YA-9As and two YA-10As were handed over to the USAF to begin a two-month flight evaluation fly-off. During the fly-off the four aircraft logged a total of 635 flight-hours.

On 18th January 1973 the USAF announced that the A-10 had been selected as Tactical Air Command's future close air support aircraft.

On 1st March 1973, Fairchild Republic received a $159 million contract to cover continued testing of the two YA-10A prototypes and the construction of ten (later reduced to six) pre-production A-10As that would be used in the flight-test programme. A $27 million order was also placed with General Electric for development and production of the A-10's power plant - the TF34-GE-100 turbofan.

Internal armament of the two YA-10As had been a single 20mm cannon but, in June 1973, the USAF awarded a $23 million contract to General Electric for development and production of 11 GAU-8 30mm cannons. This initial batch was to be used for evaluation purposes in both the prototype and pre-production aircraft although it wasn't until early 1974 that the first examples of the GAU-8 joined the flight-test programme.

During late 1973 the A-10 found itself in the centre of a political storm. Certain elements of Congress, in particular those representing Texas, were persistent in their claims that the USAF already possessed a good close air support aircraft and therefore the A-10 was not required. The aircraft in question was the A-7D Corsair, built by the Dallas-based company Vought (hence the protests from those members of Congress with a vested interest in anything that was likely to effect the state of Texas).

In order to calm the storm in Congress the USAF organised an intensive fly-off against the A-7D at Fort Riley, Kansas. The A-7D proved to be no match for the A-10 and, with the critics silenced, permission was given on 31st July 1974 to proceed with the manufacture of an initial production batch of 52 aircraft.

A-10A 80-0273/WR of the 509th TFS/81st TFW photographed during 1987. (photo: Author)

Pictured at Bentwaters in August 1980 is A-10A 77-0194/WR, still wearing the original 'grey ghost' camouflage scheme. (photo: Ashley Annis)

Part of the development programme for the A-10 involved compatibility trials with the AGM-65A Maverick air-to-ground missile and these had been successfully concluded in early-September. The 1000th flight hour milestone was reached on 14th February 1975 and at this stage of the programme only the two prototypes had flown. The next day saw the first of the pre-production aircraft (73-1664) make its maiden flight and this was followed over the next few weeks by the remaining five aircraft. With all of the pre-production A-10s now involved in the development programme the two prototypes (71-1369/71-1370) were placed into storage having flown 821 times and recording 1,139 flight-hours.

The programme continued under the control of the A-10 Joint Test Force at Edwards AFB using the six pre-production aircraft. The JTF consisted of USAF personnel representing a number of Commands including Tactical Air Command (TAC), Air Training Command (ATC) and Air Force Logistics Command (AFLC). The JTF's task was to formulate operating procedures for the type and to assess its operational suitability and effectiveness in a combat scenario. The JTF continued this evaluation work until December 1977. The first production aircraft (75-0258) took off from Farmingdale on its maiden flight in November 1975 and this was followed some three months later (February 1975) by the first deliveries of the type to TAC. The first unit to receive the A-10 was the 355th Tactical Fighter Training Wing at Davis Monthan AFB, Arizona, followed in July 1977 by the 354th Tactical Fighter Wing at Myrtle Beach AFB, South Carolina.

The A-10 may not be an aesthetically pleasing aircraft to some but its unique rugged design allows it to withstand a considerable amount of battle damage. This was demonstrated during the Kosovo Crisis when an A-10 pilot managed to return his aircraft to base having had an engine nacelle shot off by anti-aircraft fire. Other factors taken into consideration when designing the A-10 were low operating costs, ease of maintenance and interchangeability of major components. The latter factor allows items such as the main undercarriage, ailerons, rudders, elevators, vertical stabilisers and engines to be installed on either the port or starboard side. 95% of the A-10's airframe is made of aluminium alloy whilst the cockpit and other vulnerable areas are protected by titanium armour plating.

The A-10 is powered by two General Electric TF34-GE-100 high bypass turbofans positioned on the upper rear fuselage. Locating the engines in this position reduces the possibility of sustaining damage from enemy AAA due to the fact that they are protected from most angles by either the wings or tailplane. An added advantage of locating the engines in this way is that it dramatically reduces the aircraft's infra-red signature and therefore makes it less susceptible to being targeted by an infra-red homing missile.

A-10A (81-0981/WR) assigned to the commander of the 81st TFW, Col Tad L. Oelstrom, seen on display at Air Friendship '89 on 16th July 1989. (photo: Author)

In order to carry out its 'tank-killing' mission the A-10 is built around the awesome General Electric GAU-8/A Avenger 30-mm, seven-barrelled gatling gun. Weighing in at a little under two tons and some 20-feet long, the Avenger is the largest gun to be fitted to any aircraft. The hydraulically driven gun can operate at two firing rates, either 2,100 or 4,200 rounds per minute, spinning up to the latter rate in 0.55 seconds. The GAU-8/As incredible power can be further appreciated when you realise that a firing rate of 4,200 rounds per minute equates to 70 rounds per second. The ammunition is fed from a drum that has a maximum capacity of 1,350 rounds, onto a continuous belt to the gun, while spent cartridges and unfired rounds are returned via the belt to the drum.

Three types of ammunition can be used by the GAU-8/A. The first is the PGU-13/B HEI (High Explosive, Incendiary) round, which is designed for use against soft targets, or lightly armoured vehicles. It has a fragmenting jacket filled with standard explosives. The second type is the PGU-14/B API (Armour-Piercing, Incendiary) round which, as its name suggests, is used against heavily armoured vehicles i.e. tanks. The PGU-14/B consists of a lightweight, aluminium body surrounding a depleted uranium core of very substantial mass and is capable of penetrating armour through kinetic energy alone. While the round is minimally radioactive, uranium is highly flammable and combusts with the heat of the impact once inside a tank. The third ammunition type is the PGU-15/B TP (Training Practice) round, with no explosive filling. The PGU-15/B closely matches the ballistic properties of the PGU-13/B and allows A-10 pilots to perfect their air-to-ground marksmanship. The GAU-8/A was demonstrated for the first time at Nellis AFB on 13th November 1975 and provided the gathered audience with a spectacular display of its unrivalled ability. Among the large number of current (as of 1975) tanks and other armoured vehicles reduced to scrap metal was the Soviet T62 main battle tank, which at that time equipped most of the Warsaw Pact countries.

In addition to the GAU-8/A, the A-10 can carry a wide variety of external stores. The principle weapon is the AGM-65 Maverick missile. Two versions of the 8-feet 2-inch missile are used: the AGM-65B with TV scene magnification guidance, and the AGM-65D with an imaging infra-red (IIR) seeker. A third version is occasionally used, this being the AGM-65G. Like the 'D' this is an IIR weapon but is fitted with a much-improved seeker that enables the pilot to designate a specific aiming point within a larger heat source.

The AIM-9L Sidewinder has become a standard fitment for self-defence, a requirement that was not anticipated when the A-10 first entered service. The Sidewinder is usually carried on a twin rail launcher on either the port or starboard outboard stores station. An electronic countermeasures (ECM) pod - usually an AN/ALQ-131 - balances the twin rail launcher on the opposite wing station.

Fine air-to-air study of a pair of 81st TFW 'Warthogs' over the Suffolk countryside. Both aircraft are carrying AGM-65 Maverick missiles and an AN/ALQ-119 electronic countermeasures (ECM) pod.
(U.S. Air Force photo via Bentwaters 'Cold War' Museum Archives)

Four stores stations are located under each wing (two inboard of the main undercarriage) along with three under the fuselage. The centreline station and its two flanking hardpoints cannot be used simultaneously due to their close proximity to each other. The A-10 can carry a maximum load of 10 AGM-65 or 28 Mk 82 500lb Low Drag General Purpose (LDGP) bombs, or 16 Mk 84 1,000lb bombs, or eight CBU-87 cluster munitions, or 16 CBU-52/71 cluster munitions. Other stores that can be carried are SUU-23/25/30/65 dispensers, BDU-33 practice bombs, AN/ALQ-119 and AN/ALQ-131 ECM pods, MXU-648 cargo pod and up to three F-111-style 600-U.S. gallon drop tanks (one centreline). The A-10 has also been cleared for, but very rarely carries, GBU-10/12 Laser Guided Bombs (LGB), BLU-52 tear-gas canisters, M117 LDGP bombs, and the RAF's BL755 cluster bomb.

The A-10 has remained virtually unchanged throughout its operational career. The only exception to this was the conversion of the first pre-production A-10 (73-1664) into the sole two-seat YA-10B, or N/AW A-10. This aircraft was intended for night/adverse weather missions with the addition of a weapons system officer but the project was cancelled in its early stages due to a lack of interest from the USAF.

The A-10 has never been an aircraft packed with a vast array of sophisticated avionics, in fact the avionics fitment has remained very basic for most of the aircraft's career. A Head Up Display (HUD) was fitted along with a TV screen used in conjunction with the AGM-65B Maverick missile. A Pave Penny laser seeker was mounted on a pylon under the forward fuselage and this was used to locate targets illuminated by a laser source. The majority of A-10s remaining in operation today have received an autopilot as part of the Low Altitude Safety and Targeting Enhancements (LASTE) modification. The LASTE modification also provided an improvement in gun accuracy while the most visible feature is the addition of a number of formation strip lights on the airframe.

Unquestionably the most important theatre of operations for the A-10 was Europe. Here the 81st TFW initially flew six squadrons from the twin-base complex at RAF Bentwaters and RAF Woodbridge in the U.K. From early 1978, the principle objective of all USAF A-10 activity was to get the 81st operational as soon as possible. The 355th Tactical Fighter Training Wing at Davis Monthan AFB, Arizona, conducted the pilot training programme known as 'Operation Ready Thunder' (later 'Operation Ready Bentwaters'). Once fully operational the 81st TFW continued to be the priority A-10 unit becoming the first to have all of its A-10s fitted with an Inertial Navigation System (INS) and other important modifications.

The arrival of the A-10 at Bentwaters and Woodbridge caused a few problems for RAF personnel stationed at the Holbeach and Wainfleet ranges. The immense power of the A-10's GAU-8/A 30mm cannon caused the destruction of a number of the structures that supported the targets as well as the targets themselves. The support structures had to be specially reinforced to withstand the punishment dealt out by the Warthog.

The debate relating to the A-10s vulnerability - something that has continued since the type was first introduced- went some way to fuelling the USAF's decision to withdraw a number of the older airframes and replace them with the F-16. As a result of this, some A-10s ended up replacing the elderly OV-10 Bronco in the forward air control (FAC) role.

The FAC role did not involve any modification to the aircraft only a redesignation to OA-10A. Armament for this new-found mission, apart from the GAU-8/A, are AIM-9s for self-defence and LAU-68 rocket pods. The pods can carry up to seven Mk 66 rockets with phosphorus warheads that are used for target marking.

With the A-10 fleet in decline, both as a result of USAF policy and of more general military cutbacks resulting from the end of the 'Cold War,' the Warthog suddenly found itself going into battle. As mentioned earlier, the A-10 was a major player in Desert Storm wreaking havoc amongst Sadaam Hussein's army. 144 A-10s from U.S. and U.K. based units, operating under the control of the 354th TFW (Provisional), were tasked with anti-armour, air defence suppression and 'Scud' hunting missions. During the conflict a pair of A-10s made air-to-air kills by shooting down two Iraqi Helicopters.

With an original planned service life of 8,000 hours, equating to approximately to FY2005, the end of 1998 saw the first of the remaining A/OA-10A fleet commence a Service Life Extension Programme (SLEP). The SLEP included the fitting of a Missile Approach Warning System (MAWS) and a Global Positioning System (GPS). The revised service life was projected out to 12,000 hours, equating to approximately FY2016 although the most recent long-range plan has the A/OA-10 in the USAF inventory until FY2028, which equates to approximately 18,000-24,000 hours.

Although the sight and sound of the Warthog at Bentwaters and Woodbridge is now a distant memory, the type is destined to remain an important part of the U.S. war machine for several years to come.

A-10A Specifications

- Primary Mission: Close Air Support.
- Manufacturer: Fairchild Republic Corp.
- Crew: One.
- Power Plant: Two General Electric TF34-GE-100 each rated at 9,065lbs static thrust.
- Performance: Never-Exceed Speed - 450kts (518mph; 834km/h), Maximum Level Speed ('clean' at sea level) - 381kts (439mph; 706km/h), Maximum Rate of Climb at Sea Level - 6,000ft (1,828m) per minute, Takeoff Run - 4,000ft (1,220m) at maximum take-off weight or 1,450ft (442m) at forward strip weight, Landing Run - 2,000ft (610m) at maximum weight or 1,300ft (396m) at forward strip weight.
- Dimensions: Wingspan - 57 feet 6 inches (17.53m), Wing Area - 506.00 square feet (47.01m^2), Length - 53 feet 4 inches (16.26m), Height - 14 feet 8 inches (4.47m), Tailplane Span - 18 feet 10 inches (5.74m), Wheel Track - 17 feet 2.5 inches (5.25m).
- Weights: Basic Empty - 21,541lbs (9,771kg), Operating Empty - 24,959lbs (11,321kg), Forward Airstrip Armed - 32,771lbs (14,865kg), Maximum Takeoff - 50,000lbs (22,680kg).
- Fuel and Load: Internal Fuel - 10,700lbs (4,853kg), External Fuel - up to three 600-U.S. gallon (2,271-litre) drop tanks, Maximum Ordnance - 16,000lbs (7,258kg) or, with full internal fuel, 14,341lbs (6,505kg).
- Range: Ferry Range - 2,131nm (2,454 miles; 3,949km) with drop tanks, Combat Radius - 540nm (620 miles, 1,000km) on a deep strike mission or 250nm (288 miles; 463km) on a close air support mission with a 1.7-hour loiter.
- Ceiling: 45,000 feet (13,636m).

81st TFW A-10A Thunderbolt II Accidents

Date of Accident	Serial Number	Location	Additional Info
07 Jul 1979	77-0253	RAF Chicksands, Bedfordshire	Crashed whilst performing at an airshow. Pilot, Col Tom Thompson, was killed.
18 Nov 1980	78-0588	Nr. Itteringham, Norfolk	Collided with 78-0590. Pilot ejected safely.
18 Nov 1980	78-0590	North Sea, off Gt. Yarmouth, Norfolk	Collided with 78-0588. Pilot ejected but drowned along with the RAF SAR winch man attempting to rescue him.
09 Jan 1981	77-0258	North Sea, off Donna Nook range, Lincolnshire	Pilot killed.
08 May 1981	79-0083	Wainfleet range, Lincolnshire	Crashed during bombing run. Pilot killed during ejection.

22 Sep 1981	80-0182	Gambassi Terme, Italy	Pilot ejected safely.
24 Sep 1981	79-0160	Aviano AB, Italy	Crashed during landing. Pilot ok.
22 Mar 1982	80-0148	Nr. Herford, West Germany	Engines stalled, pilot ejected safely.
28 Jul 1983	79-0222	Ahaus, West Germany	Lost control during air combat manoeuvring (ACM). Pilot ejected safely.
12 Dec 1983	80-0193	North Sea, off Gt. Yarmouth, Norfolk	Collided with 80-0202. One pilot killed, one rescued.
12 Dec 1983	80-0202	North Sea, off Gt. Yarmouth, Norfolk	Collided with 80-0193. One pilot killed, one rescued.
17 Apr 1989	80-0183	Fen Ditton, Cambridgeshire	510th TFS aircraft. Pilot, Capt Donald R. Roberts, was killed.

The author wishes to acknowledge the help received from Andrew Horrex during the preparation of this list.

GENERAL DYNAMICS F-16C FIGHTING FALCON

F-16C Block 30A (85-1453/WR) of the 527th AS/81st TFW heads for Runway 25 at Bentwaters during 1989. (photo: Trevor Rose)

The arrival of the first 'Aggressor' General Dynamics F-16C Fighting Falcons at Bentwaters on 14th June 1988 added a new dimension to the role of the Suffolk base. The F-16Cs were to play the role of the 'bad guys' during air combat manoeuvring (ACM) training against fighters belonging to many of NATO's air forces. This had the prospect of being an interesting period for any avid aircraft 'spotter' as many of the aircraft participating in training with the 'Aggressors' would be based at Bentwaters for the duration of their respective courses. Sadly this was only to be the case for some eighteen months before the unit was deactivated and its F-16s transferred to other USAFE squadrons. Despite this, Bentwaters played host to numerous aircraft types from several NATO countries for this short period making the 'Aggressor' F-16Cs very welcome residents at the base.

The F-16 was originally designed as a small, low cost fighter for air-to-air combat but evolved into a versatile and effective multi-role aircraft. Designed to compete for the USAF's Light Weight Fighter requirement, the prototype YF-16 was first flown on 20th January 1974 and successfully defeated Northrop's rival YF-17 in the fly-off competition. Although the YF-17 lost the fly-off, the design attracted the interest of the U.S. Navy and it was eventually developed into the McDonnell Douglas F/A-18 Hornet.

The first of eight full-scale development F-16As flew on 8th December 1976 with the first two-seat, combat-capable F-16B making its maiden flight on 8th August 1977.

The F-16, otherwise known as the 'Viper' or 'Lawn Dart,' is instantly recognisable due to its unique shape, with its shock-inlet air intake located under the forward fuselage below the cockpit. The F-16 also features wing/fuselage blending and large leading-edge root extensions (LERX) to increase lift at high angles of attack and, coupled with its very high thrust to weight ratio, fast roll rate and high lift wing, it is a very agile fighter. The unique design of the F-16 makes it aerodynamically unstable, relying totally on a computer and fly-by-wire controls to keep it airborne. The sophisticated cockpit of the F-16 is fitted with a zero-zero capable McDonnell Douglas ACES II ejection seat reclined at 30° to increase the pilot's g-tolerance. The reclined seat necessitates provision of a limited-movement pressure-sensing sidestick controller instead of a conventional control column. The cockpit is equipped with a Head Up Display (HUD) and multi-function displays and is enclosed by a one-piece blown polycarbonate canopy providing unobstructed forward and upward vision and greatly improved vision over the side and to the rear. This feature provides the F-16 pilot with a distinct advantage during air-to-air combat.

Internal armament of the F-16 consists of a single General Electric M61A1 Vulcan 20mm cannon with 511 rounds, located on the port wing/fuselage blend. In addition to this the aircraft has the capability of carrying up to 16,700 lb (7575 kg) of ordnance, including the majority of bombs and missiles in the USAF inventory.

Initial deliveries of the F-16A/B to the USAF commenced in January 1979 to the 388th Tactical Fighter Wing at Hill AFB, Utah. Production for the USAF totalled 674 F-16As and 121 F-16Bs. Although the F-16A was (and still is) a superb fighter it did have limitations, largely due to the fact that it was not ideally suited to all-weather operations and could not carry missiles such as the AIM-7 Sparrow or AIM-120 AMRAAM for beyond-visual-range (BVR) engagements. In order to address these deficiencies a programme of modifications, known as Multinational Staged Improvement Program (MSIP) II was incorporated into F-16s beginning from production Block 25. These aircraft were redesignated as the F-16C (single-seat) and the F-16D (two-seat). A number of the modifications included in MSIP II have been retrofitted to A and B-model aircraft.

The first F-16C (83-1118) made its maiden flight on 19th June 1984, in the capable hands of company test pilot Kevin Dwyer and this was followed on 14th September by the first flight of the F-16D (83-1174), flown by John Fergione and Jim Smolka.

The F-16C is virtually identical in appearance to the earlier A-model; the most noticeable feature that distinguishes it from the 'A' is an extended base to the vertical fin complete with a prominent blade antenna. The space made available by extending the fin base was to be occupied by an internal airborne self-protection jammer (ASPJ) but this was abandoned by the USAF in favour of the continued used of a variety of external ECM pods. An additional recognition feature is the distinctly golden tint to the F-16C's canopy which is due to a lining of radar reflecting materials; although some A-model aircraft have since been retrofitted with this canopy. The F-16C is fitted with the Hughes AN/APG-68(V) multi-mode radar which provides better range, improved resolution, and expanded operating modes and is a considerable technological advancement over the APG-66 of the F-16A. The system provides numerous air-to-air modes, including range-while-search, uplook and velocity search, single target track, raid cluster resolution, and track-while-scan for up to 10 simultaneous targets. An improved GEC wide-angle HUD was also fitted in addition to a weapons interface for the AGM-65D Maverick, AGM-45 Shrike and AGM-88A HARM anti-radiation missiles and AIM-120 AMRAAM missiles. Progressive changes have been introduced to the F-16C throughout the various production blocks; some incorporated at the factory and others part of MSIP II (avionics, cockpit and airframe changes) and MSIP III (further systems installation) programmes, aimed at enhancing the Fighting Falcon's ability to carry out combat missions at night.

'Aggressor' F-16C-Block 30C 86-0219/WR taxies for takeoff at Bentwaters in March 1989. (photo: Author)

F-16C Block 30C (86-0224/WR), of the 527th AS/81st TFW parked at its dispersal at Bentwaters in August 1989. (photo: Trevor Rose)

Early F-16Cs (Block 25/MSIP II) were delivered with the A-model's Pratt & Whitney F100-PW-200 engine, which had suffered from a number of problems ever since it was first flown in the F-16A. The most common (and most serious) of these problems were compressor stalls. At the time of the introduction of the F-16C, Pratt and Whitney had been working for several years on improving their F100 engine but could not produce a satisfactory solution for the compressor stalls. In early 1984 the USAF, unhappy with this situation, officially launched an Alternative Fighter Engine (AFE) programme to look for an alternative engine for both the F-16 and the F-15 (as this aircraft used the same power plant and hence was suffering from the same problems). The USAF selected two engines, namely General Electric's F101 DFE (later redesignated F110) and an improved Pratt & Whitney F100. There would be a competition every fiscal year between General Electric and Pratt & Whitney for engine orders for both the F-15 and the F-16. Competition between these two companies would enable the unit cost to be kept to a minimum as well as providing a second source for engines, thus ensuring a steady supply. Eventually it was decided that the small number of F-15 orders could not justify such a split order, so the competition between General Electric and Pratt & Whitney was therefore confined to the F-16.

In February 1984, the USAF announced that General Electric had been awarded 75 percent of the total engine contracts for the FY 1985 run of F-16Cs. The remaining FY 85 aircraft would use the upgraded Pratt & Whitney F100, known as the F100-PW-220. The F110 was to be phased into the General Dynamics production line as soon as production engines became available, but it was decided that no USAF F-16 unit would operate a mix of aircraft using both engine types. The F100-PW-200 equipped aircraft were later retrofitted with either the F100-PW-220 engine (a 'new-build' power plant) or the F100-PW-220E (a rebuild of an existing -200 engine). These newer engines were equipped with a Digital Electronic Engine Control (DEEC), which enabled stall-free performance and improved reliability.

The first F-16C version to accommodate both engines was the Block 30/32 (sometimes known as MSIP III), with Block 30 aircraft having the F110 and Block 32 aircraft having the F100. The Block 30/32 F-16Cs share a common engine bay that can accommodate either engine but, due to differing engine airflow requirements, it is not practical to fit a Block 30 F-16C with an F100 engine or to fit a Block 32 F-16C with an F110 engine.

The Block 30 F-16 was powered by the 28,984lbs static thrust General Electric F110-GE-100 engine. This engine is physically larger than the F100 and about 770lbs heavier. The F110 does, however, provide about 5,000lbs more thrust than the F100. For this reason, it requires a larger amount of air. This in turn required that the diameter of the air intake be increased by about 1 foot to admit the extra air. However, this change was not made at first, and early F-16C/D Block 30s (Block 30A and 30B) are 'small inlet' aircraft, the 'large inlet' being made standard for F110-powered Fighting Falcons from serial number 86-0262 onward. The larger diameter intake allows air mass flow to increase from 254 to 270lbs per second. Apart from the intake size the two engines can be distinguished by differing exhaust nozzles. The engine exhaust nozzle for F110-powered aircraft is slightly shorter and more rounded than that of the F100-powered F-16s.

The Block 32 F-16 was powered by the F100-PW-220 engine, which offered a thrust rating of 23,770lbs. This engine was slightly less powerful than the F100-PW-200 it replaced, but had a new, more reliable compressor and a digital engine control system which made the engine more reliable and less prone to compressor stalls. A modification kit was developed to bring earlier -200 engines up to a similar standard to the -220, these converted engines being designated as F100-PW-220E. From Block 30/32 on, a major block designation ending in '0' signified a General Electric engine and one ending in '2' signified a Pratt & Whitney engine.

Following initial deliveries to overseas based USAF units, the 61st TFTS of the 56th TFW at MacDill AFB, Florida, became the first continental U.S. unit to receive the F-16C/D, acquiring its first examples in April 1986 and becoming operational in October 1988.

On 9th December 1992, it was announced that Lockheed had bought out the Fort Worth Division of General Dynamics for $1.525 billion. The plant became known as the Lockheed Fort Worth Company and, although this marked the end of aircraft production by General Dynamics, the F-16 would continue to be built at Fort Worth but would now be known as the Lockheed F-16. The production total for Block 30/32 F-16C/Ds reached 469 aircraft, comprising 416 F-16Cs and 53 F-16Ds.

In addition to equipping numerous USAF tactical squadrons, the F-16C Block 30 was flown by the USAF's Adversary Tactics Division on aggressor duties, and the F-16C Block 32 is currently operated by the 'Thunderbirds' air demonstration team. USAF F-16C/Ds were deployed to the Persian Gulf in 1991 in support of Operation Desert Storm along with a number of F-16A/Bs from NATO air arms. The F-16 flew more combat missions than with any other aircraft type and were used to attack airfields, military production facilities, Scud missile sites and a variety of other targets.

Active USAF units no longer operate Block 30/32 F-16Cs; Block 40/42 and Block 50/52 F-16Cs being current front-line equipment. Block 25 and Block 30/32 aircraft are now used solely by Air National Guard and Air Force Reserve units.

F-16C Block 30/32 Specifications

- Primary Mission: Multi-role Fighter.
- Manufacturer: Lockheed Martin Corporation. (ex-General Dynamics)
- Crew: One
- Power Plant: One General Electric F110-GE-100 rated at 28,984lbs static thrust with afterburning or one Pratt & Whitney F100-P-220 rated at 23,770lbs static trust with afterburning.
- Performance: Maximum Level Speed ('clean') - at 40,000ft (12,190m) in excess of 1,320mph and at sea level - 915mph, Maximum rate of climb at sea level - more than 50,000ft per minute, Typical Takeoff Run - 2,500ft (762m) at maximum take-off weight, Typical Landing Run - 2,500ft (762m) at normal landing weight, g limit - +9.
- Dimensions: Wingspan (without tip-mounted AAMs) - 31 feet (9.45m), Wing Area - 300 square feet (28.87m^2), Length - 49 feet 4 inches (15.03m), Height 16 feet 8.5 inches (5.09m), Tailplane Span 18 feet 3.75 inches (5.58m), Wheel Track - 7 feet 9 inches (2.36m), Wheel Base - 13 feet 1 1/2 inches (4.00m).
- Weights: Empty - 19,100lbs (8,663kg) with F110 turbofan or 18,335lbs (8,316kg) with F100 turbofan, Typical Combat Takeoff - 21,585lbs (9,791kg), Maximum Takeoff - 25,071lbs (11,372 kg) for an air-to-air mission without drop tanks or 42,300lbs (19,187kg) with maximum external load.
- Fuel and Load: Internal Fuel - 6,972lbs (3,162kg), External Fuel - up to 6,760lbs (3,066kg) in three 300-, 370-, 450- and 600-U.S. gallon (1,136-, 1,400-, 1,703- and 2,271-litre) drop tanks, Maximum Ordnance - 20,450lbs (9,276kg) for 5-g manoeuvre limit or 11,950lbs (5,421kg) for 9-g manoeuvre limit.
- Range: Ferry Range - in excess of 2,418 miles (3,891km) with drop tanks, Combat Radius - 340 miles (547km) on a hi-lo-hi mission with six 454-kg (1,000-lb) bombs.
- Service Ceiling: In excess of 50,000ft (15,240m).
- Armament: One M-61A1 20mm multi-barrel cannon with 500 rounds, external stations can carry up to six air-to-air missiles, conventional air-to-air and air-to-surface munitions and electronic countermeasure pods.

527th Aggressor Squadron - F-16Cs Assigned

GD F-16C Block 30A Fighting Falcon	85-1479/01
GD F-16C Block 30A Fighting Falcon	85-1453/02
GD F-16C Block 30C Fighting Falcon	86-0209/03
GD F-16C Block 30C Fighting Falcon	86-0229/04
GD F-16C Block 30C Fighting Falcon	86-0249/05
GD F-16C Block 30C Fighting Falcon	86-0219/06
GD F-16C Block 30C Fighting Falcon	86-0254/11
GD F-16C Block 30C Fighting Falcon	86-0216/12
GD F-16C Block 30C Fighting Falcon	86-0231/13
GD F-16C Block 30C Fighting Falcon	86-0227/14
GD F-16C Block 30C Fighting Falcon	86-0224/15
GD F-16C Block 30C Fighting Falcon	86-0237/16

REPUBLIC F-84G THUNDERJET

F-84G-1-RE (51-0909) of the 79th FBS/20th FBW, photographed at RAF Manston 'Armed Forces Day' on 21st May 1955. (photo: via L Bachelor and David Baker)

Not long after the Second World War the U.S. aviation industry was busy producing a number of designs that were to take advantage of the revolutionary jet engine - a power plant that was still in its infancy. Many of these designs never made it off the drawing board but those that made it into production went on to have lengthy operational careers.

Probably the most outstanding U.S. fighter from this period was the North American F-86 Sabre, this type's performance as an interceptor during the Korean War is now legendary. Although overshadowed by the F-86, there was another type that gained widespread acclaim in the same theatre of operations. This aircraft was the Republic F-84 Thunderjet and it achieved its success not as an interceptor but in the close air support role. The F-84 eventually became a main player in the U.S. Mutual Defence Assistance Programme (MDAP), serving with many allied air forces during the 1950s.

On 11th September 1944 the USAAF issued a General Operational Requirement for a mid-wing day fighter aircraft with a maximum speed of 600 mph, a combat radius of 850 miles and armament consisting of eight .50 calibre or six .60 calibre machine guns. It soon became apparent that these requirements were not possible and the USAAF were forced to modify the GOR by reducing the armament to six .50 or four .60 calibre machine guns along with a reduced combat radius of slightly in excess of 700 miles. The power plant specified was a single General Electric TG-180 (J35) which, at the time, was being developed by the Army Air Force's Air Technical Service Command. The engine was later manufactured by the Allison Division of General Motors.

The Republic design team led by Alexander Kartveli began work on a design to satisfy the GOR and saw it as a chance to produce a jet-powered successor to the company's highly regarded P-47 Thunderbolt. The outcome of the team's work was a cantilever low-wing monoplane with straight, laminar-flow wings and cantilevered horizontal tailplanes located midway up the vertical tail. The design also included a nose-mounted air intake for the jet engine and a pressurised cockpit equipped with an ejection seat and enclosed by a tear-drop canopy.

In early November 1944, Republic Aviation submitted a proposal for the manufacture of three flying prototypes, a static test airframe, a full-size mock-up and a number of models for research and development work. The AAF granted authorisation to proceed with the project, by now designated P-84, on 11th November 1944.

On 4th January 1945, a contract was issued for a further 25 test and evaluation aircraft and 75 production examples, although this was later amended to 15 test YP-84As and 85 production P-84Bs. A formal AAF inspection of the mock-up took place at Republic's Farmingdale factory during early February and conditional approval was granted pending the completion of some minor changes deemed necessary to meet safety and tactical suitability demands.

The project suffered a setback during early 1945 when a series of high-speed wind tunnel tests identified a serious longitudinal stability problem. This, together with an increase in the aircraft's gross weight required the design team to set about the task of modifying the airframe. The series of changes devised by Kartveli and his team were to be incorporated in the third prototype. Designated as the XP-84A (the first two prototypes were designated XP-84), the third prototype had a design-limited gross weight of 13,400lbs imposed on it. Republic's problems were not confined to the airframe as the development of the J35 engine had also run into difficulties, so much so that the start of flight-testing was delayed. By the end of 1945 the company had to admit that they were unable to meet the original target date for the maiden flight of the prototype.

The first XP-84 (45-59475) was eventually fitted with a General Electric J35-GE-7 turbojet rated at 3,750lbs static thrust. It was partially disassembled and flown from the factory at Farmingdale to Muroc (now Edwards AFB) in California on board a Boeing XC-97. With Major William A. Lien at the controls, the XP-84 took to the skies on its maiden flight on 28th February 1946 and in doing so became the first new U.S. fighter to have its maiden flight after the end of the Second World War.

The second XP-84 (45-59476) made its maiden flight in the following August and, on 7th September 1946, this aircraft set a new U.S. speed record of 611mph. This was to be short-lived though because on the same day the record was broken by the Gloster Meteor, which achieved a top speed of 616mph.

The General Electric J35-GE-7 turbojet that powered both XP-84s was replaced by the Allison J35-A-15 in the XP-84A, offering an increase in static thrust by 250lbs to 4000lbs. This engine was also fitted in the 15 YP-84A flight-test aircraft together with all of the production P-84Bs.

Republic received two further letter contracts during 1946 for a total of 412 aircraft but due to subsequent problems with the project, largely due to a shortage of engines, these contracts were not confirmed until June 1947, by which time the number had been reduced to 332 aircraft. A third contract for the P-84 was approved and issued to Republic during October 1947; this covered an additional 154 aircraft.

The 15 YP-84As were handed over to the USAAF in February 1947, these aircraft differing from the XP-84A by having the provision for wing-tip fuel tanks and a fixed armament of six .50 inch machines - two in the wings and four in the forward fuselage.

The P-84 was formally named 'Thunderjet' in late 1946 and initial deliveries of the P-84B commenced in August 1947 when the 14th Fighter Group at Dow Field received the new type. This unit's introduction to the P-84B proved to be a frustrating one as it soon became apparent that the aircraft still had a number of inherent problems. Among these were fuselage skin wrinkling and a reversal of trim resulting in the 14th FG's Thunderjet operations being restricted until the problems could be ironed out.

Maintenance of the P-84B was also proving to be a real headache due to lack of spare parts and the inadequate training of personnel. These shortcomings earned the type the nickname 'Mechanics Nightmare.' Worse was to come on 24th May 1948 when the entire P-84B fleet was grounded after a number of serious structural failures. Following rigorous inspections the fleet was returned to operation but were again subject to limitations pending modification by Republic.

The last P-84B was delivered in June 1948 and on the 11th of that month the newly formed U.S. Air Force adopted a new nomenclature system, which included use of the 'F' prefix for fighter aircraft. Henceforth, the Thunderjet was to be known as the F-84.

The problems encountered during development and the early months of operations meant that the USAF only ever received 226 of the 345 F-84Bs on order. The remaining 119 would eventually be delivered to the USAF as 'C' and 'D' models. In an attempt to iron out the flaws of the F-84B a major modification programme was initiated and this did go some way to improve the operational capability of this model. The F-84B had a relatively short career and never saw action in the Korean War - all remaining examples were retired by December 1952.

Deliveries of the next variant, the F-84C began in May 1948, the first units to receive this type being the 20th Fighter Group at Shaw AFB, South Carolina and the 33rd Fighter Group at Roswell, New Mexico.

The 'C' was not dissimilar to its predecessor and hence still suffered from a number of inherent problems. The major differences were a completely new electrical system and a new version of the Allison J35 engine, the J35-A-13, although the thrust rating of this unit was identical to that of the J35-A-15 fitted in the 'B.'

The USAF received 191 F-84Cs and, in common with the F-84B, all were subjected to major modification during their service life. The last F-84C was retired by the end of 1952.

Not much had changed with the introduction of the F-84D as Republic were concentrating their efforts on the much improved F-84E. The 'D' model did, however, introduce a thicker skin on the wings and ailerons, a winterised fuel system compatible with JP4 fuel and mechanical undercarriage linkages instead of the previous hydraulic type. Despite these improvements, the fate of the F-84D was placed in considerable doubt during September 1948 whilst the USAF conducted a complete review of the F-84 project to date. The USAF decided to proceed with the 'D' fearing that a decision to cancel it may jeopardise the introduction of the eagerly awaited 'E' model. Production of the F-84D was, however, limited to just 154 aircraft, these being delivered between November 1948 and April 1949. The 'D' model later became the first Thunderjet to reach Korea, arriving in theatre during December 1950. Like its predecessors, it too underwent improvement whilst in service, modifications being made to the A-1B gunsight, the tailpipe and the wing leading edges. The last F-84Ds were retired during 1957 having spent their last years of service with the Air National Guard.

The F-84E was the first Thunderjet variant to realise the full potential of the original design in terms of performance and reliability. On 29th December 1948 the USAF confirmed an earlier order for 409 F-84Es, one of which would later serve as the prototype for the swept-wing F-84F Thunderstreak. An additional 100 were ordered for overseas air arms under the Mutual Defense Assistance Programme. By the time the last F-84E had been delivered in July 1951, 843 had rolled off the production line.

Amongst the improvements incorporated into the 'E' were a Sperry APG-30 radar ranging gun-sight, a stronger wing structure and an increase in fuselage length by 12 inches. The latter enabled the provision of a larger cockpit and hence more room for the pilot. A more powerful Allison J35-A-17 rated at 5000lbs static thrust was fitted and an extended range of around 1,950 miles was possible due to the fitment of two 230 U.S. gallon wing-tip fuel tanks and the ability to carry an additional two 230 U.S. gallon underwing fuel tanks. Retractable jet assisted take-off (JATO) racks were added to the rear fuselage, increasing the maximum takeoff weight to 22,460lbs.

The first flight of a production F-84E (49-2022) took place on 18th May 1949 with the first two examples being handed over to the USAF on 26th May. Although a vast improvement over all of the previous models, the F-84E was not without its problems particularly with the A-1B gunsight. This problem was overcome fairly quickly with the fitting of a modified A-1C unit.

The F-84E's operation career did not get off to a particularly good start due to the unreliability of the J35-A-17 engine. This, coupled with a lack of spares to rectify the problems, resulted in more than 50% of the entire fleet being unserviceable in April 1950. Once these problems had been overcome the F-84E was found to be very good in the close air support role leaving the role it was originally designed for, that of air superiority and escort, to the F-86 Sabre.

The F-84E was the version that equipped most of the six USAF wings using Thunderjets when the Korean War began. The type was first taken into combat on 7th December 1950 by the 27th Fighter Escort Group. The 27th's F-84Es were initially assigned to B-29 escort duties, during which they were regularly engaged in combat with MiG-15s. The first F-84 MiG kill took place on 21st January 1951. The F-84E was, however, no match for the MiG-15, being too slow to adequately protect itself or the B-29s it was escorting, from the Russian-built fighter. The MiG-15s superiority over the F-84E during the Korean conflict can be illustrated by the loss ratio of 2:1 in favour of the MiG.

The final and definitive variant of the Thunderjet was the F-84G and this was produced in far greater numbers than the rest of the other variants combined. The F-84G was the first fighter capable of in-flight refuelling using the 'flying boom' system in addition to being the first single-seat fighter-bomber capable of delivering nuclear weapons. The 'G' was also fitted with a more powerful and reliable J35-A-29 engine capable of producing 5,600lbs static thrust and a multi-framed, reinforced cockpit canopy which replaced the clear unframed canopy of earlier versions. This variant was only intended to be an interim type pending the introduction of Republic's F-84F Thunderstreak. As it turned out, delays in the F-84F programme saw F-84G production continue until 27th July 1953, the final day of the Korean War.

Woodbridge-based F-84G-1-RE (51-0923) of the 79th FBS/20th FBW, pictured during an engine change competition at Wethersfield 'Armed Forces Day' on 15th May 1954. (photo: George Pennick)

The first operational unit to convert to the F-84G was the 31st Fighter-Escort Wing at Turner AFB in August 1951. Deliveries to the Far East Air Forces began during summer 1952, these quickly entering combat over Korea and continuing the good work that had already been accomplished by the earlier F-84E. Deployment to USAFE began in mid 1952 when the LABS (Low Altitude Bombing System) equipped F-84Gs of the 20th Fighter-Bomber Wing moved from the U.S. to RAF Wethersfield. One of the 20th FBW's squadrons, the 79th FBS, relocated to RAF Woodbridge due to a lack of space at Wethersfield.

Some 3,025 F-84Gs rolled off the Farmingdale production line, taking the total of all Thunderjets built to 4,455. Of these, 1,936 of the 'G' models purchased by the USAF went directly to those nations participating in the MDAP.

In common with most other USAF tactical aircraft, the Thunderjet saw extensive service with second line units of the Air Force Reserve and the Air National Guard following replacement in the front-line inventory by more modern types such as the F-100 Super Sabre. In the case of the F-84E, some remained with the ANG until mid 1959 whilst the F-84G remained in service, albeit in limited numbers, until late 1960.

By 1953, Thunderjets were serving with several air forces worldwide including many NATO air arms. The F-84G was operated by the air forces of Belgium, Denmark, Norway, the Netherlands, France, Italy, Greece, Turkey, Portugal, and Taiwan. F-84Gs were also exported to Yugoslavia, Iran, and Thailand. The type continued to serve with some of these air arms, notably Portugal and Iran, until the late 1960s.

F-84G Specifications

- Primary Mission: Fighter-bomber and long-range escort.
- Manufacturer: Republic Aircraft Corporation.
- Crew: One.
- Power Plant: One Allison J35-A-29 Turbojet rated at 5,600lbs static thrust.
- Dimensions: Length - 38 feet 1 inch, Height - 12 feet 7 inches, Wingspan - 36 feet 5 inches, Wing Area - 260 square feet.
- Maximum Takeoff Weight: 22,146lbs.
- Speed: 622mph at sea level.
- Ceiling: 40,500 feet (An altitude of 35,000 feet could be attained in 9.4 minutes).
- Range: 2000 miles.
- Internal Armament: Six 0.50-inch M-2 machine guns, four mounted in the nose and two mounted in the wing roots.
- Date in Service: June 1951.

NORTH AMERICAN F-100D/F SUPER SABRE

Quartet of 79th TFS/20th TFW F-100Ds cross the Suffolk coast at Orford whilst heading inbound to RAF Woodbridge, circa 1958. (U.S. Air Force photo via David Baker)

The 1950s were a prosperous decade for U.S. aircraft manufacturers. Companies like Convair, Boeing, Douglas and Lockheed were all doing well with sales of civil airliners around the world in addition to producing military types for the U.S. armed forces. The decade in question witnessed the creation of the famed 'Century Series' of fighter aircraft, the first of which was the North American F-100 Super Sabre.

The F-100, otherwise known as the 'Sled' or 'Hun', was a logical development of one of the greatest fighters of all time, the F-86 Sabre whose combat record during the Korean War remains legendary. The F-100 began life as the 'Sabre-45,' this designation referring to the proposed sweep angle of the wing. Development of the Super Sabre originally began on 3rd February 1949 and was essentially a redesign of the earlier F-86. The new design had one main objective and that was to produce an aircraft capable of sustained level flight at speeds in excess of Mach One.

Starting as a private venture, the Sabre-45 was granted U.S. Air Force approval and, more importantly, was successful in gaining a production contract although this was not finalised until almost three years later. Formally signed on 1st November 1951, the initial contract was for two YF-100A prototypes and 110 production examples of the F-100A, these being destined as day fighter interceptors.

Construction of the first YF-100A was completed in a particularly short period of time and this aircraft (52-5754) gave a clear indication of its potential when it achieved supersonic flight on 25th May 1953 during its maiden flight. The pilot on this occasion was George Welch, who was later to die in a tragic accident whilst flight-testing a production aircraft. The second YF-100A (52-5755) joined the flight test programme on 14th October 1953 and, like the first YF-100A, was fitted with a single Pratt and Whitney XJ57-P-7 turbojet engine complete with afterburner unit. Two weeks later, on 29th October, the first production F-100A-1-NA (52-5756) made its maiden flight, this being powered by a standard J57-P-7 engine rated at 9,700lbs static thrust. Flight-testing of the prototypes and early production machines was, as usual, conducted at Edwards AFB in the Mojave Desert and took approximately 16 months, resulting in the type being cleared for operational service in late September 1954.

The 29th September saw the activation of the first operational unit at George AFB, located near Edwards. The unit was the 479th Fighter Day Wing and it was equipped with a small number of early production F-100As.

On 11th November 1954, the flight-test programme suffered a major setback when the type was indefinitely grounded after a series of unexplained accidents. A number of these accidents had resulted in loss of life, among them North American's Chief Test Pilot, George Welch. The subsequent investigation lasted for several months before the cause was established. The investigation concluded that the accidents were attributed to the fact that the vertical tail surface could not cope with the pitch and yaw forces experienced during a rolling manoeuvre. Failure of this surface resulted in a loss of control that proved impossible for the pilot to recover from. Fortunately for North American the remedy was a simple one, involving an increase in fin area of 27% together with an increase in wingspan of 26 inches. The modification was carried out on the 25th F-100A (53-1530) and after successful flight-tests it was incorporated on the line from the 71st production aircraft onwards. The earlier machines were retrofitted with the 'mod' and re-issued to the Air Force who then carried on with the re-equipment programme.

The next version of the Super Sabre was the F-100B, although this was soon redesignated as the YF-107A. Intended as an all-weather interceptor and strike aircraft, the F-100B was powered by a single J75 engine fed by an air intake that had been relocated on the upper fuselage behind the cockpit. Only three of the original nine ordered were completed, the first making its maiden flight in September 1956. The F-100B/YF-107A programme was abandoned during the course of 1957.

Although the F-100B proved unsuccessful, the F-100C was produced in large numbers, with 476 being built at two factories, one at Inglewood, California and another at Columbus, Ohio. The 'C' version was the first of the type to possess dual strike/interceptor capability. It featured a strengthened wing with provision for eight external stores stations compared to the six of the earlier F-100A, and it was also the first version to incorporate in-flight refuelling equipment. The first production example of the F-100C (53-1709) made its maiden flight on 17th January 1955. The performance of the F-100C was a slight improvement on the 'A' although, like its predecessor, its frontline USAF career was relatively short with the majority being transferred to reserve units during the sixties.

One F-100C (54-1966) was modified to two-seat configuration as the TF-100C and this served as an aerodynamic test bed for the F-100F, which would later be produced in quantity. The TF-100C modification required the addition of a 36-inch section in the forward fuselage to accommodate the second cockpit and deletion of two of the four M-39E cannons.

The continuing evolution of the Super Sabre eventually led to the appearance of the definitive version - the F-100D. The first 'D' version (54-2121) made a successful maiden flight on 24th January 1956 in the hands of Dan Darnell and was the first of no less than 1,274 built by the time production terminated in 1958. The Inglewood facility produced 940 of these with the remaining 334 being manufactured at Columbus.

F-100D-65-NA Super Sabre (56-3014) of the 79th TFS/20th TFW, 19th September 1959. (photo: via Mick Sudds)

In common with the F-100C, the 'D' version was also intended to fulfil the dual strike/interceptor role although it soon became dedicated to the former role as more sophisticated interceptors became available. Powered by the Pratt and Whitney J57-P-21A rated at 11,700lbs static thrust dry and 16,050lbs static thrust in afterburner, the F-100D introduced several modifications of which probably the most notable was the addition of inboard landing flaps. Other improvements included provision of a Minneapolis-Honeywell MB-3 autopilot, further modifications to the tail, jettisonable cantilever external store stations and wing fences.

Weapons-carrying capability was essentially identical to the F-100C but the F-100D became the version to possess the ability to operate with missile armament (although this had initially been tested on six modified F-100Cs). This was aimed at improving both intercept and strike potential and it could use either the AIM-9B Sidewinder infra-red air-to-air missile or the AGM-12A Bullpup air-to-surface missile, this being carried on the inboard pylons. Also introduced with the 184th F-100D was a provision for centreline-mounted fuselage attachment points.

Nuclear weapons could be carried on the left wing intermediate attachment point or on the fuselage centreline attachment points. The nuclear weapons that could be carried included the Mk 7, Mk 28 EX, Mk 28 RE, Mk 43, TX-43, and TX-43 X1, with yields ranging from a kiloton to nearly ten megatons. For delivery of these nuclear weapons, the F-100D carried the improved AN/AJB-1B low-altitude bombing system (LABS). This system was used in conjunction with information provided by the A-4 gyro sight to calculate aiming and release information for the toss-bombing of nuclear weapons. Other weaponry compatible with this model of the Super Sabre included conventional and retarded bombs, rocket packs and napalm canisters.

The F-100D was not without its share of problems. Defective engine bearings and problems with the afterburner fuel system were encountered. A particularly serious problem was the inadvertent release of bombs from the underwing stores pylons although this was traced to improper bomb-loading procedures and not directly attributed to a defect with the aircraft. In-flight refuelling probes also had a tendency to snap off during high-g manoeuvres making it necessary for most aircraft to have their refuelling probes removed pending reinforcement of the underwing structure.

By the early 1960s, the F-100D had been retrofitted with so many in-service modifications to correct its obvious deficiencies that no two F-100Ds were alike, making for a logistical nightmare in terms of maintenance and spares.

The last F-100D rolled off the production line at Inglewood in August of 1959. Production of the F-100D at Columbus had ended in December of 1957.

The final 148 production examples of the F-100D possessed Zero Length Launch (ZELL) capability, this involving the use of a jettisonable rocket motor and a flat-bed trailer. A series of successful trials of this concept was conducted during 1958 with the first launch taking place on 28th May of that year. These aircraft featured additional stressing to cope with the loads, which would have been encountered in such launches, power being provided by a single Astrodyne rocket motor capable of generating some 150,000lbs of thrust. It was intended to house these aircraft in hardened bomb-proof shelters although in the event this system was never used operationally.

79th TFS F-100F-10-NA Super Sabre (56-3800) photographed at Woodbridge on 4th August 1969.
(photo: S Bond via Mick Sudds)

Deliveries of the F-100D to operational elements within Tactical Air Command began in the latter half of 1956 and it very soon became the workhorse of that Command, as well as joining the U.S. Air Forces in Europe and the Pacific Air Forces in considerable numbers. In addition to the USAF, the 'D' model was also exported as part of the Mutual Defense Assistance Programme with numerous examples being delivered to Denmark, France and Turkey over a considerable period of time. The F-100D was progressively retired from USAF service beginning in the mid-to-late sixties. The last fully operational unit was the 48th TFW at RAF Lakenheath which disposed of its final machines in 1972 after re-equipping with the F-4D Phantom.

The final derivative of the Super Sabre to attain quantity production was the two-seat F-100F. A total of 339 were built, all at Inglewood, between 1957 and 1959, with the first example (56-3725) making its maiden flight on 7th March 1957 flown by North American test pilot Gage Mace. This had, of course, been preceded by the TF-100C but the 'F' model was more closely related to the F-100D and, in addition to its combat proficiency training duty, it also possessed genuine strike capability although it only carried two internal cannons. The F-100F could utilise identical weapons to those of the F-100D, up to a maximum of 6,000lbs externally, but it was somewhat heavier, this having a slightly detrimental effect on the overall performance. Deliveries to USAF units began during the latter half of 1957, most squadrons receiving a small number of two-seaters, which were operated alongside the single-seat F-100D model. By the end of 1958 F-100Fs had reached most of the overseas units that were operating F-100Ds. The last F-100F that rolled off the production line was delivered in October of 1959.

The F-100F was found to be of great value in Vietnam where it was used as a high speed FAC (Forward Air Control) aircraft for target marking and control of friendly strike forces; the extra pair of eyes in the back enabled the pilot to get on with the job of actually flying the aircraft.

Beginning in 1962, about 700 F-100Ds and Fs were subjected to a series of modifications under Project High Wire, a major standardisation and upgrading programme. The main aim of this programme was to increase the variety of conventional weapons that could be carried, remove excess weight from the aircraft and to standardise the cockpit layout. Perhaps the most noticeable modification produced by the High Wire programme was the addition of a spring-steel arrestor hook located underneath the rear fuselage. This was intended to engage wires at the end of runways to prevent overshooting during bad landings or brake failures. These modifications were completed in 1965.

Even after Project High Wire was completed, some problems persisted. Malfunctions of the landing gear and the unreliability of the drag chutes accounted for a number of accidents. A high number of compressor stalls of the J57-P-21 engine still occurred although this was eventually remedied by installing the same afterburners as used on the Convair F-102 Delta Dagger.

When the production lines eventually closed, the total Super Sabre production had reached 2,294, including 359 built at Columbus. The F-100 Super Sabre was the first aircraft possessing genuine supersonic performance to enter service with the USAF and, as such, is assured of a permanent place in any history of that air arm. The 'Sled' or 'Hun' pointed the way ahead for the remarkable century series and will surely be remembered with affection by many.

F-100D Specifications

- Manufacturer: North American Aviation Corp.
- Power Plant: One Pratt & Whitney J57-P-21/21A turbojet, 10,200lbs static thrust dry and 16,000lbs static thrust with afterburning.
- Performance: Maximum Speed - 770mph at sea level (clean) and 864mph (Mach 1.3) at 36,000 feet (clean), Initial Climb Rate: 19,000 feet per minute (An altitude of 35,000 feet could be attained in 2.3 minutes).
- Dimensions: Wingspan - 38 feet 9 inches, Length - 50 feet, Height - 16 feet 2 inches, Wing Area - 400 square feet.
- Ceiling: Service - 36,100 feet, Combat - 47,700 feet, Absolute - 50,000 feet.
- Range: Normal - 534 miles, Maximum - 1,995 miles.
- Fuel Capacity: 1,739 U.S. gallons internally, total of 2,139 U.S. gallons if maximum external fuel is carried.
- Weights: Empty - 21,000lbs, Gross - 28,847lbs, Maximum Takeoff - 34,832lbs.
- Armament: Four 20-mm Pontiac M-39 cannon. Six underwing pylons for up to 7,040lbs of bombs, fuel tanks, or rockets. A MK-28 or Mk-43/57/61 nuclear weapon could be carried. Four AIM-9B/E/J Sidewinder air-to-air infrared homing missiles could also be carried.

79th TFS F-100D/F Super Sabre Accidents

Date of Accident	Model	Serial Number	Location	Additional Info
09 Jul 1957	F-100D-65-NA	56-3021	Nouasseur AB, Morocco	Crashed whilst unit was transitioning from the F-84F to the F-100. Fate of the pilot unknown.
20 Oct 1958	F-100D-65-NA	56-3012	RAF Woodbridge, Suffolk	Crashed close to runway following horizontal stabiliser malfunction. Pilot escaped uninjured.
29 Dec 1958	F-100D-65-NA	56-2985	Kesgrave, Suffolk	Crashed onto site of Falcon Caravans in Kesgrave following an engine fire shortly after take-off. The pilot, Lt Charles Prescott ejected safely but two people on the ground were killed in the accident (a female employee of Falcon Caravans died at the scene and a man living in a nearby house died later in hospital due to injuries sustained from flying debris).
14 Jun 1960	F-100D-65-NA	56-2998	1 mile NNW of Wheelus AB, Libya	Crashed following engine failure. Pilot was seen to eject and land in the sea, but was never found. Pilot was not from the 79th TFS.
21 Mar 1962	F-100F-10-NA	56-3888	23 miles W of Chateauroux AB, France	No further details known.
17 Jul 1962	F-100D-65-NA	56-3014	5 miles W of RAF Woodbridge, Suffolk	No further details known.
05 Sep 1962	F-100D-65-NA	56-2976	24 miles SW of Wheelus AB, Libya	No further details known.
01 Oct 1962	F-100D-65-NA	56-2990	3 miles N of Southwold, Suffolk	Pilot, 1/Lt James Counce was killed.
04 Mar 1963	F-100D-25-NA	55-3693	58 miles SE of Wheelus AB, Libya	Pilot ejected safely.
18 Apr 1969	F-100D-65-NA	56-3004	Possibly at Spangdahlem AB, West Germany	Suffered unspecified damage on 18 April 1969. Transferred to Sacramento AMA two weeks later and struck off charge on 13 January 1970.
13 May 1969	F-100D-65-NA	56-2986	RAF Marham, Norfolk	Crashed on final approach to RAF Marham whilst operating out of RAF Lakenheath. Pilot ejected safely.

The author wishes to acknowledge the help received from Andrew Horrex during the preparation of this list.

KAMAN HH-43B/F HUSKIE

Kaman HH-43B Huskie (62-4521) assigned to Det. 12 of the 40th ARRW, photographed at Woodbridge on 7th August 1969. (photo: George Pennick)

The Kaman HH-43 Huskie was the first helicopter purchased by the USAF specifically for airborne firefighting and airfield crash rescue. The twin intermeshing, counter-rotating rotors made the Huskie very stable in flight. The HH-43 carried an under-slung pod containing a foam fire suppressant when it was airborne and would use the combination of the foam and the downwash from the rotor blades in order to put out fires or burning aircraft.

The U.S. Navy first bought the Huskie (designated HOK-1 for the Marines and HUK-1 for the Navy) as a general-purpose helicopter. The initial Air Force version, the H-43A, could only carry four passengers as much of the cabin space was taken up by its 600-hp engine. This problem was remedied with the introduction of the HH-43B which, due to its smaller, roof-mounted turboshaft, increased the amount of available interior space. Deliveries of the HH-43B began in 1959, and the type was used for base crash rescue by all flying commands within the USAF. A number of Huskie crews set time-to-climb, altitude, and distance records in 1961 and 1962. A Huskie crew could become airborne within a minute, taking 30 seconds to get airborne and 30 seconds to pick up the fire suppression kit (foam and water bottle, nitrogen pressure bottle, and hose), and would often beat the fire trucks to a crash scene.

In mid 1964, three units were transferred from the Philippines and Okinawa to South East Asia for combat rescue. The 33rd Air Rescue Squadron assigned to Nakhon Phanom RTAB, Thailand, was the first to begin combat rescue operations, in June 1964.

The HH-43F (nicknamed Pedro) featured 800 pounds of titanium armour plating, an up-rated engine, and could carry a flexible-mount .30 calibre machine gun for combat search and rescue missions. Most of the 'B' model aircraft were later brought up to HH-43F standard. After the introduction of the Jolly Green Giants (HH-3s), the HH-43s reverted to air base crash rescue duties. HH-43s were also flown by Burma, Colombia, Morocco, Pakistan, Thailand, and Iran. The last of the USAF HH-43s were retired by the early 1970s.

HH-43B Specifications

- Manufacturer: Kaman Aircraft Corp.
- Primary Mission: Utility/Rescue/Fire Fighting.
- Crew: Four (Pilot, co-pilot and two firefighters).
- Power Plant: One 860 hp Lycoming T53-L-1A engine.
- Performance: Maximum Speed - 120mph, Cruising Speed - 105mph, Climb Rate - 2,000 feet per minute.
- Dimensions: Rotor Diameter - 47 feet, Length - 47 feet, Height - 17 feet 2 inches.
- Maximum Weight: 9,150lbs.
- Ceiling: 25,700 feet
- Range: 235 miles
- Armament: None
- First Flight: 27th September 1956.

A rare photo of two Kaman HH-43B Huskies (62-4516 & 62-4537)) assigned to Det. 12, 40th ARRW in formation over Woodbridge on 7th August 1969. (photo: George Pennick)

SIKORSKY HH-3E JOLLY GREEN GIANT

Sikorsky HH-3E Jolly Green Giant (67-14716) of the 67th ARRS, photographed at RAF Bentwaters Open House in 1970. 67-14716 was delivered to the USAF on 20th May 1968 and remained in use until 1980 when it was written off after a heavy landing. (photo: Alan Haynes)

The CH/HH-3 was a long-range, amphibious transport helicopter that remained part of the U.S. Air Force's inventory for more than 30 years. The H-3 was based on Sikorsky's highly successful S-61 design and was developed initially as an anti-submarine warfare platform for the U.S. Navy (S-61A), acquiring the designation SH-3.

The H-3 was first used by the USAF to fill a requirement as a support helicopter for its 'Texas Tower' radar sites located in the Atlantic and to recover drones in the Gulf of Mexico. The USAF borrowed six SH-3s from the U.S. Navy for this task and redesignated them as CH-3Bs.

The first USAF-specific version, the CH-3C (S-61R) retained the amphibious capability of the SH-3 but featured a redesigned fuselage, a hydraulically operated rear-loading ramp, stabilising sponsons and retractable tricycle landing gear.

The initial USAF order for 22 CH-3Cs, placed on 8th February 1963, was followed by contracts for 111 more after the type had been selected in July 1963 to fill a new USAF requirement for a long-range support helicopter. The first S-61R flew on 17th June 1963 and this civil prototype was followed a few weeks later by the first CH-3C. Deliveries to the USAF began on 30th December 1963 and in February 1966 production was switched to the CH/HH-3E with up-rated 1,500shp T58-GE-5 engines. All aircraft delivered as CH-3Cs were modified to CH-3E or HH-3E standard with more than 1000lbs of titanium armour-plating, an Auxiliary Power Unit for self-starting, jettisonable fuel tanks, rescue hoist and an in-flight refuelling probe. By the beginning of 1970 deliveries totalled 83 CH-3Es and 35 HH-3Es, the latter type being operated by the USAF Air Rescue Service.

The HH-3Es were probably best known for their numerous rescue missions in South East Asia. 496 of the 980 aircrew rescues made between 1966 and 1970 involved the HH-3E. It was during this conflict that the HH-3E became known as the 'Jolly Green Giant' due to it's green and tan camouflage scheme.

On 31st May/1st June 1967, two USAF crews flying HH-3Es made the first non-stop flight across the Atlantic by helicopter. The 4,271mile flight took 30 hours, 46 minutes and required nine in-flight refuellings. Lt Col Herbert E. Zehnder, the pilot of one of the HH-3Es on the transatlantic flight, flew that same aircraft in the raid on the Son Tay prisoner of war camp near Hanoi on 20th/21st November 1970.

The HH-3Es had a number of limitations and as a result were mostly replaced by the HH-53. The Jolly Green Giant continued to serve in the Air National Guard, Air Force Reserve and Air Force Special Operations Forces into the 1990s. One Reserve HH-3 unit served in Operation Desert Storm but all HH-3s were retired by 1995.

Sikorsky HH-3E Specifications

- Primary Role: Combat search and rescue.
- Manufacturer: Sikorsky Aircraft Corp.
- Crew: 2 or 3 (pilot, co-pilot, and flight engineer/loadmaster) plus gunners and pararescue personnel when required.
- Power Plant: Two General Electric T58-GE-5 turboshafts producing 1,500 shaft horsepower each.
- Maximum Speed: 162mph.
- Ceiling: 11,100 feet.
- Dimensions: Fuselage Length - 57 feet 3 inches, Height - 18 feet 1 inch, Rotor Diameter - 62 feet.
- Gross Weight: 22,050lbs.
- Payload Capacity: 25 troops or 5,000lb of cargo.
- Armament: Up to three .50 calibre machine guns or three 7.62mm M60 Miniguns.

Sikorsky HH-3E Jolly Green Giant of the 67th ARRS pictured at Woodbridge on 7th August 1969. (photo: George Pennick)

LOCKHEED HC-130H HERCULES

Lockheed HC-130H Hercules (64-14861) of the 67th ARRS awaiting its next mission at RAF Woodbridge on 21st April 1971. This aircraft had recently transferred from the 57th ARRS and still carries that unit's markings on the nose. (photo: Don Gilham)

On 8th December 1964 Lockheed flew the first of 66 HC-130Hs with the USAF receiving its first example (64-14852) on 26th July 1965. This extensively modified version of the standard C-130 was primarily tasked with search and rescue missions, but also performed tasks related to the U.S. space program. The HC-130H could be fitted with up to two 1800-gallon fuel tanks inside the fuselage in addition to the standard pair of wing-mounted tanks. This increased fuel capacity boosted the range of this version of the Hercules by a further 500nm.

Perhaps the most interesting addition to the 'H' version was the Fulton surface-to-air recovery (STAR) system. The system comprised a set of forks, or yoke, on the nose of the aircraft and a winch mounted in the rear fuselage. The addition of the yoke necessitated the fitting of a squarer radome than that fitted to a standard C-130. The purpose of the Fulton STAR system was the airborne retrieval of personnel from the ground. A recovery kit containing an overall-type harness attached to a 30ft balloon on a 525ft lift line was dropped to the person to be retrieved. After the harness was fitted to the person the balloon was inflated with helium and made its ascent taking the lift line with it. The line was fitted with coloured markers to aid visibility during daylight retrievals and lights for night operations. The HC-130H would intercept the lift line with its nose yoke and once the line was caught the hydraulic winch retrieved the person on to the back of the cargo ramp. The HC-130H was fitted with fibreglass cables that extended from each wing tip to the nose, these prevented the lift line from fouling the propellers during retrieval operations. The system was used to good effect in the Vietnam conflict saving the lives of many downed pilots and was equally well suited to the retrieval of packages. The recovery kits eventually proved impractical for most rescue purposes but they remained available for use by the U.S. special operations forces.

Training with the Fulton STAR system began in 1966 at Edwards AFB, California. The first person to be retrieved with the system was Capt Gerald LyVere on 3rd May. Later that day Col Allison C. Brooks, commander of the USAF Aerospace Rescue and Recovery Service, and A3C Ronald Doll carried out the first human test of the two-man recovery suit. On 5th May 1966, a training exercise in the Pacific, which saw the recovery of three men, proved the system's ability to recover the crew of an Apollo spacecraft.

A fatal accident in 1982, the only fatality in 17 years of live pick-ups, damaged the credibility of the Fulton STAR system for personnel retrievals. That fatal accident together with the increased use of search and rescue helicopters resulted in a reduction in the use of the system over the following years. The Fulton STAR system remained in use with a single unit, the 8th Special Operations Squadron at Hurlburt Field, Florida, until 14th September 1996 when it was withdrawn from service.

At the request of NASA, the HC-130H was also fitted with a Cook Electric AN/ARD-17 re-entry tracking system that was to be used in conjunction with the Gemini, and later, Apollo spacecraft. The antenna was housed in a distinctive fairing on top of the forward fuselage and was capable of a complete 360-degree coverage in the horizontal plane. The system was designed to lock on to the UHF signals transmitted by the spacecraft as it emerged on re-entry through the ionosphere. The received signals would then used to accurately plot the bearing of the spacecraft from the HC-130H and affect a safe pick up of the returning astronauts. This was never to be put to the test as no spacecraft recovery missions involving the 'H' ever took place and consequently no astronauts were ever recovered. The HC-130H proved invaluable during the Vietnam conflict for airborne coordination of combat search and rescue missions. Using its AN/ARD-17 tracker it was able to receive signals from the Personal Locator Beacons (PLB) of downed aircrew and either perform a retrieval itself using the Fulton STAR system or direct rescue helicopters to the scene.

This version of the Hercules was used for the mid-air retrieval of many different items that had been in space, including data and film containers. The operation was a highly complicated, but precise one and 18 of these specialist versions of the Hercules could, with their advanced communications and navigation equipment, provide coverage around the world across a wide strip on either side of the equator. Four HC-130Hs were modified to JC-130H standard with added equipment for aerial recovery of re-entering space capsules.

Additional modifications included a radio operator position against the aft cockpit bulkhead in place of the crew bunks, which were relocated within the main fuselage, and an observation window installed on each side of the forward fuselage to aid visibility during rescue missions. A stowage area was provided inside the fuselage for three MA-1/MA-2 rescue kits which contained life rafts and waterproof supply capsules. Ten launch tubes were fitted to the rear-loading ramp to enable the use of flares, marine location markers or smoke and illumination signals.

Out of the work of the HC-130Hs in recovering downed airmen and pieces of the space programme grew the use of the Hercules for refuelling helicopters, a task which had previously been considered too dangerous to attempt. The Sikorsky HH-3C was acquired by the Aerospace Rescue and Recovery Service as part of a plan to make the task of picking up returned astronauts more efficient and less costly. The combination of Hercules and helicopter would, it was thought, replace the deployment of large naval task forces to the splashdown areas, and although this scheme never became a reality, the refuelling of HH-3s by HC-130Hs was proved to be a practical proposition. A total of 20 HC-130Hs were converted into tankers for the HH-3, and the later HH-53 Super Jolly Green Giant, and were designated HC-130P.

HC-130H Specifications

- Primary mission: Aerospace rescue and recovery
- Manufacturer: Lockheed Aircraft Corp.
- Crew: Three officers (pilot, co-pilot, navigator) and six enlisted (flight engineer, airborne communications specialist, loadmaster and three pararescuemen).
- Power Plant: Four Allison T56-A-15 turboprop engines producing 4,910 shaft horsepower each.
- Dimensions: Length - 98 feet 9 inches (30.09 metres), Height - 38 feet 6 inches (11.7 metres), Wingspan - 132 feet 7 inches (40.4 metres).
- Maximum Takeoff Weight: 155,000lbs (69,750 kilograms).
- Maximum Speed: 289 miles per hour (464 kilometres per hour) at sea level.
- Ceiling: 33,000 feet (10,000 metres).
- Range: Beyond 4,000 miles (3,478 nautical miles).
- Date in Service: 1965

LOCKHEED HC-130N HERCULES

Lockheed HC-130N Hercules (69-5827) of the 67th ARRS on approach to Greenham Common, 22nd June 1979. (photo: Don Gilham)

The HC-130N version of the Hercules was identical to the HC-130P except that it was not fitted with the Fulton STAR system. This meant that the 'N' did not have the capability for in-flight retrieval of personnel or packages but was used mainly for the in-flight refuelling of combat search and rescue (CSAR) helicopters such as the HH-3E and the HH-53C. Fifteen HC-130Ns were delivered to the USAF, beginning with 69-5819. The HC-130N, in common with the HC-130H and HC-130P was fitted with the Cook Electric AN/ARD-17 re-entry tracking system. In later years some of the Space Shuttle launches and recoveries were supported by HC-130Ns.

The progress of time found that the HC-130N's role was switching from search and rescue to special operations. In February 1996, as a direct result of this change of roles, those HC-130Ns (and HC-130Ps) assigned to special operations units were redesignated MC-130P Combat Shadow thus aligning the type with other M-series special operations mission aircraft.

2000 saw the completion of several modifications to the entire fleet of MC-130Ps, which were required to enhance its special operations role. The modifications to the Combat Shadow included a fully integrated inertial navigation and global positioning system and night vision goggle compatible interior and exterior lighting. In addition the fleet was fitted with forward looking infrared (FLIR), radar and missile warning receivers, chaff and flare dispensers, night vision goggle compatible head-up displays, satellite and data-burst communications, as well as in-flight refuelling capability as a receiver (on 15 aircraft).

In the process of its transformation from HC-130N to MC-130P the now obsolete Cook Electric re-entry tracking system, complete with fuselage fairing, was removed.

Some search and rescue HC-130Ns remain in service and, along with the HC-130P, are the only dedicated fixed-wing combat search and rescue platform in the USAF inventory. The 71st Rescue Squadron in Air Combat Command, the 102nd RQS, 129th RQS and 210th RQS in the Air National Guard, and the 39th RQS and 303rd RQS in the Air Force Reserve operate the aircraft in this role.

HC-130N Specifications

- Primary mission: Air refuelling for combat search and rescue helicopters.
- Manufacturer: Lockheed Aircraft Corp.
- Crew: Three officers (pilot, co-pilot, navigator) and six enlisted (flight engineer, airborne communications specialist, loadmaster and three pararescuemen).
- Power Plant: Four Allison T56-A-15 turboprop engines producing 4,910 shaft horsepower each.
- Dimensions: Length - 98 feet 9 inches (30.09 metres), Height - 38 feet 6 inches (11.7 metres), Wingspan - 132 feet 7 inches (40.4 metres).
- Maximum Takeoff Weight: 155,000lbs (69,750 kilograms).
- Maximum Speed: 289 miles per hour (464 kilometres per hour) at sea level.
- Ceiling: 33,000 feet (10,000 metres).
- Range: Beyond 4,000 miles (3,478 nautical miles).
- Date in Service: 1969.

HC-130N Hercules (69-5827) of the 67th ARRS photographed at Woodbridge in 1984. (photo: Author)

LOCKHEED HC-130P HERCULES

Lockheed HC-130P Hercules (66-0220) of the 67th SOS photographed at Bentwaters in 1989. (photo: Author)

First flown in 1964, the HC-130P was identical to the HC-130H except for the addition of a pair of wing-mounted pods containing hose-drogue units. This gave the 'P' the added capability of in-flight refuelling combat search and rescue helicopters such as the HH-3E and the HH-53C. The HC-130P retained all of the HC-130H's equipment such as the Fulton STAR system and the Cook Electric AN/ARD-17 re-entry tracking system.

Secondary mission capabilities included operations with the U.S. Special Forces. This involved performing tactical airdrops of pararescue specialist teams, zodiac watercraft, or four-wheel drive all-terrain vehicles, providing direct assistance to a survivor in advance of the arrival of a recovery vehicle. Other capabilities were extended visual and electronic searches over land or water, tactical airborne radar approaches and operations from temporary airstrips. A team of three pararescue specialists, trained in emergency trauma medicine, harsh environment survival and assisted evasion techniques, were part of the basic mission crew complement.

The increased use of the type by special operations units resulted in those HC-130Ps assigned to Air Force Special Operations Command (AFSOC) being redesignated as MC-130P 'Combat Shadow' in February 1996.

The MC-130P primarily flies missions at night to reduce probability of visual detection and intercept by airborne threats. Improvements to enhance the aircraft's special operations role were made to the fleet of MC-

130Ps and these were completed by 2000. All aircraft now feature a fully integrated inertial navigation and global positioning system, and night vision goggle compatible interior and exterior lighting. In addition the Combat Shadow fleet was equipped with forward looking infrared (FLIR), radar and missile warning receivers, chaff and flare dispensers, night vision goggle compatible head-up display, satellite and data-burst communications, as well as in-flight refuelling capability as a receiver (on 15 aircraft).

In the process of conversion from HC-130P to MC-130P the now obsolete Cook Electric re-entry tracking system, complete with fuselage fairing, and the Fulton STAR system were removed. The latter resulted in the standard C-130 radome being fitted to the aircraft.

A number of HC-130Ps remain in active service with the USAF as dedicated search and rescue platforms. Air Combat Command's 71st Rescue Squadron along with the 102nd RQS, 129th RQS and 210th RQS in the Air National Guard and the 39th RQS and 303rd RQS in the Air Force Reserve operate the aircraft in this role.

The HC-130P deploys worldwide to provide combat search and rescue coverage for U.S. and allied forces. Combat search and rescue missions include flying low-level at night aided with night vision goggles, to a target area where aerial refuelling of a rescue helicopter is performed or pararescuemen are deployed.

The secondary mission of the HC-130P is peacetime search and rescue. HC-130P aircraft and crews are uniquely trained and equipped for search and rescue in all types of terrain including arctic, mountain, and maritime. Peacetime search and rescue missions may include searching for downed or missing aircraft, and locating missing boats or people. The HC-130P can deploy pararescue personnel or escort a rescue helicopter to a survivor. The HC-130P can also airdrop survival equipment if required.

HC-130P Specifications

- Manufacturer: Lockheed Aircraft Corp.
- Crew: Three officers (pilot, co-pilot, navigator) and six enlisted (flight engineer, airborne communications specialist, loadmaster and three pararescuemen).
- Power Plant: Four Allison T56-A-15 turboprop engines producing 4,910 shaft horsepower each.
- Dimensions: Length - 98 feet 9 inches (30.09 metres), Height - 38 feet 6 inches (11.7 metres), Wingspan - 132 feet 7 inches (40.4 metres).
- Maximum Takeoff Weight: 155,000lbs (69,750 kilograms).
- Maximum Speed: 289 miles per hour (464 kilometres per hour) at sea level.
- Ceiling: 33,000 feet (10,000 metres).
- Range: Beyond 4,000 miles (3,478 nautical miles).
- Date in Service: 1965

Lockheed HC-130P Hercules (66-0220) of the 67th ARRS photographed at Woodbridge during 1985. (photo: Author)

SIKORSKY HH-53C SUPER JOLLY GIANT

Sikorsky HH-53C (68-10364) of the 67th ARRS seen participating in the flying display at Bentwaters during 'Air Friendship 84.' (photo: Author)

The HH-53 was derived from Sikorsky's S-65A that had been developed to satisfy a U.S. Marine Corps requirement for a heavy assault helicopter to replace the Sikorsky CH-37 Mojave.

A contract for a mock-up, a static test airframe and two flying prototypes was placed in August 1962, under the designation CH-53A. The prototype CH-53A was first flown on 14th October 1964 and entered service in September 1965. Powered by two T64 engines mounted either side of the upper fuselage, driving the transmission proven by the CH-54 Tarhe, the CH-53 featured a large boxlike cabin with a rear loading ramp and forward side doors. The main undercarriage retracted into large sponsons slung low on the fuselage sides. The sponsons were provided to permit emergency water landings.

There can be no denying that the CH-53A was a big helicopter and, on delivery to the war zone in South East Asia, it quickly established a reputation for carrying outstanding loads either internally or under-slung from its cargo hook. These included 1-ton trucks, Honest John missile systems, and 105mm howitzers. Known as the Sea Stallion, the CH-53A was to become the USMC's principal heavy-lift helicopter, a position it still holds today, albeit as one of a number of completely updated versions. One hundred and forty-one CH-53As were built but none remain in U.S. service. The last examples served with USMC training and reserve units, but were retired in July 1993.

USAF interest began with the loan of two CH-53As from the USMC in late 1966. This led to the purchase of 8 HH-53B and 44 HH-53C 'Super Jolly Green Giants' for the USAF Air Rescue Service in September 1966. The HH-53s were fitted with 3,435shp T64-GE-7 engines, external jettisonable fuel tanks, an in-flight refuelling probe and a rescue hoist and were a replacement for the HH-3E in the search and rescue role. The USAF also purchased 20 CH-53Cs, similar to the HH-53B/C but lacking the in-flight refuelling probe. The CH-53C was used for training, general transport duties and for the support of ground-based Forward Air Control (FAC) teams.

In late 1969, the Pave Low I system was applied to one HH-53 to provide some measure of night capability. A single HH-53B was converted to YHH-53H Pave Low II standard, which added a terrain-following radar in a nose radome, offset to port, and other night/adverse-weather equipment.

Subsequently, eight HH-53s and two CH-53Cs were upgraded to HH-53H Pave Low III standard, featuring an AN/APO-158 terrain-following radar, Marconi Doppler navigation, Litton Inertial Navigation System (INS), AAQ-10 Forward Looking Infra Red (FLIR) in a turret under the nose fairing, map display system and numerous electronic countermeasures. When a Special Forces role was added under the 'Constant Green' programme, the designation changed to MH-53H, one major change being the adoption of a Night Vision Goggle (NVG) compatible cockpit.

Under a programme beginning in 1986 and ending in 1990, the surviving HH-53B/C/H and CH-53C airframes were all upgraded to MH-53J Pave Low III Enhanced standard.

Sikorsky HH-53C Specifications

- Primary Role: Combat search and rescue
- Manufacturer: Sikorsky Aircraft Corp.
- Crew: Six (Two pilots, two flight engineers, two aerial gunners).
- Power Plant: Two General Electric T64-GE-7 engines producing 3,435 shaft horsepower each.
- Maximum Speed: 165mph (264km/h).
- Dimensions: Length - 92 feet (28 metres), Height - 25 feet (7.6 metres), Rotor Diameter - 72 feet (21.9 metres).
- Maximum Ceiling: 16,000 feet (4,849 metres).
- Maximum Takeoff Weight: 46,000 pounds (18,900 kilograms); (can be increased to 50,000 pounds in emergencies).
- Range: 630 statute miles (550 nautical miles); unlimited with air refuelling.
- Armament: Any combination of three 7.62 miniguns and .50 calibre machine guns.

Sikorsky HH-53C Super Jolly Green Giant of the Woodbridge-based 67th ARRS carrying out its display routine at Bentwaters during Air Friendship '84. (photo: Author)

SIKORSKY MH-53J PAVE LOW IIIE

*Woodbridge-based MH-53J of the 21st SOS on a training mission over the North Sea.
(U.S. Air Force photo by MSgt Dave Nolan)*

Under a programme that began in 1986 and ran for four years, all of the surviving HH-53B/C/H and CH-53C airframes were upgraded to MH-53J Pave Low III Enhanced standard with the first examples reaching Special Operations units in 1987. The upgrade programme included terrain-following radar (TFR), forward looking infrared (FLIR), night vision goggle (NVG) compatible cockpit and titanium armour plating. Also incorporated were mounts for 0.50 calibre machine guns and/or 7.62mm miniguns, AN/ALQ-162 continuous-wave radar missile jammers, ALE-40 chaff/flare dispensers, ALQ-157 infrared missile jammers, ALR-69 missile warning receivers, global positioning system (GPS), projected map display and a powerful searchlight mounted under the nose. In addition to this the power plant was up-rated from the T64-GE-7 to T64-GE-100, which provided an extra 500shp per engine.

The addition of an advanced avionics suite, combined with its ability to in-flight refuel for increased range, meant that the MH-53J could penetrate hostile airspace undetected at very low level in all weathers, to infiltrate or extract Special Forces teams and their equipment. Apart from supporting U.S. Special Forces the MH-53J was assigned two other missions, namely combat search and rescue and assisting civilian rescue agencies.

The MH-53J fleet underwent a service life extension programme (SLEP) at the U.S. Navy's aviation facility at Pensacola, Florida, which modernised the basic airframe structure, hydraulics and wiring. The structural modifications increased gross weight by 8,000lb (3629 kg) to give an effective increase of 45% in payload capability. Operationally, this meant that the MH-53J could carry an additional 3,970 lb (1800 kg) of fuel, which extended the time between refuellings from three hours to five hours. A further modification known as Shipboard Operations (SBO) was funded in light of the failed rescue attempt in Iran in 1980, and aimed to improve shipboard stowage by adding fully automatic rotor blade and tail pylon folding. An additional benefit of this modification was that it made the task of preparing the MH-53J for transport by C-5 Galaxy far less time consuming. All 41 MH-53Js had undergone the SLEP by July 1995.

In November 1993 IBM/Loral was awarded a contract to integrate and test new avionics and systems on two MH-53Js. These included an Integrated Defensive Avionics System via a Mil Std 1553 databus (incorporating the AAR-47 missile plume detector and the ALQ-136 missile jammer) and a Multi-Mission Advanced Tactical Terminal (IDAS/MATT). The latter included a receiver, which could uplink threat information from a classified database known as 'Constant Source,' and display this data on a cockpit digital map system. These modifications were subsequently applied to the rest of the MH-53J fleet.

During 1998/1999 the MH-53J underwent a further transformation, which resulted in a redesignation to MH-53M Pave Low IV. This latest version of the MH-53 is externally identical to its predecessor but internally the cockpit has undergone a major upgrade. The MH-53M has been equipped with a 3D-colour moving map display, which can be relayed from the cockpit to other crewmembers located in the rear of the helicopter. This has the distinct advantage of allowing each crewmember to see their exact position whilst on a mission thus improving situational awareness. The MH-53M has also benefited from a new Lockheed Martin AP-102A weapons systems computer, updated avionics and new Multi-Functional Displays. The MH-53M Pave Low IV is currently the largest and most powerful helicopter in the USAF inventory, and the most technologically advanced helicopter in the world.

MH-53J Pave Low IIIE Specifications

- Primary Role: Long-range infiltration and extraction of Special Operations Forces under adverse weather conditions
- Manufacturer: Sikorsky Aircraft Corp.
- Crew: Six (Two pilots, two flight engineers, two aerial gunners).
- Power Plant: Two General Electric T64-GE-100 engines producing 4,330 shaft horsepower each.
- Dimensions: Length - 92 feet (28 metres), Height - 25 feet (7.6 metres), Rotor Diameter - 72 feet (21.9 metres).
- Maximum Speed: 165mph (264km/h).
- Maximum Ceiling: 16,000 feet (4,849 metres).
- Maximum Takeoff Weight: 46,000 pounds (18,900 kilograms); (can be increased to 50,000 pounds in emergencies).
- Range: 630 statute miles (550 nautical miles); unlimited with air refuelling.
- Armament: Any combination of three 7.62 miniguns and .50 calibre machine guns.

5. Thoughts about Wheelus

By Mike Lynam (Crew chief, F-4C 64-0888, 92nd TFS/81st TFW)

F-4C-24-MC 64-0872 of the 92nd TFS/81st TFW pictured during Temporary Duty (TDY) at Wheelus AB, Libya in 1969. This photo was taken by John Czarnota who was the crew chief on this particular jet.

Wheelus Air Base was located just west of Tripoli, Libya on the coast of the Mediterranean Sea. It had one very long, 11,000 + ft. runway and was surrounded by an 8-10 foot stone wall fence that had jagged colored glass sticking up from the top. The reason for the colored glass (or so we had heard) was that if an Arab tried to climb the wall to get into the base and was cut by colored glass, he would not go to paradise (or wherever it is they believe they go after death). The base was very long east-to-west but was not very deep north-to-south.

The 81st TFW consisted of the 78th TFS, the 91st TFS, and our unit - the 92nd TFS. Our three squadrons went TDY to Wheelus on a rotating basis. Actually, squadrons from all over Europe and even Navy squadrons off carriers in the Med used Wheelus for bombing and gunnery practice. There was a huge bombing and gunnery range out in the Sahara desert.

The 92nd, I remember, usually went for 30 days every January, April, July, and October (except for one very interesting exception). Not everyone in the squadron went on every TDY, although I managed to go on 8 of them in 3 years. As I recall, usually about half the unit went down with roughly 10/12 aircraft and the necessary crew chiefs, munitions troops, field maintenance guys, etc. We all stayed (except the pilots, of course) in a dusty old 3 story barracks about 2/3 miles from our flightline. Our flightline was located at the far western edge of the base in front of a large maintenance hanger that was usually empty.

Wheelus was sandy, dusty, and usually hot. Summertime temps could easily top 120 degrees, which made the flightline seem like 150 degrees. There were salt pill dispensers in the hanger and heaven help you if you ever got on the wrong side of the jet when it taxied out and you got caught in the jet wash. The already roasting temps on the tarmac and the extra heat of the jet exhaust would almost make you faint!

One redeeming feature of the base was the beach. There was a very long sandy beach on the Med and in the center was a beach house/snack bar place called

"The Halfway House". Many off duty hours were spent hanging around Halfway House and swimming in

the very clear warm waters of the Med. Being able to get a suntan was a nice bonus for the troops who came down TDY from Northern Europe or England. Having a nice deep tan didn't hurt when you got back to your home base and went to town to chase the local girls!

Usually, at least once each trip, the pilots would throw a beach party near the Halfway House and invite the crew chiefs. Everyone would let their hair down and drink the pilot's version of grog and everyone would get falling down drunk. It was great for morale and camaraderie.

The pilots liked to treat us well in Wheelus because when they had their nightly beers at the Officers club they often wound up making bets about their prowess on the bombing range with pilots from other squadrons from Germany, etc. The key to our power in this situation was that they lost the bet if their jet aborted and they never even got to the range! Now, there ain't a crew chief alive that couldn't find some reason to "Red X" a jet for something if he set his mind to it. So, while the vast majority of our pilots were normally pretty good guys, they got even nicer in Wheelus. This was especially true when they made bets with the Navy pilots that were TDY off the aircraft carriers in the Med.

There was a great rivalry there. They never said so, but I think it really galled the Air Force pilots that on landing, the Navy jets would already be turning off the runway at the touch down point for the Air Force guys! Those Navy pilots had no idea what to do with 11,000 feet of runway! It must have looked like landing on an interstate highway in Kansas to them.

As you can guess, the weather was almost always hot and dry, although one time I did see what was probably the heaviest downpour of rain I'd ever seen in my life. I don't know what conditions caused it, but I remember it to this day. It didn't last long but it looked like the sky had opened up into a huge waterfall and it hit right during engine start of an 8-plane launch. So the pilots closed the canopies but the poor crew chiefs were just getting hammered! I remember this because my jet wasn't part of the launch and I was just standing in the door of the flight shack laughing at the poor bastards getting drenched! It was the closest thing to a monsoon I'd seen but it seemed so out of place in Libya.

Another time I was witness to a weather event that is not out of place in Libya but was quite impressive also, a sandstorm. It was like a blizzard of sand. We saw it rolling in from the desert. A great, billowing cloud of sand that stretched from one horizon to the other and when it hit it just sand blasted everything in it's path. We were off-duty at the time and we scampered for the cover of the barracks, but that didn't seem to help much. That sand found its way into every crack and crevice of the rickety old wooden structure we lived in and managed to coat most everything inside. When we were out in it, the sandstorm invaded every part of your body. It not only gets into every part of your hair, but into your eyes, ears, up your nose and even your teeth! If we hadn't had pants on it would have packed sand into other places as well! That storm lasted most of the night and the next day there were sand drifts all over.

There was a hamburger joint/beer parlor called 'The Snake Pit" about ¼ mile from the barracks that was used quite heavily. It was on base, of course, this being a Moslem country. It wasn't very fancy, more like a beat-up, dusty little snack bar that served beer. I remember some of the Arabs that grilled the hamburgers. They had only one eye, the left one, and a membrane (no eye patch, here) covered the right one. The story was (once again, so we had heard) that the mothers of some Libyan boys would have the kid's right eye poked out so that they couldn't aim a rifle and therefore wouldn't be drafted into the Libyan army, because if you got drafted, it was for life! I don't know how true this story was, but I did notice quite a few Arab workers on base had no right eye!

And all the Arabs called every GI, "sedeki", which in Arabic meant friend. Of course, it was a generic term, as I don't think any of them wanted to be our friend unless we were going to buy something from them. Of course, we had to change our greenbacks in for scrip when we got there, as that was all that was used on base. But, there was the usual black market for US dollars off base.

I remember that we would wake up at dawn every morning to the sound of the call of the muezzins from the minaret at the local mosque not far off base. The haunting, lowing sounds of "Allah Akbar" drifting across the desert air. Made you think you were in a movie about "The Arabian Nights" !

The exception to the squadron rotation pattern I mentioned earlier occurred in the late summer of 1969. For reasons that I don't remember we switched months with the 78th and went from mid-August to mid-

September. It was a normal, uneventful TDY at first but on September 1st, 1969 when the King of Libya was on vacation in Crete or Cyprus (I can't remember which) an unknown 28 year old Libyan Army captain named Mohamar Kadafy staged a little coup-de-etat. We all laughed about it at first. We thought, hell, this ain't going to last long! As we all now know, Kadafy has managed to keep his hold on Libya for over 30 years! Old Mohamar wasn't too fond of Americans then or now and rescinded all Libyan/American base agreements and told us all to leave ASAP. Not only TDY personnel, but all permanent party personnel also.

Well, things got interesting after that. The base dependents were naturally the first evacuated as many C-130 and C-141 cargo planes showed up to take them out. The TDY squadrons were next to go and when it came to our turn to fly the F-4's out and for the troops to leave on the C-130, I got to say good bye to all the 92nd guys and stand on the tarmac and watch them taxi out, and take-off on their return to England. I had the privilege to be left behind with a smattering of field maintenance types as my jet, good old 64-0888 was in that normally empty hanger on the flightline with a fuel cell problem. It was all torn apart and not even close to being fixed yet, so somebody had to stay behind and take care of it and get it out of Wheelus as soon as it was finally fixed. This took about 5 days with the help of the field maintenance guys left with me. Well, we finally fixed the jet and the pilots who stayed to fly it out finally did so (I found out later they only got as far as Torrejon AB in Spain before they had to land with another problem!). So, now I could attempt to get back to RAF Bentwaters from Libya and

Shot from the back seat of 63-7646, this photo shows a 92nd TFS F-4C on approach to Wheelus AB in 1969. (photo: John Czarnota)

The 92nd TFS flightline at Wheelus in 1969. 64-0872 is in the foreground with 64-0888, otherwise known as Fred, next in the line. Mike Lynam was crew chief on the latter jet. (photo: John Czarnota)

John Czarnota pre-flights F-4C 63-7646 during TDY at Wheelus. (photo: John Czarnota)

A 92nd TFS F-4C is marshalled from the flightline at Wheelus in 1969. (photo: John Czarnota)

I had no clue how I was going to do that, except to take the first plane north I could get.

This turned out to be rather more difficult than expected. I had very low priority on getting a seat on any northbound plane and they were all northbound ! I was staying in the barracks with the field maintenance troops and every day I would pack my duffel bag, grab my canvas bag of tools and head out the door for the transit terminal only to wind up sitting around all day trying to catch a hop. Everyday, same story. After a couple of days doing this, it became a running joke with the field maintenance boys. As I trudged back into the barracks every night they had great fun busting my balls and even started making bets with each other as to when I would finally get out and back to England. They were stuck staying to fix another aircraft and would be leaving in about a week. One day about 5 days after I began trying, I finally managed to grab a seat on a Coast Guard C-123 that was only going to the Navy base at Naples, Italy. But, it was a chance to leave and I took it, hoping I could get a Navy plane north from there.

Well, to make a long story short, it took me five days just to get to Rhein Main AB in Germany, via Naples; the Navy base at Rota, Spain; and Torrejon AB, Spain. When I walked into the transit barracks in Rhein Main and was checking in, I noticed a stack of TDY orders on the counter that were for 81st TFW troops and then noticed some of the names. It was the same group of guys that had been making bets on me getting out of Wheelus! So, I requested to be billeted with them and when I walked into the huge room they were bunked in you couldn't believe the blank looks of disbelief on their faces! They assumed I had been back on base in England for 5 days. Turns out their C-130 had a mechanical problem and had to land at Rhein Main over night. We had an uproarious time laughing about the weird set of circumstances and the arguments about the bet, because they had already paid each other off and the bet wasn't officially over yet! So, I finally got back to Bentwaters the next day on their plane and called my flight chief to tell him I was back. He started hollering about "Where the hell have you been, etc., etc." I just told him, "Sarge, it's a long story!" The upshot is that 64-0888 was still not back; it was still in Spain!

'Fred' awaits its next mission at Wheelus in 1969. (photo: John Czarnota)

6. The Ultimate Dilemma: a reflection on Victor Alert at Bentwaters

by Mike Lynam (Crew chief, F-4C 64-0888, 92nd TFS/81st TFW)

It's not the kind of problem that most people have to consider and Gleason didn't want to be considering it either. Deeply disturbing thoughts had begun creeping into his mind about the guilt and karma crushing horror that would consume him for his part in the stunningly sudden annihilation of so many people. Culpability in the deaths of hundreds of thousands has a way of making a man face an awful truth about himself.

Gleason knew that the dreaded abhorrence that churned inside him would just have to stay there. No one ever talked about it. Not in his world. If he was smart he'd keep his mouth shut. The least that would happen would be his removal from his current assignment. If his conscience ever forced him to act on his guilty worries he'd be up on charges, if he lived, which would be doubtful. He had to follow orders - that was what he was trained to do. He knew he should keep his mouth shut but the beer got the best of him.

"I was just following orders. Where have I heard that before?" Jack Gleason chuckled to himself.

"What the hell are you talking about?" Hutch burped.

Yeah, he knew he should keep his mouth shut but Gleason and Hutch were hanging around the NCO club and it was damn near closing time. The beer had flowed and the English floozies that were bused in from Ipswich had come and gone. Hutch and Gleason weren't in the mood to try to net the same old birds again. This Saturday night they were just tired and drunk.

"Nukes." Gleason said.

"Nukes? What about 'em? We see them all the time." Hutch replied.

"Don't you ever wonder about how you'd feel if we actually launch our nuclear armed jets during an alert?" Gleason said.

"No, why would I?" Hutch replied while belching and reaching for his beer.

Steve Hutchinson was Gleason's roommate, fellow Air Force crew chief and best friend. They had been together from the time they had arrived overseas. They had worked together, drank together and whored together. If Gleason couldn't tell Hutch how he felt it would just keep eating at him, so he took a chance.

"Jesus, Hutch! Think about it. We'd be part of helping to kill thousands and thousands of people. Has that concept ever crossed your mind?"

"It'd be war. That's what we do."

It was that simple to Hutch but Gleason was trying to deal with an internal mental problem and felt drunkenly confident enough to pursue the subject with his buddy.

"Yeah, I know it would be war and they'd be killing thousands of us so we'd have to kill thousands of them. It's just that sometimes I wonder how I'd feel about helping to nuke all those civilians." Gleason said quietly.

"Wonder all you want. There'd be nothing you could do about it, anyway." Hutch said. Hutch was blond haired, strong jawed and confident in his youth and invulnerability. He loved his beer and he was a great friend but he wasn't the least bit bothered by any internally derived moral dilemmas.

"Well, theoretically, I suppose someone could if he ever had the mind to do it." Gleason stupidly continued.

"Do what?"

"Do something about it. Imagine if one of the crew chiefs just could not deal with launching his jet under those circumstances."

"Deal with it? What's to deal with?" Hutch huffed.

"Suppose all of a sudden his conscience got the best of him and he decided not to help kill hundreds of thousands of people?"

"You just do it. That's what we're supposed to do."

"Yeah, just like the Germans. 'Just following orders.'" Gleason pointed out.

Ironically, the hundreds of thousands of people they might help kill could very possibly be German - East German. Not Nazis now, but Communists instead. They might even be Poles, or Romanians, or even Hungarian. Gleason and Hutch didn't know as they weren't privy to actual target information although it was common knowledge that all the targets were in Eastern Europe, not the Soviet Union, due to fuel range.

"Yeah, orders. You just launch the jet like we do everyday on the flightline. What is up with you?" Hutch asked.

Jack Gleason had always been your basic stable Air Force crew chief. He had been overseas on this foggy English outpost for almost three years and was one of the veterans on the flightline. His jet almost always went up when it was supposed to and when it did, it came back down in one piece - every time. He'd never lost a pilot or injured a ground crewman, except himself.

Gleason was involved in the Cold War in the late sixties and was only 21 years old. He had no moral dilemma about the Air Force bombing and killing hundreds of the enemy in Vietnam so he wondered why he was bothered by the idea of helping to wipe out 500,000 or so people.

"Maybe it's the number. But what's the difference between X amount of people getting bombed conventionally and Y amount of people getting nuked? Dead is dead." Gleason said.

"Yeah, dead is dead. So what?" Hutch asked, wondering why Gleason had brought this up.

"Well, It's an interesting situation, don't ya' think?

"And just what the hell would the guy do? Beg the pilots not to taxi out and take off?" Hutch snickered and belched again.

"Disable the jet before it taxied out."

"He'd have to be nuts! They'd hang him for that and then they'd get serious."

"What's the difference? We'd all go up in smoke in a nuclear Armageddon. You realize that our little base here is one of the largest nuclear weapons storage depots in all of Europe. We'd be ground zero for a few dedicated Soviet nukes. There'd be nothing left of the guy to hang and no one to do it either."

"Hell, Jack. I can't think of anyone of us chiefs that would do that, except maybe that creep Huffington, he's sort of a lefty weirdo and hell, sometimes so are you, but even he ain't stupid enough to sabotage a jet. We'd all launch our jets and anyway how the hell would you know that any one particular scramble is the real thing? They're not going to tell us."

That was the one major problem Gleason couldn't quite get past. How the hell do you know when it's the real thing? But, he had an idea about it so he threw the question back at Hutch.

"Well, in all the time we've been here and all the time we've pulled VA duty waiting for World War III, what's the one thing that's never happened?"

"What's never happened? What kind of stupid question is that? How am I supposed to figure out something that's never happened? You're a dope!" Hutch chuckled.

"Well, the sirens go off and we all run out to the jets and put the codes into the bombs and get ready to go but the jets have never taxied out of the aircraft shelters." Gleason helpfully pointed out.

"So what?"

"So what I've always heard is that if we ever do taxi out and go airborne those Russian agents that are always hanging around the farm fields around here would spot it and assume that we were actually going after them, since we haven't ever launched with nukes from here before, even for practice."

"Well, yeah. Sure, I've heard that too but I don't think I'd put too much stock in that shit. How long have you been in, numbnuts? This is the Air Force. They do all sorts of stupid things." Hutch chuckled.

Hutch certainly had a point there - Gleason had to agree. Gleason also knew that even the Air Force was pretty damn serious when it came to anything nuclear.

Now standing idle and empty, the eight Victor Alert barns at Bentwaters are symbolic for the 'Cold War' mission that the base represented. A nuclear attack on the Soviet Union would have been launched from these very buildings. As such, their importance in helping to maintain world peace throughout the Cold War cannot be underestimated. (photo: Author)

Gleason dropped his drunken semi-public ramblings at that point but his dilemma still haunted him. They finished their beers and stumbled back to the barracks. Gleason trusted Hutch but even good friends will let slip things about you that you don't want others to know.

Life on the flightline went on as normal after their conversation. Everyday flight operations kept him busy but Gleason continued to be bothered by the question. His mind would stir with the numbers. He realized that his Dad's generation and his Grandpa's, and hell - all the way back to the Civil War - his ancestors did what they had to do, despite their moral questions.

Why did the thought of helping to nuke masses of people bother him when he realized that during World War II the incendiary bombs dropped on Dresden and Tokyo burned up more people than the early nukes killed in Hiroshima and Nagasaki? Wasn't it General Curtis LeMay's theory that the act of war was to kill more of them than they do of us - until they quit? War is about death. Where do you draw the line about numbers?

Gleason had never had to face this type of judgment while looking out across a rifle barrel. In the Air force it is a very impersonal business to drop shit on the heads of people from altitude, unless, of course, the pilots are getting shot at - it then becomes very personal to the aircrew. However, the totality of the devastation imposed on people from an aircraft, shot at or not, is usually far greater than that from a rifle. Armies all over the world have great firearms but a few well-placed nukes will turn all that into a gigantic obscene joke.

Gleason hadn't mentioned the subject again and his life went on like always. Stumble out of bed and get to the flightline so early that the even the huge rats that came from the farm fields that surrounded the base were not yet running around the flightline.

Pre-flight the jet, talk to the aircrew, help them get cranked up and rolling, kill the hour or so that they would be airborne by trying to avoid the flight chief so he wouldn't find something for you to do. Meet the jet when it returned from whatever practice mission was the order of the day. Check out the plane, re-fuel it, put a new drag chute in the tail, change bad tires, get the weapon's troop to re-load it, da, ta, da, ta, da.

Do this two or three times and then get off shift. Stop at the mess hall to eat, the barracks to shower and change into civvies. Head to town and get drunk and chase women. Get back to the barracks late and sleep a few hours and get up and do it again.

Ah, there's nothing like the dulcet tones of screaming jet engines to soothe a hangover in the morning. But it was normal everyday Air Force life when you're a crew chief. Then the Russians invaded Czechoslovakia.

Those pesky Czechs taking to the streets demanding their freedom put the whole world into a huge political snit and all the military units in Europe at high DEFCON alert. The Russians, failing to see the humor in this Czech business, pissed and moaned and rolled their tanks and armored personnel carriers out of their home bases and grabbed Czechoslovakia back like a little kid, saying "Mine, mine, mine!"

Well, this caused all sorts of hell to break loose on their nice peaceful flightline and forced Gleason to make his awful choice. All the jets that could possibly get airborne were brought to the flightline and loaded with nukes. The wing already had 12 F-4 Phantom aircraft on nuclear alert. There were always that many ready to go. These aircraft were parked in the Victor Alert area, a separate highly secure compound. The regular flightline was not normally the victim of top-notch security. Gleason's old Aunt Nell and her 75-year old boyfriend could slip into there.

But when the nukes came out, the cops came out. There were Air Police troops everywhere. The crew chiefs dragged jets out of the maintenance hangers and corrosion control. Maintenance types were swarming over them trying to patch them up and get them airworthy. Fuel trucks and weapons troops and the brass were crawling all over the place. Hutch and Gleason knew they were there for the duration, which would conclude, one way or the other, when people a lot higher than them decided whether there would be war or peace.

It had been that way all of Gleason's life. He grew up with air raid siren tests, neighbors with bomb shelters, and 'duck and cover' drills in the school hallways. As if there was any chance of surviving a nuclear blast by cowering in the hallway. There was always the threat that everyone could die because of the Russians.

When Gleason was a schoolboy he could never understand why they would want to bomb us. We were the good guys, the Americans. We grew up afraid of the big bad Russian Bear, knowing there was someone over there that could decide to push a button and end everything - we were helpless. But, so were the Russian kids, and they knew it too.

By morning we had all the airplanes that could possibly fly loaded and ready. Then we waited.

"Well, whatta ya' think?" Hutch asked. They had both been assigned to the VA area and were just sitting around waiting for World War III. An odd way to spend one's time, Gleason had to admit.

"About what?" Gleason responded.

"About this Russian shit. If we launch, will any jackass try to disable his jet?"

"I hope we don't find out." Gleason said. He was primarily hoping for himself. He was afraid to find out what he'd do and he wanted it to remain unknown.

Hutch looked Gleason straight in the eye with the penetrating power of a radar beam in a storm. "What are you going to do?" Hutch asked, pointedly.

The NATO 'Cube' nuclear weapons storage igloos housed within the Weapons Storage Area (WSA) at Bentwaters. These particular igloos were also known as 'Hot Row.' (photo: Author)

"Maybe we'll find out." Gleason replied sternly, looking right back at Hutch. And they did, that afternoon.

The Russian tanks rolled into Prague and in what must of have an been an attempt by NATO to impress upon the Soviets their dissatisfaction with this blatant diplomatic faux-pas, the powers that be in the chain of command did something that Gleason considered to be really stupid. The sirens started blaring and they all started running. Ground crews and flight crews, all hustling to their jets like Pete Rose rounding second.

Gleason's heart was pounding like a teenager on his first date. He was more worried then he had ever been on a scramble. Christ! This could actually be it! He thought as he went through the procedures to help arm and prepare the airborne machine of nuclear death.

The pilots were set and ready to go in the cockpit and Gleason was ready on the ground. At that point they normally called off the exercise and the scramble was over. Just what he was hoping would happen now. He didn't want to see the pilot hold his right hand up and start a swirling motion with his index finger. That meant they were starting the engines and that would be very bad news.

Gleason just stood on the ground in front of the cockpit, waiting. It seemed like an eternity and then the pilot did it. He twirled his finger and Gleason hit the switch that sent high pressure air from the ground power unit to the engines and got them spinning. He began to get freaked as he ran over to switch the air hose from one engine to the other. No, no, no! he was screaming internally. The engines spun up and settled down into idle and he disconnected the air and power hoses and went to the front of the jet and waited again.

All this only took a couple of minutes and Gleason had been too busy to decide what to do. While he stood nervously in front of the jet waiting for the next order he had visions of huge fireballs and vaporized people and children with their skin peeling off due to radiation; a destroyed city and irradiated land and poisoned water and burned dogs. Families that would never enjoy the next day let alone the next generation. Every awful thought that had ever crossed his mind, from grade school on, about the terror and horror of the consequence of nuclear weapons was reeling through his brain.

Son of a bitch, Gleason thought, all those horrific things would happen because of the stupid godamn bomb he was standing there looking at. This bomb. This one right here in front of him - mounted under the centerline of the fuselage - and he could stop this one particular bomb from creating all of the horror it would cause. He could save hundreds of thousands of people from instant death and let them deal with what was going to be left of the world later. Gleason knew that he'd be a victim from some Russian nukes but at least he felt that he could arrive upstairs with cleaner karma.

Don't signal to pull the chocks! Gleason's mind was screaming! Then the pilot did just that!

"Jesus Christ! Jesus Christ! Jesus Christ! Gleason yelled, although no one could hear him over the screaming jet engines from all the planes in the VA area. He ran under the jet to pull the chocks wondering how to disable the plane and realized that he could throw one of the hefty wooden chocks into one of the engines. It would be like tossing a fireplace log into the intake and that would certainly screw up the turbine blades and cause the engine to do all sorts of non-standard things. The jet would never take off and he'd not be responsible for all those deaths.

Gleason grabbed the chocks from the right main gear and ran out to the front of the jet.

"Oh, shit!" Oh, shit!" he was hollering as he tossed the first set of chocks to the side of the jet and ran to grab the other set. He yanked them from under the left wheel and ran to the front again and just as his arm swung back to toss them into the intake, he whirled around and sent them flying, off to the side, away from the jet!

"Dammit!" Gleason barked. He hated himself, but he waved the jet forward and just collapsed into a sitting position on the tarmac after the plane taxied out. He watched the jets taxi to the end of the runway and take-off. He was despondent. He knew he'd be dead in a few minutes and that he had not stopped his part of the nightmare. Gleason wanted to cry but had no tears, just roiling mental anguish.

"How could I have done this? Yeah, I was just following orders and those orders are going to put me in hell!" Gleason moaned to himself.

Almost everyone on the flightline after the launch of the jets was just stunned. No one was moving. Gleason looked around and thought of a snapshot of finality. He figured he was taking his last look at the world and thought about how he was going to explain this to whomever one explained things to after they died. He began to hope that there might not be life after death. At least that way he wouldn't have to think about this horror anymore.

The minutes went on. People started to move from their stunned paralysis and Gleason looked across the flightline and spotted Hutch near where his plane had been. Hutch was looking up in the sky.

Gleason walked slowly and dejectedly over to him. Hutch spotted him and looked straight at Gleason and winked.

"Good man." Hutch said.

"Dead man, cursed man, eternally condemned man is more like it." Gleason croaked. "Shit! We're going to be dead in a few minutes!"

"Well, if we are, at least we'll be at ground zero and we'll never know what hit us." Hutch said, scanning the skies again.

"What the hell are you looking for?" Gleason asked. "You ain't going to be able to see the nukes coming down.

"I'm not looking for nukes, you jackass. I'm looking for our jets." Hutch said.

"They're long gone and won't have anything to come back to, idiot!" Gleason barked.

"Really? What's that out in the distance?" Hutch laughed as he pointed towards the eastern horizon.

Gleason looked up and saw them. Twelve black dots with smoke trails flowing behind them. They were coming back! It wasn't World War III!

"God Damn, son-of-a bitch! Look at that!" Gleason screamed with delight. He started hopping and dancing around in total glee. He would never know that kind of total and utter mind-cleansing relief again. But he would also never forget that moment.

All the jets landed, taxied in, and shut down. They stayed armed and on alert status for a few more days until NATO finally figured out that they weren't going to be able to convince or scare the Russians out of Czechoslovakia. The DEFCON alert was lifted and the nukes removed from the jets on the flightline. Normal flight operations resumed and three nights later Hutch and Gleason found themselves in the NCO club again.

Gleason was on a mission to get totally drunk and was well on the way to accomplishing his goal. "I've never been so bloody happy in my life as I was when we saw those jets coming back." He laughed, taking another drink of his beer.

"Well, I had a few moments when I wondered if it was real." Hutch said. "But, I kept thinking, why would we respond with nukes when all the Russians did was take back control of a country they already had under their thumb? Didn't make sense for us to start World War III over it."

Gleason thought this over and finally said, "I couldn't think about it politically. I had all sorts of mental horror running though my mind. I thought about disabling my jet and damn near tossed the chocks into the intake. But I couldn't do it." Gleason admitted, sheepishly.

"Damn good thing. You'd be in prison for life, if you weren't shot first!" Hutch said.

"Well, I wasn't sure what I'd do if I ever actually came up against it. But now I know and I'm not exactly proud of myself. But, I'll tell you what, I hope I never have to face this shit again." Gleason said. "And, I bet you were wondering what I'd do, too."

Hutch sighed and looked drunkenly up at Gleason and said, "Nah, I knew what you'd do. You're like the rest of us. We just follow orders!!"

7. A Pilot's Story: Flying the F-86A & F-84F from Bentwaters

By Harry Eckes – F-86A/F-84F pilot 91st FIS/FBS

2/Lt Harry Eckes stands beside a 91st FIS/81st FIG F-86A Sabre at Bentwaters during 1954. (photo: Harry Eckes)

Looking through the hedgerows after turning the corner at the Ivy Lodge and seeing F-86 Sabres at Bentwaters caught me by surprise. The motor pool had sent a jeep to Wickham Market (Campsea Ash) train station to pick up Jack Downey, Al Boughton and myself. We had recently graduated from pilot training and had completed our combat crew training in the F-84E at Luke AFB near Phoenix, Arizona, and all of us young Lieutenants were eager to start flying with the 81st Fighter Wing at RAF Station Bentwaters. The date was 24 March 1954.

My worry that we had been trained in the wrong airplane was short lived. It wasn't long after reporting in for duty that we started our training for the F-86 Sabre assigned to the 91st Fighter-Interceptor Squadron.

After some accelerated but thorough training by the 'old timers' of the squadron and the North American Co. Technical Representative (Tech Rep), we were ready to fly the Sabre.

The weekend in the middle of our training was used well for studying, reading and listening to the North American Co. Tech Rep. He gave up his weekend and came to Aldeburgh where we were living at the Jays Hotel, just down from the White Lion Hotel. Sitting on the sea wall and learning about the F-86 Sabre – it just doesn't get much better than that! There was the "unwritten" word that you were ready to fly the F-86 after you could demonstrate you could pre-flight, start the engine and taxi around the ramp with the instructor clinging to the side. If you could make the taxi route and get back to the parking spot with out dumping him on the ramp you were ready. So after only a week at Bentwaters I was flying one of the greatest fighters of its time.

That first flight was exciting and I really felt at ease from the moment I was strapped in the cockpit. After a few training flights it was up to 37,000 feet and then dive to reach supersonic flight for my first time. Supersonic flights in the Sabre took a little effort since we always flew with the 120-gallon external fuel tanks fitted.

The F-86A has hydraulically boosted controls and there was some wing rock associated with passing through the transonic speed and of course the jump in the airspeed and mach indicator as you attained supersonic flight. An interesting point is that the early serial numbered airplanes had wider cord ailerons, which would provide more roll control particularly at lower airspeed. Only one draw back was with a flight control hydraulic failure reverting back to manual control required some pretty heavy control stick forces. I was to experience this on about my tenth flight when my F-86 suffered a hydraulic failure. The crosswinds were strong at Bentwaters so I was told to divert to RAF Station Sculthorpe since they had a wider runway, which made the landing a little easier.

Progress of the new pilots was always monitored. The Squadron Commander, Operations Officer and sometimes the Group Commander would fly with us to see first-hand how we were doing. I was assigned to fly wing for Colonel Cassidy (Brigadier General Retired), the 81st Group Commander, on a flight to Weisbaden Germany. After engine start I was unable to check in on the radio. Col Cassidy, who was in his airplane about 50 yards away, shut down his engine and came running over to my airplane to see what was wrong. At about the same time he climbed up the side of my airplane I discovered that my radio mic cord had come unplugged; very embarrassed I held up the end of the plug and thought to myself how dumb could I be! He took one look at the mic cord and all he said was "let's go try it again." He was a great Commander as well as a great person and I still get a chance to talk with him now and then at our 81st Wing reunions.

One of my early flights as wing for one of the 'older' pilots on his last F-86 flight before returning to the USA, turned out to be an interesting sight seeing tour. We departed Bentwaters on a beautiful morning, stayed at low altitude (about 500 feet), proceeded south past the Dengie Flats air to ground gunnery range and turned west up the River Thames toward London. We had excellent views of the port of London, Tower Bridge and the Tower of London. After a tight left turn we went by Westminster and Big Ben, followed by a hard right toward the west. As far as I know no one spotted our tail numbers during that low pass over London but I did not rest easy for a week or two! Years later on a trip back to England I was reminded of this beautiful view when my wife Laura and I took a ride on the London Eye.

There were many fighter units, both USAF and RAF that filled the skies over East Anglia. Any time after takeoff and landing gear retracted you were 'fair game.' You learned very quickly what the term 'check six' means in fighter pilot language. Mock 'dog flights' were pretty common with other F-86A's and F's from the 81st Wing, F-84G's from the 20th Fighter Wing and numerous Vampires and Meteor F8's. It was a great, but sometimes dangerous way to learn the fighter pilot business and not good for your career if you were caught participating in unauthorised 'dog fights.' Sometimes we had good luck with our gun camera film. I got the upper hand over a Meteor F8 and with airspeed down to 105 knots and had a nice film of him lowering flaps and extending the finger speed brakes trying to lose me. After fuel began to get low and it was time to head home, I moved up on his wing and then departed with a friendly wave. I really had the feeling and confidence that I could handle myself well in this world of fighter pilots.

2/Lt Harry Eckes (third from left) pictured with fellow 91st FIS pilots at Bentwaters in 1954. (photo: Harry Eckes)

Although assigned to the 91st FBS, this photo shows 1/Lt Harry Eckes in the cockpit of an F-84F belonging to the 92nd FBS. (photo: Harry Eckes)

During the summer months night flying would start late in the evening because the sun would set late. On one of these late flights I returned to Bentwaters at about midnight and found that the nose landing gear would not lock down. My fuel was running low also. Squadron Ops and mobile control now came to my assistance in any and all ways to help me get the gear down and indicating safe. The F-86A had a hand hydraulic pump to get the gear down with a hydraulic failure but with normal system pressure that wouldn't help. Following cycling of the gear numerous times and a touch and go landing to attempt to tap the nose gear I still couldn't get the green 'locked' indication. It was recommended that I try to pump it down with the hand pump. I knew that this would be unsuccessful as I was fighting normal system pressure but I tried it anyway. I was told to "really pump it hard." This I did, resulting in breaking the pump handle (which didn't get me in good standing with the crew chief!). My maintenance background knew that replacing the pump was quite a chore. So, with fuel running low and all the other aircraft getting on the ground ahead of me in case I collapsed a gear and closed the runway, I made my approach. This too was unsuccessful as I was forced to break off the approach and go around again because the emergency vehicles were all on the runway chasing the previous landing F-86 thinking that was me! I kept the pattern in very tight, put it on the runway and rolled to a stop where the crew chief pinned the gear and all was well. When the refuelling truck refuelled my aircraft they figured I had about 10 gallons remaining. Now that is cutting it too close!!

Later in September of 1954 we had an enjoyable deployment to Aalborg, Denmark to fly simulated attacks on Norway and Denmark. I flew wing on one of the sorties for Major Moats (Maj Gen Retired), the 91st Squadron commander; we put on quite a show over downtown Oslo! Thankfully we didn't get in any trouble for our 'buzz job' because the Chief of Staff of the Norwegian Air Force was an old friend who flew with Maj Moates in England during WWII. He had been expecting the show!!

The weather in England started to deteriorate in September and since we did not have an aerial gunnery range for 'hot' firing in England, we deployed to Cazaux on the west coast of France, south of Bordeaux. On my first three air-to-air sorties with the aid of a good radar ranging gun sight in my F-86, I shot a 19%, 21% and a 27% which completed my qualification. I was quite proud of this accomplishment but later figured this was dumb on my part because I returned to Bentwaters while the other pilots all enjoyed the flying and beaches at Arcachon.

91st FBS pilots pose in front of a selection of classic British cars. Lou Canegalo, the Republic Technical Representative, is second from right, back row and Harry Eckes is second from right, front row. (photo: Harry Eckes)

Our fighter-interceptor mission for the 81st Wing was coming to an end and we were redesignated the 81st Fighter-Bomber Wing in preparation for the replacement of our F-86 Sabres with Republic F-84Fs in late 1954. We even started to do some dive bombing practice with the F-86's in preparation for the nuclear delivery capability. The F-84F was a great improvement for the new mission but never as enjoyable to fly.

That fantastic year of flying the F-86 Sabre was coming to an end and there was a certain sadness on the last few flights delivering our Sabres to Belfast, Ireland. The Sabres were to be loaded onto a cargo ship for transportation back to the US and reassigned to the Air National Guard.

My first year flying jet fighters set the stage for my passion of flying. Now with experience in the T-33/F-80C, the F-84E, the F-86 Sabre and getting ready for the F-84F it was obvious how the F-86 Sabre would be forever the 'bench mark' from which I would compare and evaluate other jets. No wonder that many a time you would hear that familiar phrase, "Back when we had 86's…

The 'Cold War' dictated a change of mission for the 81st Fighter Wing and the new fighter-bomber role would mean that the F-86's would be replaced with the more capable F-84F Thunderstreak.

The F-84F was the latest progression of the F-84D/E Thunderjet that was used during the Korean War as a fighter-bomber. Its development was delayed many times due to engine and design changes and this resulted in the F-84G model entering service before the F-84F. The 20th Fighter Bomber Wing was equipped with the F-84G and one of the squadrons, the 79th, was based at Woodbridge. The 20th wing was scheduled to receive the F-84F's after we completed our transition. Even though development of all the fighters during this time period began as air superiority aircraft capable of flights to high altitudes and supersonic speeds, the F-84F would take its place as the latest fighter-bomber more suited for low altitude, longer range, and high speed special weapons delivery. This was now the new mission of tactical fighters.

I can still remember my first impression of seeing the F-84F's arrive at Bentwaters. It was going to be exciting to check out in another new fighter aircraft even though the change over would came with many operational growing pains. It definitely would not be as enjoyable to fly as the F-86 Sabre but with time its capabilities would be realised.

The winter weather at Bentwaters was not the best for conducting transition training so it was off to Nouasseur AB, near Casablanca, Morocco.

The first few flights were in 'clean' aircraft, with all the external tanks and pylons removed. With only 3750 pounds of fuel internal, the flights were rather short in duration but the climb to 45,000ft was quite impressive and there it would indicate about .93 Mach in level flight. With a slight decent it would easily reach supersonic flight and with fully hydraulic irreversible flight controls there were no sensations in reaching supersonic flight except for the usual jump in the airspeed/mach indicator.

The Wright J-65 engine, a U.S. development from the Hawker Siddley Sapphire, was rated at 7220 pounds of thrust, and specific fuel consumption was about .85, making it well suited for longer range both at high and low altitude.

The Republic Aircraft Company, designers of the F-84's, were well known for building strong heavy airplanes. Jokingly, pilots would say "they would have built it out of lead but it was heavy enough the way it was." It was designed to withstand 9.33 G's, although the Air Force lowered this to the 7.33 G standard for fighter aircraft.

Take off weight for a clean airplane was approximately 18,500 pounds with internal fuel but grew to almost 28,000 pounds for a mission ready aircraft loaded with external weapons and fuel tanks. At temperatures above approximately 60°F, four JATO bottles would provide the much-needed additional 4000 pounds of thrust for 14 seconds during takeoff from the 7800ft runway at Bentwaters. The expended JATO bottles and rack were then jettisoned in the North Sea out from the Orford lighthouse.

The F-84F also had six 50-caliber guns, four in the nose and one in each wing root. Since we rarely fired the guns on a gunnery range anyway, one of the nose guns was later removed for the installation of the weapons delivery gyro and, on some of the aircraft, the mechanical BT-9 bombing computer. Now and then for readiness testing we would arm a few of the guns, drop dye marker in the North Sea and then practice strafing on the spot in the water. We were lucky that we didn't catch a few of our own ricochets off the water.

Most of our combat training was high and low navigation training and bombing practice on the Dengie Flats gunnery range, delivering practice bombs using the dive, toss and 'over the shoulder' delivery methods. The toss and over the shoulder were quite new as a means of delivering a nuclear weapon. The fighter v fighter tactic was fast becoming a lost art for most of us 'die hard' fighter pilots but there were still some 'fun' moments of engaging in air-to-air practice or 'dog fights' against anything that happened to be in the air. The Hawker Hunters appeared during this period and they were unbelievable once they were equipped with the all-flying tail. We learned very quickly to fly modified "defensive/offensive" tactics in these air-to-air encounters.

Our training configuration was usually with one 450-gallon tank on the right inboard pylon and a practice bomb rack on the left inboard pylon. This asymmetric load made the airplane yaw to the right and constant rudder trimming was required throughout the flight. On the longer navigation flights the two outboard 230-gallon tanks were added and then the airplane really began to fly like a 'bomber.'

We were also equipped for in-flight refuelling and that was particularly helpful on long-range deployments. Refuelling was usually scheduled for the flights to and from Africa for our annual bombing training. Of course, the F-84F was more than capable of non-stop flights to and from Nouasseur AB in Morocco but the refuelling would give us more flexibility if the weather proved to be a factor.

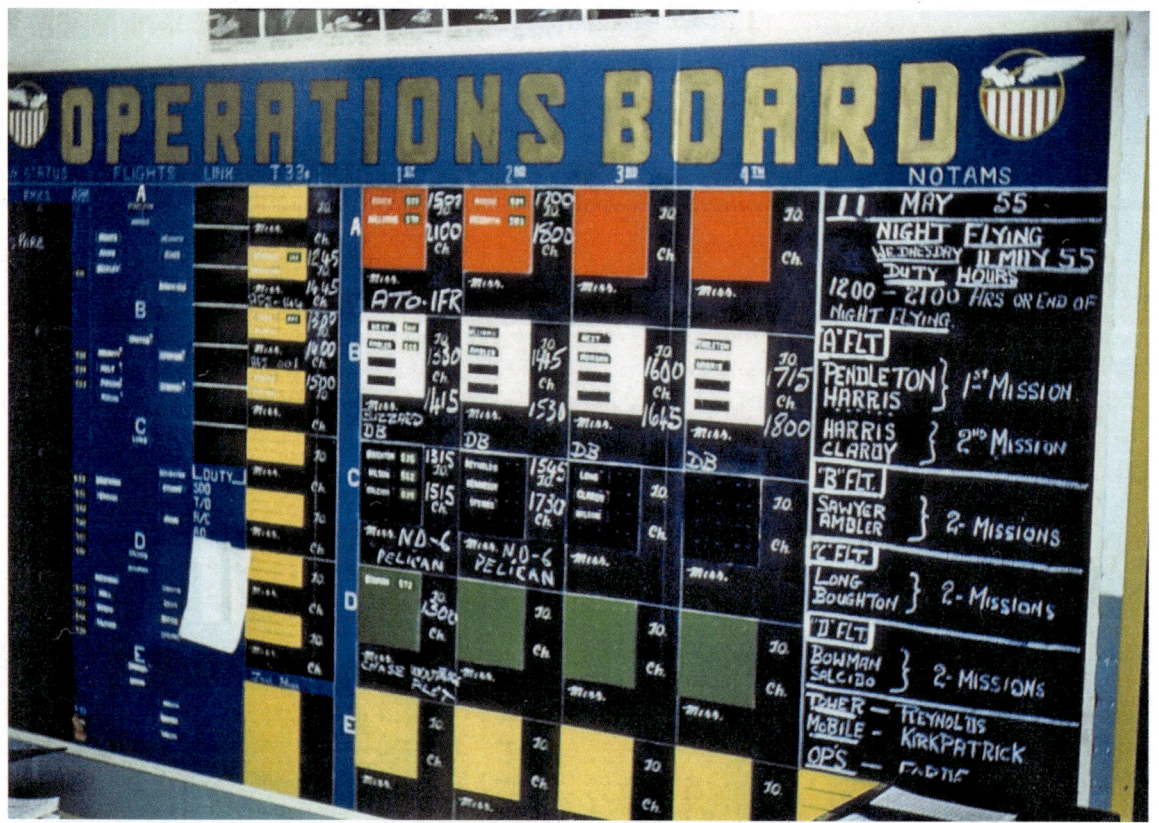

The 91st FBS ops board as it appeared on 11 May 1955. (photo: Harry Eckes)

Early 1950s aerial photo of Bentwaters. (photo: Harry Eckes)

On one of the return flights to Bentwaters from Nouasseur, I was configured with two 450-gallon drop tanks (rather than the usual three-tank configuration), and 'smokeless' JATO. It scared the other pilots when they did not see the usual large cloud of white smoke during the take-off roll. Someone forgot to tell us that the new JATO bottles would be smokeless. My two-wingmen, that I was leading back, aborted for mechanical reasons so I headed to England by myself. My radio failed passing the Straight of Gibraltar so rather than stop for fuel in France as planned, I just continued on to Bentwaters. With only a radio compass for navigation I found BBC London, turned East North East towards Bentwaters, hoping for a break in the weather. No such luck!! However, I spotted a 79th Squadron F-84F, joined up with him, and with the use of 'radio out' hand signals he dropped me off on a GCA approach to runway 26 at Bentwaters. The guys at Squadron ops were a little surprised to see me drop in having heard nothing about my expected time of arrival. I had almost 2000 pounds of fuel remaining after the 2+45 flight.

Early in our training we discovered that during the 4 G pull up required for our toss and 'over the shoulder' bomb delivery we would not have enough aileron control with the asymmetrical external loads. Republic test engineers already had worked on this problem and installed spoilers forward of the flaps that worked with the ailerons. So after the first year we had all the airplanes replaced with the later 'Dash 45' model that had the new spoilers and also a higher vertical stabilizer.

The F-84F was getting to be enjoyable to fly and with the exceptional roll rate I would get pretty bold at low altitude aerobatics. Of course this was very important since I met a young lady from Aldeburgh. She had a friend that was in the RAF and flew Meteor MK.8's out of Wattisham. He would fly the entire Aldeburgh waterfront inverted and then push up and climb into the clouds inverted. With a little practice I was doing the same thing but my timing was never very good...she was never there to see my show!

With the mission training requirements came numerous operational readiness inspections. At the most unexpected early morning hour the siren would go off and the old fashioned network of notification was activated. There were a few of us pilots living in the BOQ Quonset (Nissen) huts, and we could be at the 91st Squadron Operations in a matter of minutes to begin scheduling airplanes and crews. Some of these alerts would require all the operational ready aircraft to deploy or at least simulate deployment up to taxing the airplane out to the runway.

On one of these deployments, I was scheduled to deploy in one of the old 'Hangar Queens' and would be one of the last airplanes airborne. With my maintenance background, and being a designated maintenance flight test pilot, I always felt quite confident with these airplanes. The Hangar Queen was an 'operational ready' aircraft that was usually partially dismantled ready for a major inspection. So while the other aircraft were already taxying for takeoff this aircraft was being hurriedly put back together so it could make the required departure time.

Finally as the last airplane of the deployment, I started and taxied out for take off on Runway 26. As I lifted off the runway, at about the time the landing gear was fully retracted, I experienced an engine explosion followed by a reduction in thrust, vibration, and very high engine tail pipe temperatures. I quickly pulled up onto a left downwind passing between the Woodbridge and Bentwaters runways and dropped the full 450-gallon drop tank but retained the empty outboard 230-gallon tanks in case I landed short of the runway. I kept it in as close as I could because the engine was about to fail completely. I lowered the landing gear over the overrun, touched down and the engine seized, all within a few seconds. I rolled to a stop at the far end and Lou Canegalo, the Republic Technical Representative, was the first one to meet me. He had looked up the exhaust pipe and noticed the discoloration and indications of major internal damage. Later that day he brought me a pair of mechanic pliers that were found in the inlet of the engine. Rather than point the finger at the maintenance crew we chalked this one off to 'unknown foreign object' damage to the engine. It could have all been a lot worse! I often wondered how much crop damage I caused to the farm field where the 450-gallon drop tank impacted!

The summer of 1957 was approaching and it was time for me to move on to my new assignment back in the States. Those years at Bentwaters went by so quickly. That first and memorable assignment had come to a close after flying two great airplanes - the F-86 Sabre and the F-84F Thunderstreak - with the 91st Fighter-Bomber Squadron. It was excellent preparation to ready me for the next generation of fighter aircraft such as the F-100, F-104, and the F-4…but for some strange reason, I will always remember that it was still lots of fun "back when we had -86's!"

8. Chapter 8 – Twin Bases Wall Art

Bentwaters – 81st Supply Squadron, Fuel Operations Building. (photo: Author)

Bentwaters – 81st Supply Squadron, Fuel Operations Building. (photo: Author)

Bentwaters – Building 437, Munitions Maintenance and Assembly. (photo: Author)

Bentwaters – Building 437, Munitions Maintenance and Assembly. (photo: Author)

Bentwaters – Building 1679, 92nd TFS Weapons Maintenance Shop. (photo: Author)

Bentwaters – Weapon Inspectors Building, Weapon Storage Area. (photo: Author)

Woodbridge – MH-53 Maintenance Hangar. (photo: Author)

Woodbridge – MH-53 Maintenance Hangar. (photo: Author)

Woodbridge – 67th SOS Avionics Repair Shop. (photo: Author)

Woodbridge – 67th SOS Avionics Repair Shop. (photo: Author)

Woodbridge – 91st TFS Operations Building. (photo: Author)

Woodbridge – 67th SOS Operations Building. (photo: Author)

Woodbridge – 67th SOS Operations Building. (photo: Author)

Woodbridge – 67th SOS Operations Building. (photo: Author)

Woodbridge – 81st Component Repair Squadron (CRS) Building. (photo: Author)

Woodbridge – 81st Component Repair Squadron (CRS) Building. (photo: Author)

Woodbridge – 'Hot Pit' Filter Pad. (photo: Author)

Woodbridge – Phantom Lanes Bowling Centre. (photo: Author)

9. Around the Twin-Bases

Bentwaters – 527th Aggressor Squadron commander's Tab-Vee Hardened Aircraft Shelter (HAS). (photo: Author)

Bentwaters – 92nd Tactical Fighter Squadron commander's Tab-Vee Hardened Aircraft Shelter (HAS). (photo: Author)

Bentwaters – Control Tower and Bird Control Quonset hut. (photo: Author)

Bentwaters – Alternate Wing Operations Centre (AWOC). (photo: Author)

Bentwaters – Air Combat Manoeuvring Instrumentation (ACMI) debriefing facility. Also known as the 'Star Wars' building. (photo: Author)

Bentwaters – Field Training Detachment 'Maintenance University' building. (photo: Author)

Bentwaters – Weapons Storage Area (WSA) entrance. (photo: Author)

Bentwaters – Weapon storage igloos located in the Conventional Ammunition Store (CAS). (photo: Author)

Bentwaters – Weapon storage igloos located in the Conventional Ammunition Store (CAS). (photo: Author)

Bentwaters – Small Permanent Communications Display Segment (SPCDS) tower overlooking the Conventional Ammunition Store (CAS). The SPCDS system linked each storage igloo to alarm displays in this tower and a similar tower in the Weapon Storage Area (WSA). Guards manning the towers monitored the displays for signs of unauthorised access to the stored weapons. (photo: Author)

Woodbridge – 667th Special Ops Maintenance Squadron (SOMS) hangar. Note the four 'Jolly Green Giant' footprints. (photo: Author)

Woodbridge – MH-53 maintenance hangar. (photo: Author)

Woodbridge – C-130 maintenance hangar. (photo: Author)

Woodbridge – 78th/91st Tactical Fighter Squadron combined hardened squadron ops building. (photo: Author

Woodbridge – 78th TFS commander's Tab-Vee Hardened Aircraft Shelter (HAS). (photo: Author)

Woodbridge – 78th TFS 'Hot Pit' refuelling facility. (photo: Author)

Woodbridge – Fire station. (photo: Author)

Woodbridge – 81st Component Repair Squadron (CRS) workshops. (photo: Author)

10. Preserving the Memory: Bentwaters 'Cold War' Museum

The former Wing Command Post at Bentwaters is now the nucleus for the Bentwaters 'Cold War' Museum. (photo: Author)

Plans for a museum at Bentwaters were unveiled at the 81st Fighter Wing Association's 50th anniversary reunion, held at the base in September 2001. The reunion itself was marred by sadness as it followed in the aftermath of the terrorist attacks on the World Trade Centre in New York.

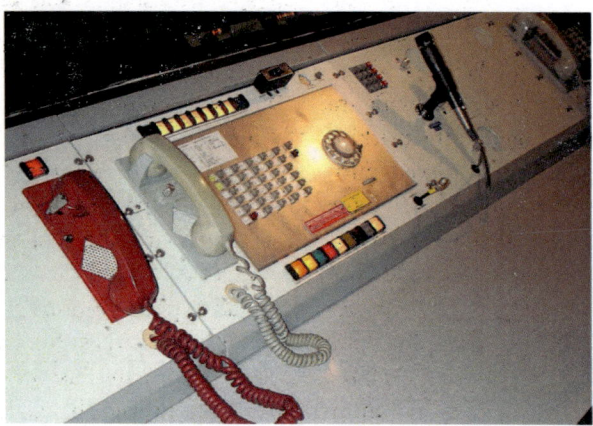

The Wing Commander's console in the Battle Cabin. (photo: Author)

The original idea was for a room in the control tower to be set aside for memorabilia and photos but this idea was subsequently changed to something that was on a much larger scale. The new plan sees the former hardened Wing Command Post as the nucleus of the museum with a number of other key buildings and areas on the base being selected for restoration and inclusion on a proposed bus tour.

The Command Post (or CP as it is also known) has an interesting history itself. The CP was manned during Operation El Dorado Canyon (the 1986 USAF raids on Colonel Gadaffi's HQ in Libya), although it is unclear as to what extent it was involved. There are unconfirmed reports that the entire operation was planned and controlled from here. The building also has a link with the UFO sightings that occurred in December 1980. Numerous books have been written about this and there is no doubt that the Bentwaters CP played a fundamental role during this period of 'unexplained' activity! The last operational milestone for the CP was during the first Gulf War in 1991. The building was manned for the duration of the conflict in support of the A-10s that were deployed to theatre.

In addition to portraying the history of Bentwaters, the Bentwaters 'Cold War' Museum, as it will be known, will also encompass the other half of the former Twin-Base complex - RAF Woodbridge.

The fully restored War Operations Room within the Wing Command Post. (photo: Author)

Work on the museum project started in earnest on 31 May 2003, when members of the newly formed Bentwaters Aviation Society began clearing unwanted fixtures and fittings from the CP.

From the very early stages of the project it was decided that two of the key rooms should be restored to an operational appearance. These rooms were the Battle Cabin and the War Operations Room and, although unmanned during normal day-to-day operations, they would have been the two most important rooms within the CP during exercise and wartime.

An amazing stroke of luck and a great deal of detective work uncovered a source of original communications consoles, alert state displays and associated equipment. This was all subsequently refitted into the Battle Cabin and War Ops rooms. Following detailed information from a number of personnel who actually worked in the CP, both rooms have been successfully restored and will undoubtedly prove to be a big attraction for visitors to the museum.

Other than the two rooms previously mentioned, most of the remaining rooms house exhibits covering various aspects of the Twin-Bases history. In addition to separate rooms dedicated to the general history of both bases, there are rooms covering Special Operations at Woodbridge and the 527th Aggressor Squadron.

Although the CP will form the centrepiece of the museum, it is by no means all that visitors can expect to see. As stated earlier, a number of other buildings have been restored and these can be seen during a bus tour of the airfield. These additional buildings include the hush-house engine de-tuner, hardened aircraft shelters and weapon storage areas. One of the hardened aircraft shelters contains the museum's collection of aircraft and visitors will be able to view these during the tour. There is also an opportunity to see restoration work on these aircraft being carried out by members of Bentwaters Aviation Society.

It is anticipated that the aircraft collection will grow steadily over the years. Currently the star exhibit is a former MoD Llanbedr-based Gloster Meteor D.16 drone, WH453. This aircraft is being returned to its original F.8 configuration and will eventually be re-painted in the markings of No. 72 Sqn, RAF, a unit with which it served during the 1950s. Although the F.8 variant has no real links to Bentwaters, the F.3 variant of the Meteor has the distinction of being the first jet-powered aircraft to be stationed at the base.

The museum project team had hoped to acquire and display some examples of USAF aircraft types that had once played such an important part in the history of both Bentwaters and Woodbridge. However, changes in the USAF Museum's 'loan' policy, post 9/11, have meant that this is unlikely ever to happen. This was a major blow for the team of volunteers, and one that could not have been predicted. It is a real shame that a museum, largely dedicated to what was once the biggest wing in the entire USAF, will not have any representative aircraft types on display for visitors to see. Hopefully this situation will change sometime in the future.

Despite this initial setback, the Bentwaters 'Cold War' Museum will still be a major attraction for aviation enthusiasts and former based personnel for many years to come. Unlike most of the other disused airbases in the U.K., Bentwaters has remained largely intact. This fact, in conjunction with the museum itself, will go some way to enable future generations to understand the important roles played by both Bentwaters and Woodbridge during the Second World War and throughout the 'Cold War' period.